Psychology and the
political experience

Psychology and the Political Experience

ALAN HUGHES

Senior Lecturer in Political Sociology
University of Melbourne

Cambridge University Press

Published by the Syndics of the Cambridge University Press
Bentley House, 200 Euston Road, London NW1 2DB
American Branch: 32 East 57th Street, New York, N.Y. 10022

© Cambridge University Press 1975

Library of Congress Catalogue Card Number: 74–12961

ISBN: 0 521 20594 8

First published 1975

Photoset, printed and bound
in Great Britain by
REDWOOD BURN LIMITED
Trowbridge & Esher

For Hans and Sophie Scholl,
and the men and women of 20 July 1944;
especially, Claus, Count Schenk von Stauffenberg

INVICTIS PAX

Contents

Preface

This study of psychological dispositions and their interrelations with political attitudes is both theoretical and empirical. In its first aspect, it dwells on themes general to advanced industrial societies; the empirical investigation is located in urban Australia.

It has had many sources of guidance, but my gratitude goes first to Professor Alan Davies and Dr Frank Knöpfelmacher of the University of Melbourne, and to Mr Talis Polis, of La Trobe University, who each, in their, shall I say, very different ways, inspired my interest in this enterprise. My thanks also go to the supervisors of my doctoral thesis at the Australian National University, Dr Don Aitkin. Professor Robert Parker and Mr Michael Kahan, for their sustained encouragement in many improbable vicissitudes. Mr David Bottomley and Mr Irving Saulwick, of the Australian Sales Research Bureau, undertook the interviewing reported in the principal survey, at cost (or possibly beneath it) and deserve my acknowledgement of their generosity to academic research.

I owe much to the friendly assistance of Dr Ken Forster, of Monash University, Miss Mary Rose, of the Australian National University, and Mr Beau Sheil, of the University of Sydney.

Most of all, my gratitude goes to my wife, Wendy, without whose support this work could not have been completed.

Melbourne, 1974   ALAN HUGHES

1 Introduction: psychology and politics

1.1. Introduction

'The subtlety of Nature', said Bacon, 'is a great many times more subtle than the subtlety of Logic.' The complexity of the actual social world demands, not merely invites, empirical methods of investigation, which are indispensable for a proper understanding. In humane studies, deduction from first principles is a path that leads directly to error. An intuitive anticipation of what kind of things may be found, on the other hand, is likely to be an aid to scholarly investigation of human activity, since our ordinary understanding of social processes is often a useful short-cut: there is no need to behave like the blind men trying to discern the shape of the elephant, if we are, in fact, sighted. This book is primarily a statistical investigation, sometimes with an aim of defining structures not previously known; but where structures are already identified, or common knowledge can be adduced, then it is addressed to a better description of the structure and an investigation of its correlations.

It is an interdisciplinary study, in one aspect concerned with four major psychological dispositions, which are regarded as already identified. These are alienation, conceived as social estrangement; the authoritarian personality tendency of the 'right'; ethnocentrism; and anxiety. Since the first three of these have not been well measured, nor their structure well described, this study is partially addressed to the development of adequate measures for them. An empirical test of the disparateness of their identity is also introduced. In part, therefore, it lies in the domain of social psychology. In considering the correlations of the dispositions and their social meaning, it dwells partly in sociology; and in investigating and identifying disparate structures of political opinion, not previously well recognized, its purpose is best described as political science. Whilst the measurement of the psychological dispositions, on the one hand, and of political attitudes, on the other, are both intended to be substantive, the focal point of the research is at the connections

1

to be discovered between the two, i.e. its central concern is with political psychology.

Greenstein[1] has suggested three divisions of heuristic utility in organizing the issues of enquiry into personality and politics: the 'individual case study', diagnosing a single actor; the 'typological study', to 'classify actors and to explain the origin and behaviour of the types in the classification'; and 'aggregative analysis', to explain features of the larger social and political system.

In its separate investigation of each of the four psychological constructs mentioned above, this study falls within the second category. It is concerned with modal psychological processes which throw light on individual functioning. The alienated man, for example, is first considered as a *possibility*, in that the connectedness of the various sentiments said to be associated with social estrangement is first tested, and their cohesiveness shown *not* to be a result of their covariance with anxiety. It is argued here, also, that alienation cannot be regarded as a social modality of anxiety. The social incidence of alienation and its statistical correlations with other psychological constructs are then elaborated, in accordance with the general strategy endorsed by Lasswell[2] of moving outwards, as it were, from 'nuclear types'. The implications of the investigation of the dispositional paradigm for an understanding of individual actors is then illustrated by introducing two men, 'John' and 'Patrick', both interviewed in depth; the first is alienated, the second not.

A general qualification to the characterization of this investigation as a typological exercise of the kind described by Greenstein should here be made. Whilst it is recognized that each of the four constructs bears upon modes of personality functioning, it is not suggested here that each wholly describes a type of person. A person may be highly alienated and ethnocentric but not anxious or authoritarian, for example. Whilst this book does not attempt a *typology* of persons, in the sense of the preceding sentence, it is also not oriented to the qualities of political actors considered as *unique* persons. The methodological approach of this research, consisting chiefly in correlational analysis of data from a mass survey, is inclined to lead the reader

[1] F. I. Greenstein, 'The Need for Systematic Inquiry into Personality and Politics: Introduction and Overview', *Journal of Social Issues*, 24 (1968), pp. 1–14; see also his book, *Personality and Politics* (Chicago, 1969).

[2] H. D. Lasswell, *Psychopathology and Politics* (New York, 1960; first ed. 1930), ch. 4.

away from an appreciation of the idiosyncratic qualities of the dispositions and political views of individuals. Its main hope is that an understanding of general processes will lead back, as it were, to finer insights into the variety of what individuals feel, think, and do.

In its concern with central tendencies, this work extends in some degree into the third division of research described by Greenstein, aggregative analysis. It attempts to define, in a limited area, some of the norms, in the statistical sense, of the interrelations of dispositions and political attitudes in an Australian urban context. Although broad in scope in this sense, it does not aim to provide anything approaching a psychological *interpretation* of all Australian political events or circumstances in the contemporary period. The argument will, indeed, emphasize many of the *limitations* of 'psychological' influences on politics, in general, and of the influence of dispositions, in particular.

The four dispositions were chosen because my primary interest, like that of many, lay in the political repurcussions of sentiments of aggression and insecurity. Its primary inspiration was drawn from the research of Adorno, Frenkel-Brunswik, Levinson and Sanford[3] into the psychodynamics of ethnocentrism, but also from the dramatic, even if methodologically unsound, intervention of Srole[4] in the chain of associated work which followed in such quantity, indicating the need to take into account social frustration and uncertainty. My attention was also excited by the comedy of errors which followed from the intrusion of acquiescence into the measures, the implications of which are reviewed *in extenso*. Anxiety was added as the psychological disposition of most general interest, apart from the first three. It is considered that these four dispositions all deserve the term 'psychological', because they are all related to features of personality functioning, and are all in some degree *opaque* to the common understanding, thus entitling them to be qualified by the name of a specialized discipline. Alienation, on which the term 'psychological' sits least easily, is so described because, conceived as social estrangement, it refers to a very large part of the individual's relations with his social environment, including some areas of which he may be unaware.

[3] T. W. Adorno, E. Frenkel-Brunswik, D. J. Levinson and R. N. Sanford, *The Authoritarian Personality* (New York, 1950).

[4] L. Srole, 'Social Integration and Certain Corollaries: An Exploratory Study', *American Sociological Review*, 21 (1956), pp. 709–16.

1.2. The structure of this book

This Introduction touches upon some theoretical considerations, including the present status of the 'behaviouralist' approach to politics, with which, in broad terms, I am in sympathy; and also on the place of the process named *Verstehen* in social inquiry. It suggests what might be considered original, or novel, in this work, considered as a research enterprise.

Chapter 2 provides a very brief sketch of the political environment within which this study is set. Beginning with the normative values (what is 'given') in Australian politics, it proceeds to some implications of the present quasi-federal system, and then to a description of the policies of the main political parties. The new electoral equilibrium established by the Labor 'split' of 1955, and the federal elections of 1963 and 1966 are discussed.

Appendix A describes the sample surveyed in 1966, and compares it with population parameters. The 1966 voter sample, the survey of which was funded by the Australian National University, was of 400 voters, 200 in Melbourne and 200 in Sydney. A 'captive' sample of 155 low-grade public servants was also surveyed in 1966 as a preparatory step to the main operation.

Chapter 3 is a selective review of some empirical work done in recent times, using 'scaling' methods, into authoritarian personality tendency, alienation and ethnocentrism.

We then proceed to elaborate some of the necessary canons of attitude scale technology, and to present new scales for the measurement of authoritarianism, alienation and ethnocentrism (in Chapter 4). The report of the results of the empirical investigation of the psychological structures is to be found in Chapter 5.

Appendix C describes the construction of the psychological measures. The extent of the corruption of research into the authoritarian personality by the defects of the first well-known measure of it, the 'California F scale'[5] is unavoidably highly technical but also very important. It is examined in Appendix E.

A book concerned in part with the relevance of psychological attitudes to politics is nothing without some discussion of political attitudes and their structure. But since these are not, in their detailed analysis, central, standardization data for the 'political' scales are to be found in Appendix D. The political attitude fabric is delineated in the broad in Chapter 6. The connections between the psychological

[5] T. W. Adorno *et al.*, *op. cit.*, pp. 255–7.

and political attitude structures are then elaborated in Chapter 7. Chapter 8 is a *jeu d'esprit*: it contains a speculative discussion of a tape-recorded political conversation in a small group, which has the advantage of portraying political opinions in conflict *in situ*, as it were, partly to recall to the reader the immense complexity of both the structure and function of political attitudes in situations of personal interaction. The chapter has the added purpose of showing how such contrived situations may be useful in suggesting hypotheses which may be testable with data from larger samples.

Chapter 9 selectively reviews some general findings, and considers their relevance to psychological interpretation of events at other times and in other places, particularly the bizarre role of anti-Semitism in the destruction of the liberal German political order in 1933 and its place in the Nazi imagination.

1.3. What is new in this book?

The main claims to originality lie, firstly, in the construction and validation of three measures of dispositions: alienation, authoritarianism and ethnocentrism. The first and last of these have satisfactory reliability coefficients, and are suitable for general research use. The reliability of the second is modest, but it is capable of being used as a 'core' instrument for the development of an authoritarianism scale with items more central to personality functioning, the desirability of which is argued throughout the text. The procedure for demonstrating, by factor analysis, the disparateness of each of the four constructs, and the substantive outcome, which is consistent with the hypothesis of disparateness, is also an original departure. So too is the test of the cohesiveness of alienation as social estrangement, when the covariance with anxiety of each element of the construct is withdrawn.

The application of these instruments to a representative mass sample in an Australian urban *milieu* is another way in which this research contributes something new. The discovery of the dimension of 'conscience' radicalism, for example, and its separateness from other dimensions of political sentiment, although specific to the Australian urban context, may have applications elsewhere. The report of the relation of the psychological dispositions to political attitudes, and the theoretical discussion of the interconnections between them varies from previous work in other places[6] in differentiating between

---

[6] For example, H. McClosky, 'Conservatism and Personality', *American Political*

the varieties of political radicalism and conservatism.

1.4. Some theoretical considerations

The reputation of political psychology has, in recent times, undergone a change for the better. This is partly through the careful balancing of the nomothetic and idiographic approaches to the problems of analysis by Greenstein[7] and others. It is now generally recognized that, without a comprehension of the special opportunities which may occur for psychological influence, which relies very often on an idiographic study, paying attention to what is peculiar to a situation, the generalizations afforded by nomothetic research resemble an armoury of weapons whose potency is uncertain from time to time and case to case.

Greenstein[8] has specified some of the circumstances in which 'personality' factors may influence political behaviour. Systematization of this kind is desirable and necessary, but there remains an irreducible residue of judgement about the quality of particular sociopolitical environments, a *Fingerspitzengefühl* for the occasions when psychological influence is likely to become not merely an accident of events but systemic. To say this implies the methodological utility of *Verstehen*,[9] of insightful 'understanding'. (The German term has a strong connotation.) The obligatory character of 'understanding', for the social scientist, is very general, and has to do with the presence of 'meaning' in the social world as opposed to the natural order investigated by scientists. It has been well put by Schutz.[10]

The world of nature, as explored by the natural scientist, does not 'mean' anything to the molecules, atoms and electrons therein. The observational field of the social scientist, however, namely the social reality, has a specific meaning and relevance structure for the human beings living, acting and thinking therein. Thus, the constructs of the social sciences are, so to speak, constructs of the second degree, namely constructs of the constructs made by the actors on the social scene, whose behaviour the social scientist has to observe and to explain in accordance with the procedural rules of his science.

Science Review, 52 (1958), pp. 27–45.

[7] F. I. Greenstein, 'The Impact of Personality on Politics: An Attempt to Clear Away the Underbrush', *American Political Science Review*, 61 (1967), pp. 628–41.

[8] *Ibid.*

[9] The most well-known analysis of this is that of T. Abel, 'The Operation Called *Verstehen*', *American Journal of Sociology*, 54 (1948), pp. 211–18.

[10] A. Schutz, 'Concept and Theory Formation in the Social Sciences', *Journal of Philosophy*, 51 (1954), pp. 266–7.

The behavioural scientist will, and in my view should, try to test hypotheses derived from human insight by empirical procedures, e.g. by operationalizing the constructs and measuring them and their correlations in a sample. But whether or not he does so, comprehension and a socio-political situation must extend beyond formal knowledge, reducible to numerical or linguistic expressions, to at least a momentary communion with the meanings of the situation in the minds of the actors therein, i.e. *Verstehen* of individual feelings; and also of the human implications for the culture, perhaps in judging what is foreseeable, i.e. cultural *Verstehen* also.

The acceptance of the meanings of situations as seen by their actors, and still more of the 'cultural implications' of empirical findings, multiplies the data of social research in a manner unnerving to the more simplistic proponents of attitude scale technology, since nomothetic generalization, or even the *construction* to be placed on described social situations, becomes difficult. The principle of parsimony, which is a fundament of science, is more difficult to apply when data of these kinds are admitted. If the concept of *intention* is also admitted, as I think it should be, the stockade containing the babbling horde of data groans and bulges under the stress. Nevertheless, since it is the explication of social reality and not some (illusory) convenience for social commentators which is the primary concern of social science, it follows that what is said in a general way about the data must be said very carefully, after looking in every direction. A difficulty in verifying a complex proposition does not reduce its epistemological status. Lafitte,[11] in arguing 'the simple proposition has no special status' remarks:

That an intense narcissistic need for personal approval is typical of the schizoid character may be hard to verify not only because of the complexity of the work involved but also because specifying the operations is rendered difficult by the terms of the proposition. 'Narcissistic need', 'schizoid character' and even 'personal approval' do not have self-evident meanings.

The *principle* of parsimony, of applying the most economical construction to the available data, is not, of course, endangered by this argument. What is being pointed out is that its *application* may be extraordinarily difficult.

It will be obvious that the methodological orientation of this work

[11] P. Lafitte, *The Person in Psychology: Reality or Abstraction* (London, 1957), p. 41.

is anti-reductionist, or 'contextualist', to use Greenstein's[12] term. But not only must the overt behaviour and sometimes dormant dispositions or attitudes of the political actors be understood within their context; *intended actions*, which usually, but not necessarily, involve a value orientation must also be taken into account. It is argued here that some phenomena are political *per se*, and have few sociological or psychological correlates. The fact that most workers in this field now acknowledge the independence of political behaviour in many of its aspects is one of the main reasons why political psychology is now more reputable. The recognition of the many factors which may be at work in shaping events is exemplified in Smith's[13] schematic map for the analysis of personality and politics, especially in his complex Figure 2, where not only feedback but the engagement, or disengagement, of dispositions and attitudes are accommodated. This may be contrasted with the work of earlier theorists, particularly Eysenck,[14] whose approach was, by implication, heavily reductionist. Figure 17 in his book[15] is an early counterpart of that of Smith, and implies a loose governance by ideology of attitudes, and, in their turn, of habitual opinions and specific opinions. Although Eysenck's argument is more sophisticated than his diagram might suggest, there is a dearth of discussion of politics *qua* politics everywhere in his work.[16]

This kind of work may bring the whole body of psychological research into politics into disrepute, and, I fear, did so. The main ground of the feeling against such research in the 1950s was that it tended to be simplistic and reductionist, and, indeed, derisory of politics: in other words, it was felt that it made a puerile and mis-

[12] F. I. Greenstein, 'The Need for Systematic Enquiry into Personality and Politics', p. 9.

[13] M. Brewster Smith, 'A Map for the Analysis of Personality and Politics', *Journal of Social Issues*, 24 (1968), pp. 15–28, esp. p. 20.

[14] H. J. Eysenck, *The Psychology of Politics* (London, 1954), chs. 4 and 8.

[15] *Ibid.*, p. 112.

[16] In advancing the conception of 'tough–tender-mindedness' as the principal dimension governing opinions on social issues apart from a *single* 'radical–conservative' political dimension, Eysenck omits (i) to describe anywhere the technical features of the factor analysis on which the conception is based; (ii) conjures up a construct validation based on James's discussion of temperamental types which is at unacknowledged and possibly unseen variance with his own: James's 'tenderminded' type is 'monistic' and 'dogmatical' as opposed to 'pluralistic' and 'sceptical'. The whole analysis reeks of confusion between larger and smaller issues: 'Abolish abortion and licensing laws' is the cryptic label attached to two points of his diagram 23 (see his pages 130–1).

guided attempt to diminish the human stature in the political domain.

This was not true of the work of Adorno and his colleagues, and it is principally to them, and those psychologists who followed up their work, and engaged the sympathetic attention and, indeed, the admiration of political scientists, that we owe the present burgeoning interest in the bearing of psychological dispositions on political attitudes. The difficult birth of the psychology of politics is, in one way, no cause for surprise, for it is a peculiar creature, having the features of both art and science. Possibly the Germans were right in giving that psychology which practises *Verstehen* and is idiographic in inclination one of their improbably long but evocative titles: *geisteswissenschaftliche Psychologie* (literally, cultural science psychology). As practised in this research, political psychology is not of this type, since it has a nomothetic intent; but it is deferential to it. 'Statistical research', said Collingwood,[17] 'is for the historian a good servant but a bad master. It profits him nothing to make statistical generalizations, unless he can thereby detect the thought behind the facts about which he is generalizing.' This is true also for the student of the psychology of politics. But it is not merely the 'thought' of the actors to which we wish to penetrate; it is to their unconscious or half-aware motivations. The measurement of psychological dispositions makes this possible. Moreover, statistical research has the great virtue of putting a distance between the analyst's prejudgements and the eventual outcome of his analysis: it makes it easier for him, in Collingwood's own phrase, 'to work against the grain of his own mind'.[18]

1.5. A central idea: the 'alienation triptych'

This book advances towards various conclusions in the method and substance of looking at psychology in politics. Since it is not a mystery story, there is no need to delay to the reader one main finding of the empirical work. On the contrary, it is better to advance it immediately, as a guide to a better understanding of the complexities to be explored later on. A 'triptych' is a three-part panel painting, each panel forming part of a whole. The expression here is used to describe a tripartite system of dispositions. Alienation is the centrepiece. Following from it is irrational hostility, often '*targeted*' upon

[17] R. G. Collingwood, *The Idea of History* (London, 1946), p. 228.
[18] *Ibid.*, p. 305.

out-groups. When hostility finds this form of expression, it is called 'ethnocentrism'. The third disposition, anxiety, is caused not only by threatening circumstances, but also by alienation itself. In turn, it may reinforce alienation, because, at high levels, it reduces 'drive', renders the individual a psychological cripple, and deprives him of the strength to combat the social frustrations which help create a felt alienation. This system of sentiments is illustrated in Figure 1.1.

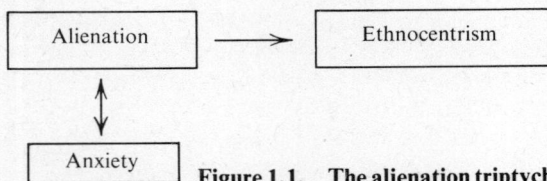

Figure 1.1. The alienation triptych

Alienation is a term used variously. Here, it is used to refer to an enduring *sentiment* of separation from the larger and smaller social environs of the individual, involving frustration, mistrust, and doubt about commonly accepted social verities. It can be both malignant and creative: the social scientist, for example, has, as part of his business, a duty to be sceptical of even what most people regard as axiomatically true. In doing so, he takes up a burden: for most people, it is a burden thrust upon them. Most generally, frustration and mistrust result in irrational hostility. Frustration often leads to misdirected aggression; and mistrust is a close cousin of hostility.

Irrational hostility may be general, or, frequently, focussed upon out-groups, such as ethnic minorities. The 'out-group', of course, may be ethnic, communal, or otherwise: capitalists, communists or probation officers. As with air pollution, which often creates visually interesting twilights, it is possible to imagine beneficial side-effects. A shared resentment of a common enemy can be a basis for fraternity. One has only to reflect on war experience to see this. On the other hand, it is as well to be sure that the 'enemy' is, in fact, 'shared'. That is why conversations dealing in bigotry often begin in a guarded fashion.

No independent relation was found between anxiety and ethnocentrism, possibly because retreat and the avoidance of combat are as common as hostility in anxious people. This would lead to the null relation. However, *repressed* anxiety, which may not reveal itself on the anxiety scale used here, may be at the root of the 'authoritarian personality'; but *overt* anxiety seems to have no discernible role to play in energizing hostility.

It should be said here, parenthetically, that the critique of the concept of the authoritarian personality is by no means peripheral to this research. It is one of its central concerns. In some degree the problems attendant upon the delineation and measurement of authoritarianism are well known, but unresolved. Hence the analytical attack and summation of its outcome, in Chapters 3, 4 and 5, and Appendix E.

Yet this part of the work represents, to put the point bluntly, only fresh light on a familiar story. It is not novel to conclude, as I do, that authoritarianism is an important cause of ethnic bigotry. But so, too, is alienation, in varying force, although on the whole, equally operative as a cause. What comes as more of a surprise is that the feed-in, so to speak, of authoritarianism to ethnocentrism is isolated and apparently unrelated to either alienation or anxiety at the manifest level. The closely bound system of alienation, anxiety and ethnocentrism, is theoretically more salient, more a dominant theme and one to which authoritarianism is best considered an adjunct.

To return to this tripartite system: one of its habitual locations in the social structure is amongst the poor. It is important to note that, whilst all three dispositions are more marked amongst the poor, they do not go together merely because of their common relation with poverty. This can be shown by holding socio-economic variables constant. When this is done, the interplay of the three remains substantially the same, with some modifications, for example: the lead-on to ethnocentrism may be dampened in a higher educational group.

These interconnections of alienation, ethnocentrism and anxiety are central tendencies. Whilst the relations described are strong enough to speak of a system, they are not at all one-to-one relations. There will be many exceptions, and it is better to think in terms of ethnocentric people being disproportionately more frequent amongst alienated people, than to make a mental equation of the two dispositions: the same goes for alienation and anxiety.

In measuring dispositions, and studying the correlations of scale scores, what we are doing is moving from the actual social world, where the data have been gathered, to an analysis of a symbolic world, with a different logic, governed by the rules of applied mathematics. This is not as unusual a procedure as it may at first seem: a similar one occurs in every day life, when things and events are often translated into words, linguistic symbols, which have their own order in linguistic structures. The very exercise of 'conceptualization' involves entry into a symbolic universe, related to, but logically distinct from, the outer world.

The empirical method, despite its necessary brutalization of raw data, has great power in discovering general trends. But in the humanities, it is necessary to return to direct observation to appreciate the complexity inherent in the data. Therefore, we may consider illustrative 'case studies', to observe the way in which dispositions are displayed in the behaviour of individuals. But one can also move upwards, as it were, to a consideration of how the interrelationship of dispositions can aid an understanding of some critical historical episodes, such as the collapse of the German Weimar Republic at the onslaught of Nazism. This is done in the Conclusion.

2 The political context

2.1. Introduction

This chapter fulfils the promise of Chapter 1 in providing a very brief sketch of some features of the Australian political scene. It should be remembered that this period was the peak of the conservative ascendancy, from 1950 until 1972. But it is by no means uncharacteristic: the post-1972 federal Labor government has merely tilted the balance of Australian politics.

Some crucial features of the system as it functions may not emerge in surveys of the mass public. A notable case in point is the central role of the Democratic Labor Party and its social base in a section of the Victorian Catholic Vote, mobilized by the National Civic Council. The highly compressed presentation here can hardly do justice to its significance, not to say its theatrical potential, as a highly successful, at times semi-clandestine operation, led by a lay organizer and publicist, Mr B. A. Santamaria. But we must first turn to what is most, not least, obvious in Australian politics.

2.2. Legitimacy: what is 'given' in Australian politics

Gallup Poll (Australian Public Opinion Polls: hereafter, APOP) findings are of some interest here, and an admirable guide to them has been provided by Goot.[1] However, as is so often the case, the socio-political character of Australia has been better described by historians, of whose works the most generally highly regarded is perhaps that of Hancock,[2] and by writers offering a general commentary, such as the brilliant autobiography by Horne,[3] describing his boyhood in an Australian country town, than by political scientists.

---

[1] M. Goot, *Policies and Partisans: Australian Electoral Opinion, 1941 to 1968*, Occasional Monograph No. 1, Department of Government and Public Administration, University of Sydney (Sydney, 1969).

[2] W. K. (Sir Keith) Hancock, *Australia* (Brisbane, 1961; first ed. 1930).

[3] D. Horne, *The Education of Young Donald* (Sydney, 1967).

Davies and Encel[4] have produced a general sociological commentary, and Davies'[5] studies in depth of five second-rank political activists gives a vivid impression of the *ambience* of Australian politics.

During this period, as through almost its entire history, the constitutional government of Australia was at once 'effective' and regarded as 'legitimate' in the senses described by Lipset.[6] Considered in relation to other countries, it was a very stable system. Australia has never faced the prospect of civil war, and only once the prospect of invasion (by the Japanese, in 1942). Only a few towns in the far North-west (for example, Darwin, in 1942) have ever been subjected to aerial bombardment. Parliamentary government and the prerogatives of a strong, independent judiciary are so much a matter of course that no APOP question about their desirability was asked of the public in the period. Australians are wedded to the federal system and to the present structure of the constituent States. An APOP question about the desirability of the present number of states found overwhelming support for it (of the order of 75 per cent)[7] in 1967. Federal elections are held frequently (every three years) and there is overwhelming support for this also,[8] as well as for voting being compulsory.[9] About the desirability of the federal upper house, the Senate, which represents the states equally, there is a more even division of opinion, but still a majority in support (1961 and 1965).[10]

The nature of Australian patriotism is a curious one. The Australian Labor Party (hereafter, ALP) has been less of an enthusiast for the Imperial idea than the conservative parties (presently the Liberal and Country Parties), but the generally accepted concept of a wider loyalty has impeded the growth of a parochial chauvinism. The notion of Empire and its obligations has impelled this small nation to send a variety of military expeditions abroad, beginning with a small contingent sent to fight the 'Mad Mahdi' in the Sudan in the 1880s, a

---

[4] A. F. Davies and S. Encel (eds.), *Australian Society: A Sociological Introduction* (Melbourne, 1965).

[5] A. F. Davies, *Private Politics: A Study of Five Political Outlooks* (Melbourne, 1966).

[6] S. M. Lipset, *Political Man* (London, 1963), ch. 3.

[7] M. Goot, *op. cit.*, p. 126.

[8] *Ibid.*, p. 126.

[9] *Ibid.*, p. 126.

[10] *Ibid.*, p. 126.

larger one to the Boer War, and a huge volunteer army of 400,000 (for a nation with a population then approaching 5,000,000) in support of the 'mother country' in the First World War. The idea of the military expedition, embarked upon to protect some threatened interest far away, had a high place in the Australian imagination. 'War' did not carry much sense of immediacy to the Australian locale: it was A Great Moment when the men volunteered, embarked, and sailed away, some to return as heroes. Voting is compulsory, but war, until recently, was not. But a moral imperative was involved. The young Donald Horne is asked anxiously by his father in the 1930s: 'You'd go if you had to, wouldn't you, son?' Only after the threat of Japanese invasion was a limited form of conscription for overseas service introduced, even then with great reluctance. Conscription for the war in Vietnam came as something of a shock to the public. Australia has always cast itself in the role of a plucky ally, and this partly explains the early general support for the Vietnam commitment.

Australians combine republican manners and an affection for the crown of England, which is nearly always seen as a symbol of the country's British inheritance. Support for continuing our present ties with Britain rather than becoming an entirely separate republic waned from about 65 per cent to 55 per cent between 1966 and 1968.[11] However, the celebration of the principle of constitutional monarchy is prominent in the rituals of the armed services, the churches, the law, the independent and state schools and all state as well as federal parliaments. Indeed, it was a practice of some states, such as Victoria, still to invite distinguished Englishmen to act as Governor, the Queen's representative; but the habit of doing the same in the federal sphere died during the period, and it seems most unlikely that any future Governor-General will be an Englishman.

Australia tends to see itself as a kind of social microcosm of the United Kingdom and Ireland, with the English upper class left out, and a higher proportion of Scots and Irish. Englishmen, Scotsmen and Irishmen are not regarded as foreigners. Despite the increasing economic, political and academic orientation to the USA, Americans are regarded with more curiosity and some resentment. The national anthem was still 'God Save the Queen', in spite of the seemingly perpetual public debate on the desirability of a purely Australian alternative.[12] The nature of Australia as an immigrant

[11] *Ibid.*, p. 125.

[12] The APOP found overwhelming popular support for 'keeping the Union Jack in

15

polity is a subject to which we shall return.

The federal government had been formed by a coalition of the Liberal and Country Parties (the former the larger partner) since 1949, without interruption, and these had gradually taken on the appearance of being the normally ruling parties, despite a vigorous Labor opposition. This had split in 1955, when the 'Anti-Communist' (later, the 'Democratic') Labor Party was formed, but the ALP maintained a very large (40 to 50 per cent) share of the vote throughout the period.

We shall now briefly consider the 'effectiveness' of the federal government during this period. Its chief implication, as of this discussion of 'legitimacy', is of stability and confidence in the regime.

2.3. 'Effectiveness' of government: economic growth

Australian society is an affluent one, especially by comparison with its neighbours in Asia. The Gross National Product per head in 1967, in 1967 US dollars, was $2143, compared to $326 in Malaysia, and $1158 in Japan.[13] It is also one growing steadily more affluent. After a minor recession in 1960–1, the annual growth of the GNP per head at constant prices was 3·7 per cent, between 1962 and 1967.[14] This was achieved despite a population growth of from 10·3 million in 1960 to 11·6 million in 1966.[15] Moreover, consumer prices rose only moderately during this period: if the financial year 1952/3 is taken as a base of 100, the Consumer Price Index was 125·7 in 1963/4 and 138·9 in March 1967.[16] Personal consumption expenditure showed a marked increase per head, and a smaller proportion devoted to basic necessities, such as food and drink.[17] In terms of selected indicators of economic growth, production of steel increased from 1·5 million tons in 1951/2 to 5·6 million tons in 1965/6, an annual growth rate of 9·8 per cent.[18] The number of motor vehicles per 1000 of population increased from 187 in 1951/2 to 331 in 1965/6, reflecting an annual growth rate of 4·2 per cent.[19] Expenditure on education by all public

our flag' in 1967. Cf. M. Goot, *op. cit.*, p. 125.

[13] *ANZ Bank Quarterly Survey*, 19 (1969), no. 1, p. 23.

[14] *Ibid.*

[15] *Trends,* 7 (published by the Rural Bank of New South Wales), 1966, no. 1, p. 8.

[16] Reserve Bank of Australia, *Statistical Bulletin* (June 1967), p. 292.

[17] *Trends*, 7 (1966), no. 1, p. 8.

[18] *Ibid.*, p. 8.

[19] *Ibid.*, p. 8.

authorities rose (at current prices) from $280 million (Australian dollars) in 1959/60 to $530 million in 1965/6, a considerable increase even when deflated for rising costs and the growth in population.[20] Australia was not, however, a heavily taxed country, compared with other Western nations. In 1965, total taxes were 29·9 per cent of National Income in Australia, compared with 33·6 per cent in the USA, 37·9 per cent in the United Kingdom, and 51·2 per cent in France.[21]

This brief review indicates an economic situation in which consumers' rising aspirations were steadily fed, where no rentier class was enraged by galloping inflation, where immigration could be sustained without greatly retarding the growth of real income per head and demands for more spending in the public sector, on services such as education, were being met with some degree of satisfaction; in short, where social change was gradual, orderly, and favourably regarded by the community at large. This is not to say that there was contentment with, for example, the level of spending on public services. It could have been, and was, in fact, argued that public expenditure should have been rising more rapidly than it did. Indeed, this issue penetrated the mass consciousness both at the level of individual experience and public debate. There was a vociferous demand for more and better educational facilities, and as the analysis of the 1966 sample suggests (see Appendix A) the younger generation were indeed becoming better educated than their elders. But there was little in the overall socio-economic situation to provoke a radical challenge to the bases of the established system; rather, proposals for gradual reforms were given a slowly widening circulation in an increasingly well educated and financially more 'comfortable' political public. The left-of-centre fashion was for reformism, not extreme proposals, and the data of the survey of 1966 should be considered in this light. The general improvement in living conditions was not entirely uniform, but such pockets of poverty as remained in Australian society were not easily politically mobilized: they were amongst pensioners, handicapped people, deserted wives with families, and recent immigrants from Southern Europe. 'Poverty' as a global issue was not to be raised until 1968–9.[22]

[20] *Ibid.*, p. 8.
[21] *ANZ Bank Quarterly Survey*, 18 (1969), no. 2, p. 13.
[22] See, e.g. R. J. A. Harper, 'Survey of Living Conditions in Melbourne – 1966',

It is not hard to see why most Australians regard their politics as almost a light-hearted game, to be played with detachment and some cynicism. When an affair of state becomes *important*, it ceases, in common parlance, to be 'political'; it becomes a 'public' or 'national' issue. There is no dispossessed ruling class, which history has passed by, longing for a restoration of an *ancien régime*; no Great Pretender; no local equivalent of the *Action Française*. The grand issues of style, capable of arousing great emotion, had been settled long ago. Modernists in Australia often feel, indeed, that the *ancien régime* is too long with us; but they would scarcely trouble to cross the street in the cause of a republic. The main issues in internal politics are socio-economic: who is to get how much of the growing cake of national production. These are matters fought over by political syndicates of interested groups, organized as political parties; but before we consider them we must note an ironical feature of the Australian federal system.

2.4. An implication of the federal system

A federal system is one in which power is divided between a central authority and political authorities for the constituents, in such a way that neither can, by its own *fiat*, withdraw powers from the other. It is sometimes remarked that by virtue of this inbuilt inflexibility, federations tend to conservatism. I wish here to argue the reverse for Australia. The Constitution spells out the powers of the Commonwealth parliament, leaving the residue to the states. In 1942, through its power to levy taxes, which it holds concurrently with the states, the Commonwealth parliament passed four acts, later held to be *intra vires* in peace time, which had the effect of taking over all taxation of incomes, previously levied by the states. The Commonwealth, now in possession of this principal 'growth' tax, makes grants to the states from its consolidated revenue, which account for about 55 per cent of their total receipts of revenue.[23]

Since they have few 'growth' taxes of their own, the states are thus heavily dependent upon Commonwealth generosity to finance the services they are constitutionally empowered to provide, in the field of education, for example. Section 96 of the Constitution permits,

---

Economic Record, 43 (1967) pp. 262–88. Harper concludes that about 5 per cent of Melbourne's population were then living in 'poverty', by Australian standards.

[23] Commonwealth Bureau of Census and Statistics, *Official Year Book of the Commonwealth of Australia* (Canberra, 1966), no. 52, p. 765 and pp. 786–8.

but does not compel, the Commonwealth to attach any conditions it pleases to the grants to the states. Conditions were, in fact, applied to about one fifth[24] of these grants. But notice the implication here: should the Commonwealth wish to *usurp* the policy-making functions of the states, it could apply the conditions to *all* its grants, including ones requiring their expenditure to be matched, dollar for dollar, by the states. The Commonwealth would then have *de facto* withdrawn, unilaterally, powers now in the hands of the states. Since this extraordinary capability lies with the Commonwealth, it follows that Australia does not have, in the strict sense, a federal system, but one better described as quasi-federal.

The result of the present financial relations between the Commonwealth and the states is that the governments of the states, whatever their political complexion, will be mendicants pressing the Commonwealth for more funds for public projects in great demand, especially in education, whilst at the same time avoiding the odium attached to levying extra taxation. It follows that (a) actual policy-making discretion is, in most fields, really in the hands of the Commonwealth, on to which the survey of 1966 is, therefore, properly focussed; and (b) that since the pressure from the States is always for *increased* spending, the quasi-federal system, as it now functions, has a *radical*, and not a conservative bias.

As we shall see, policy alignments between the major parties are more distinct than in the USA, for example. The ALP applied continuous pressure for greater expenditure in the public sector, and the then government parties had to fend off its electoral challenge by an apparently good performance, which was measured in the eyes of the press and the public largely by the degree to which it satisfied the demands of the states. It is seldom recognized how closely the ALP and the governments of the states, then nearly all[25] conservative in party complexion, were associated in pressing for increased public expenditure.

2.5. The main political parties and the elections of 1963 and 1966.

The structure of parliamentary government within which the parties operate has been described, *inter alia*, by Davies,[26] Crisp[27] and

---

[24] R. J. May, *Federalism and Fiscal Adjustment* (Oxford, 1969), pp. 56–66, esp. p. 66.

[25] In 1970, *all* were governed by non-Labor Ministries.

[26] A. F. Davies, *Australian Democracy* (Melbourne, 1958).

[27] L. F. Crisp, *The Parliamentary Government of the Commonwealth of Australia*,

19

Miller.[28] The House of Representatives is pre-eminent, and, as British constitutional principles have been received, a federal government which does not command a majority in this House must resign. The survey on which this research is based was accordingly taken during the elections for the House of Representatives in 1966. The Australian political party system has a mild family resemblance to its British relative, as the analyses by Jupp[29] and Overacker[30] make clear, although it should be noted that the creation and rise to power of the ALP antedated its British counterpart by about twenty years, and the British system contains no counterparts of the Country Party and the Democratic Labor Party.

All Australian parties of significance are oligarchies. Their mass membership is small, and has very little influence on policy. This fact probably contributes to the detachment and mildness of interest on the part of the Australian voter.[31] The Liberal and Country Parties are coalitions of urban and rural capital, with an electoral base in the urban middle class and the general country population. The ALP has its electoral base in the urban working class, and its state and federal conferences are heavily dominated by the representatives of its affiliated trade unions.[32] Australian politics is the politics of class and interest group, well understood to be so by the public. The interest group struggle is carried on continuously through strikes and collective bargaining between unions and employers, within a framework of arbitration tribunals and 'conciliation' commissions. But neither party, nor a coalition of parties, can hope to govern without obtaining voters from the 'other side of the class fence', and this fact is widely supposed to account for a convergence in their domestic policies. Labor no longer proposes nationalization, but instead concentrates on proposals for new or revived public corporations, or redistributive proposals which would, on balance, favour the working class, and improved public facilities, by, for example, greatly in-

---

third ed. (London, 1961).

[28] J. D. B. Miller, *Australian Government and Politics: An Introductory Survey*, second ed. (London, 1959).

[29] J. Jupp, *Australian Party Politics* (Melbourne, 1964).

[30] L. Overacker, *The Australian Party System* (London, 1952).

[31] See A. F. Davies and S. Encel, *Australian Society*, pp. 110–13.

[32] However, in 1968, there was an infusion of parliamentary leaders into the ALP federal conference.

creased grants to the states for their education systems. The Liberal and Country Parties' habit is to propose more modest increases in public spending, limited income redistribution, and to emphasize the American alliance and the British connection. Although the ALP stands neither for a republic nor for any change in Australia's system of alliances with the USA, its refusal to support the sending of troops to combat the insurgency in Malaya, in 1955, or to Vietnam in 1965, was taken up by the government of the day as symbols of a weak defence policy.

From 1960 until 1967, the ALP was led by Mr Arthur Calwell, who although clearly devoted to social justice, seemed indifferent to middle-class support and suspicious of intellectuals. From 1949, the Prime Minister was Sir Robert Menzies, the darling of suburban middle-class matrons, an orator of the grand style, devoted to both the Imperial connection and the American alliance. He resigned in January 1966, and his place was taken by Mr Harold Holt, an amiable team leader, well regarded but scarcely 'the man Mr Menzies was'. (The title is almost always overlooked in common conversation: 'Mr' Menzies is a title with a dignity all its own.)

The 1963 elections were dominated by issues of domestic policy, with the parties taking well-defined stands of the kinds outlined above. They were won handsomely by the Liberal–Country Party coalition. The Australia-wide results are set out in Table 2.1.

TABLE 2.1   *1963 House of Representatives elections*[33]

	Lib. Party	Country Party	ALP	DLP	Other	Total
Votes	37·1%	8·9%	45·5%	7·4%	1·1%	100%
Seats	52	20	52	0	0	124

The electoral system for the House is based on single-member constituencies and preferential voting. If no candidate has a majority of votes on the first count, the second preference votes of the least successful, at the full value of one vote, are successively allotted until a majority for one candidate is attained. It can be seen that the second preferences of the Democratic Labor Party (hereafter, DLP), of

[33] C. A. Hughes and B. D. Graham, *A Handbook of Australian Government and Politics, 1890–1964* (Canberra, 1968), p. 416.

which 80 to 90 per cent[34] went to the government parties, were important in this outcome. Had they gone the other way, the ALP might well have won.

In 1966, the elections were, at the level of public debate, very much concerned with issues in external policy, particularly Australia's commitment of troops to the war in Vietnam and conscription of a proportion of twenty-year-olds for service in that war. There was some conflict over economic issues, but they assumed much less public prominence than in 1963. The issue of the American alliance was dramatized by a pre-election visit to Australia by the President of the USA, Mr Lyndon Johnson, from 20 October to 22 October, during which he was lionized by the public. At both elections, the DLP was a vociferous proponent of a 'strong' defence policy posture, with an ideological pace in its rhetoric matched only by the miniscule Communist Party, alleging Communist influence in the ALP, particularly in Victoria. There was some substance in this latter claim, but not a great deal.[35] The government parties inflicted a crushing defeat on the ALP (see Table 2.2), which was probably partly a result of growing public impatience with Mr Calwell's leadership.

TABLE 2.2   *1966 House of Representatives elections*[36]

	Lib. Party	Country Party	ALP	DLP	Other	Total
Votes	40·1%	9·9%	40·0%	7·3%	2·7%	100%
Seats	61	21	41	0	1	124

The government parties would have won the 1966 elections even if the DLP had amalgamated with the ALP, but the DLP's support was clearly vital to the Liberal and Country Parties when their electoral stocks were low, as they were in 1961, and were again to be in 1969.[37]

[34] C. A. Hughes, 'Political Review', *Australian Quarterly*, 36 (1964), no. 1, p. 103.

[35] For a more extended discussion of the Byzantine situation in Victorian Labor politics, see A. Hughes, 'Political Review', *Australian Quarterly*, 41 (1969), no. 2, pp. 103–6.

[36] D. Aitkin, 'Political Review', *Australian Quarterly*, 39 (1967), no. 1, p. 87.

[37] For a discussion of the 1969 elections, see A. Hughes, 'Political Review', and B. A. Santamaria, 'Struggle on Two Fronts: the DLP and the 1969 Election', *Australian Quarterly*, 41 (1969), no. 4, pp. 15–24 and pp. 33–42.

A note on the genesis of this unusual party and the general balance of electoral power may here be useful.

2.6. The Labor split of 1955 and the balance of electoral power

From the early 1940s until 1954, a lay Catholic movement led by Mr B. A. Santamaria[38] worked within Australian trade unions to combat Communist influence. The 'Catholic Social Movement', as it was called, was a semi-clandestine affair, for fear of raising Protestant hackles, but operated with non-'Movement' allies in 'Groups' officially endorsed by the ALP. After gaining control, with their allies, of a number of key unions in Victoria and New South Wales in the late 1940s and early 1950s, the 'Groupers' found themselves, willy-nilly, in a position of power within the ALP. At the height of its influence, there were actually some *eighty* members *of the 'Movement' itself*[39] as delegates at the Victorian state conference of the ALP, the total number of delegates being about 350. This was a cohesive body large enough, with its allies, to command control of the party in that state. However limited its aims may have been, its militancy alarmed many ALP members, particularly as it seemed to be behaving as a party within a party. Late in 1954, the then federal leader of the ALP, Dr H. V. Evatt, possibly fearing that the 'Movement' was seeking to replace him, organized intervention in the affairs of the Victorian branch of the ALP by the party's federal bodies, which culminated in the departure of the 'Groupers' (the 'Movement' and their allies) from the ALP in 1955 to form a body first known as the 'ALP (Anti-Communist)' and later the 'Democratic Labor Party'.[40] The DLP and the 'Movement', now renamed the

[38] For a brief history of the 'Movement' see B. A. Santamaria, '"The Movement": 1941–60 – an Outline' in H. Mayer (ed.), *Catholics and the Free Society: An Australian Symposium* (Melbourne, 1961), pp. 54–103.

[39] Interview by the writer with Mr B. A. Santamaria, 2 November 1956.

[40] A somewhat unsatisfactory account of the history of the 'Movement' and the split in the ALP has been given by T. Truman, *Catholic Action and Politics* (Melbourne, 1959). The title is misleading, since the 'Movement' was never officially 'Catholic Action', i.e. a lay body whose policy is directed by the bishops, who bear responsibility for its actions. The 'Movement' was in the category *'action of Catholics'*, i.e. a lay body whose policy was directed by its lay leaders, who bear the entire responsibility for it, although it received *personal* support from influential members of the Catholic hierarchy in Victoria. Other Catholics could, and did, oppose it. A more reliable account of the Labor 'split' is contained in R. A. Murray, *The Split: Australian Labor in the Fifties* (Melbourne, 1971).

23

'National Civic Council', have been in implacable opposition to the ALP ever since. This is a central fact of Australian politics, since it was the DLP voters' second preference votes which sustained the Liberal and Country Party federal government in every crisis, and prevented ALP victories. In electoral terms, it seems that about half the Victorian Catholic community voted for it. It had little Protestant support. To put the point baldly, these events had the effect of detaching a large part of the Irish working class and *petit bourgeois* vote from the ALP, a section of its electoral base which had previously been amongst its most loyal supporters. Since the basic position of the DLP has been to allege a Communist threat to the country from without and within, and to concentrate on external politics, the result of this fragmentation of the Labor social infrastructure was to shift the balance of electoral power in favour of the conservative parties, which are more in harmony with the DLP in external affairs. This new electoral equilibrium thus had the paradoxical effect of settling domestic economic policy questions on quite other grounds, i.e. defence policy. Nobody can understand the course of Australian politics without knowing this. However, although it is a fact of crucial importance, it can almost escape notice in a mass survey of the electorate, such as that described here. It has therefore been imperative to describe this contextual feature of Australian politics separately.

Even had the ALP not suffered this critical loss of support, it would probably have seen its electoral strength ebbing during this period. There was a long-term sociological drift against the ALP, brought about by the expansion of the middle class and the contraction of the working class. This is a reflection partly of the changing structure of the work force,[41] in particular the growth of its professional and higher clerical components, and partly of the rising tide of affluence, which has encouraged middle class identification amongst higher income manual workers. The *embourgeoisement* of the Australian urban electorate, manifest in the occupationally mixed streets of the prosperous outer suburbs, gave an old-fashioned ring to working-class politics and a contemporary air to being middle class in life-style and outlook. The ALP, especially when led by Mr Calwell, could not easily keep pace with this changing situation. Its

[41] See *Trends*, 6 (1964), no. 3, where the occupational census data for 1947 and 1961 are compared.

24

corporate image, built around conferences chiefly of semi-skilled and unskilled manual workers, was simply all wrong. Its policy position on domestic affairs was more in harmony with the electorate's mood (as both the APOP surveys and that reported here confirm) but the advantage was, at this time, difficult to exploit, mainly because of the unpopularity of its 'Left' position on foreign policy. There was an overwhelmingly strong conviction that Communism in Asia was a danger to this country, and issues where the government's policy was clearly unpopular (for example, in its decision to send conscripts to Vietnam) were encapsulated in the larger defence issue, on which the ALP was not trusted by the electorate. The ALP's electoral position was partly retrieved in 1969 by its new-look leader, Mr G. Whitlam, but in the period to which we are addressed, its support was comparatively low. The formation of an ALP federal government in 1972 was never widely anticipated.

Of all the disparate political sentiments most surely identified in this book, in Chapter 6, the left–right continuum in foreign policy is the one most free of sociological and psychological correlates, and the most susceptible to influence by political leaders, who must sometimes act in ways dictated by external events. It is, therefore, the one most liable to future flux, not having its roots in any secure sociological or psychological ground. The implications of the changing nature of Australia's international position will be noted in this political introduction; but it might be as well, before doing so, to return to Australia's nature as an immigrant polity.

2.7. Australia as an immigrant polity

Most Australians, and their fathers, are not immigrants, but the polity was in its first style a colonial one, with institutions transplanted from the United Kingdom. The period after the Second World War saw a flood of immigration from Southern Europe, as well as the traditional British source, a phenomenon which at first nearly raised the hair on the heads of British Australians. (All Australians are, by law, still both 'Australian citizens' and 'British subjects'.) After the first shock-wave of immigration from the Continent, Australians came to accept their new multiplicity. As Table 2.3 suggests, they were much less resistant to migration of Jewish people, Greeks, Italians or Negroes (but not Chinese) in 1964 than in 1948.

TABLE 2.3   *Opposition to immigrants of four race or nation groups,
1948 and 1964*[42]

	1948	1964
Negroes	77%	47%
Jews	58%	17%
Greeks	32%	18%
Italians	45%	23%
Chinese	24%	33%

The percentages refer to the proportion of all respondents expressing antipathy.

In the case of Jews, Italians and Greeks, the pattern has been one of integration rather than assimilation. That is to say: these three groups have formed communities with marked internal links, and also connections with the host society; each group therefore retains a special character which has not been dissolved. In the case of Italians and Greeks, this has been as much the result of happenstance as of deliberate policy, these migrants having settled mainly in the inner-city areas, giving them a changed and distinctive atmosphere.

In many Australians, of British, Irish and European stock alike, there is often faintly discernible in their outlooks a nostalgia for their countries of origin. The Anglican Church is still, officially, 'The Church of England in Australia'. A Kiplingesque 'public school' tradition persists. 'Land of Hope and Glory' is still sung occasionally at school concerts. Irish folk songs are played to small drinking groups of Irish descent. Illustrated maps of Italy adorn the walls of 'espresso' cafés. Australians bring to each other, sometimes with great feeling, the images of their homelands far away. The dominant British tradition is overtly passionate only on rare occasions. When Sir Winston Churchill died, in 1965, an enormous fund was raised for fellowships in his memory. A memorial service to him was held in St Paul's Anglican Cathedral, in Melbourne, at which the Lieutenant Governor, Sir Edmund Herring, delivered the oration. When he quoted the famous speech of determination to fight on, and came to the sombre passage contemplating defeat, the struggle to be carried on by 'our Empire beyond the seas', his voice broke with emotion.[43]

[42] The 1948 sample is a Melbourne one (*n*=370) reported in O. A. Oeser and S. B. Hammond (eds.), *Social Structure and Personality in a City* (London, 1954), p. 55. The 1964 sample is Australia-wide (*n*=474), reported in A. Huck, *The Chinese in Australia* (Melbourne, 1967), p. 93. The characteristics of the sample, which appears adequately representative, are discussed on pp. 98–100 of his book.

[43] Observation of the writer.

It was no wonder, when the British decision to withdraw troops East of Suez was announced, that many Australians, particularly the older generation, felt strangely bereft.

2.8. External events

The war in Vietnam was the first in which Australia participated without Britain as an ally. The American orientation presented new problems. Australia is a much smaller nation in relation to the USA than it is to Britain. Moreover, Australians were not sure of how they were viewed by this mighty power: whether or not the great flood of affect disgorged upon President Johnson in 1966 was to be requited. If the USA were to retreat into isolationism, as the British were withdrawing from the Indian Ocean, what would become of us? Within the British Empire, in which Australians had felt themselves first-class citizens, there was an intrinsic 'overseas' commitment. The reality of the disintegration of the Imperial system in the 1950s was partly concealed from Australians by continuing British military activity in South-east Asia, first in suppressing the Communist insurgency in the Malay peninsula, and then in the defence of Malaysia during 'confrontation' by Indonesia. Both of Australia's 'great and powerful friends' (as Sir Robert Menzies liked to call them) were still seen to be active in the region. When Sir Robert Menzies retired, the Imperial mantle seemed to vanish with him. An active debate arose about the Australian–British relation in 1967. In April, the *Bulletin*, a weekly which had been a strident advocate of the new American orientation, spread over its cover: 'Britain: The End of the Affair?'[44] When, on 18 July, Britain announced withdrawal of its forces East of Suez by the mid 1970s, there was a nation-wide sigh of regret. The *Sydney Morning Herald* ran three editorials on the subject in one week. On 20 July it said: 'Britain perhaps has been no bad guide for us in the past, but we must find our own sign posts for the future.' On 22 July, in an editorial headed 'Twilight of an Empire', it spelt out the general mood: 'To anyone with the slightest sense of history, this week has been of profound and moving significance. For the announcement that Britain will withdraw her troops East of Suez by 1975 means the formal end of the British Empire.'

There can be no doubt, however, that many of the close associations between Britain and Australia will continue. The mixture of amusement and affectionate fascination with which Australians

[44] *Bulletin*, 8 April 1967.

regard their monarchy was admirably captured by a columnist[45] in the Melbourne *Herald*, 10 July 1967:

> Imperial Grandeur east of Suez has now rubbed thin. Back in London, the splendid fairytale continues in the sonorous unchanging language of the Court Circular. Listen–
> The Queen this evening visited the new Jewel House and the Chapel Royal of St Peter Ad Vincula at the Tower of London. Her Majesty was received upon arrival by the Constable (Field Marshal Sir Gerald Templer) who presented to the Queen the Keys of the Tower, which Her Majesty was graciously pleased to return. . . .

The point of this short account of Australia's inheritance and its international position, which was, in 1966, somewhat uncertain, and later, in the light of American withdrawal from Vietnam, increasingly so, is threefold. Firstly, if this multiplicity of national inheritances is to continue to exist with internal harmony, then the psychological grounds of harmony and disharmony have to be understood. This work, which is in large part an analysis of the antecedents of disharmony, of ethnocentrism, is directed towards that end, as part of its more general purposes. Secondly, it bears upon the nature of the Australian outlook, and on Australians' conception of themselves and others, in the new and strange external situation which was emerging when the attitude survey reported here was carried out. The attitudes have therefore to be understood in this context.

Thirdly, this introductory sketch of the Australian political scene is meant to provide the reader with some contextual understanding of the structure of dispositions and attitudes to be explored. No work on psychology and political attitudes can *omit* 'politics'.

But the empirical findings in the Australian situation are by no means intended to be of use only in understanding Australia. The central purpose of the investigation is to use the Australian urban sample as a vantage point for the scrutiny of questions general to advanced industrial societies. To many, it will be superfluous, but it has been offered in the conviction that the stuff of politics is in only some aspects related to psychological disposition, and that no study of political attitudes can be complete without some account, however brief, of the environment in which they are held.

---

[45] Geoffrey Tebbutt.

3 Authoritarian orientation and alienation: some previous research

3.1. A general point

The purpose of the research reported in this book is to test the hypothesis that some psychological factors, such as authoritarian personality orientation, may be important in influencing political attitudes and decision-making.

This suggestion obviously could not apply equally to all kinds of political decisions. In the case of domestic economic policy, for example, the movements of the political actors may be chiefly related to the kinds of class or group pressures to which they are subject; there may be no need at all to refer to the peculiarities of individual functioning in explaining the political process. However, special studies of the attitudes of groups and individuals may have particular point in explaining decisions on issues of foreign policy, and such domestic matters as capital punishment or migrant assimilation, because attitudes on these questions cannot readily be related to clearly defined interests. In these areas, an approach that seeks to interpret political events in terms of antecedent social and economic conditions, or institutional conflicts, cannot be expected to provide the answers.

This argument is in part accessible to empirical verification. If it can be shown that voters' attitudes on these kinds of issues are liable to be influenced by psychological factors, then it becomes plausible to maintain that dispositions among politicians are also likely to be affected by them, either directly or through sensitivity to the climate of opinion in the electorate.

The rationale of the measurement of dispositions is considered more fully at the beginning of Chapter 4. The purpose of this chapter is threefold: firstly, to review selectively the respective roles of authoritarian personality tendency, on the one hand, and alienation, on the other, in relation to ethnic prejudice (hereafter, ethnocentrism); secondly, to evaluate the scales used in their measurement; and thirdly, to chart links which have been disclosed by empirical research between all three and political opinions.

3.2. Authoritarian personality tendency

The concept of the authoritarian personality was evolved by a group of American and German psychologists and sociologists on the basis of empirical research amongst samples of highly prejudiced subjects in the USA after the last war.[1] Their research was related to earlier work by Fromm,[2] and parallel findings by Dicks in a sample of German prisoners of war were simultaneously reported in 1950.[3] The term 'authoritarian' is here used in a technical sense. It relates to a personality pattern, or syndrome, widely diffused in Western societies, which combines a number of interrelated characteristics commonly regarded as unpleasant by liberal intellectuals: the authoritarian type is aggressive, inflexible, submissive to in-group authorities and generally punitive. These personality characteristics have been shown to be systematically related to each other and frequently to have their roots in emotional relationships experienced in infancy, as well as in later institutional or class conditioning. The psychodynamic basis of the syndrome is hypothesized to lie in conflicts between strong, thrusting instinctual impulses towards aggression and destructiveness, and a rigid set of moral norms perceived as binding by the authoritarian personality but as external to the self. The conflicts are controlled by the relatively weak 'ego' only by resort to a number of unconscious defence mechanisms, notably 'projectivity' (the tendency to impute one's own repressed desires to others), 'anti-intraception' (rejection of the subjective, the imaginative and the tender-minded) and stereotypical thinking. These in turn facilitate the more conscious defence 'stratagem' of ethnocentrism, which may be loosely described as irrational hostility to, or intolerance of, out-groups, combined with exaggerated glorification of the in-group.[4] The syndrome is dubbed 'authoritarian' because it predisposes the individual to recruitment to an authoritarian movement of the 'right'; but as Shils and others have

[1] T. W. Adorno *et al.*, *The Authoritarian Personality*.

[2] E. Fromm, *The Fear of Freedom* (London, 1942).

[3] H. Dicks, 'Personality Traits and National Socialist Ideology', *Human Relations*, 3 (1950), pp. 111–54.

[4] A more precise definition and discussion of 'ethnocentrism' is to be found in Chapter 4. The discussion of 'alienation' in this chapter is also necessarily somewhat cursory, and the nature of this disposition, conceived as social estrangement, is also discussed in more detail in that chapter, as well as Chapter 5.

pointed out,[5] similar psychological characteristics are concentrated also on the extreme 'left'.

Numerous dispositional scale surveys have lent support to the findings of the original researchers that authoritarian personality characteristics are linked with hostility to minority groups.[6] However, much empirical work done with the standard device for measuring authoritarian orientation, the California F scale,[7] has been shown to be of dubious value because of an important method-ological weakness in scale construction. The F scale is *all-positive* in form, that is, every 'item', or statement, with which the interviewee is asked to agree or disagree, is phrased in such a way that the 'auth-oritarian' response is in every case agreement. It is therefore possible to score highly merely by virtue of having a generalized tendency to agree with questionnaire items. The importance of this deficiency was clarified in a study by Chapman and Bock,[8] who analysed eight studies which had employed both positive and 'reversed' F scales (ones where *disagreement* with the items registered authoritarianism) and concluded that, on the positive scale, for college populations in the USA, 'content variance' (reflecting authoritarianism) probably accounts for only 30 to 40 per cent of the total variance, the remain-ing reliable variance (the upper and lower limits of which were fixed at 70 and 85 per cent) being divided between agreement tendency and the interaction between agreement tendency and content variance, in proportions which varied markedly from sample to sample. In short, agreement tendency was, apparently, often nearly as important as authoritarian orientation in determining scale scores.[9]

---

[5] E. A. Shils, 'Authoritarianism: "Right and Left"', in R. Christie and M. Jahoda (eds.), *Studies in the Scope and Method of 'The Authoritarian Personality'* (Glencoe, 1954).

[6] Cf., for example, E. Campbell and B. McCandless, 'Ethnocentrism, Xenophobia, and Personality', *Human Relations*, 4 (1951) pp. 185–92; A. W. Siegman, 'A Cross-Cultural Investigation of the Relationship between Ethnic Prejudice, Authoritarian Ideology, and Personality', *Journal of Abnormal and Social Psychology*, 63 (1961), pp. 654–5; and studies reported in R. Christie and P. Cook, 'A Guide to Published Litera-ture relating to "The Authoritarian Personality" through 1956', *Journal of Psycho-logy*, 45 (1958), pp. 171–99.

[7] T. W. Adorno *et al.*, *op. cit.*, pp. 255–7.

[8] L. J. Chapman and R. D. Bock, 'Components of Variance due to Acquiescence and Content in the F Scale Measure of Authoritarianism', *Psychological Bulletin*, 55 (1958), pp. 328–33.

[9] This brief discussion of the problem of infection of scores by acquiescence is also

It follows that where researchers have reported significant correlations between two all-positive scales, purporting to measure, for example, authoritarianism and ethnocentrism, these may be interpreted in some cases as meaning simply that two imperfect measures of agreement tendency will correlate with each other, which is not very remarkable.

An earlier study by the present writer (described below) attempted to avoid this difficulty by using 'balanced' scales, i.e. ones where half the items are positive, and the other half reversed. On this type of scale, respondents with very high agreement or disagreement tendency will have their scores driven towards the distribution mean, but this kind of contamination of the variance should not seriously distort correlations between the scales.

3.3. Authoritarianism and political opinion

There has been remarkably little research on the relation between authoritarian orientation and political opinion. Eysenck[10] has provided some evidence on its relationship to opinion on capital punishment and harshly punitive treatment of sex offenders, as did the original American researchers; but his T measure is of dubious validity. Lipset[11] has suggested that the apparent tendency of working-class samples to score higher than middle-class samples on measures of authoritarianism should lead us to shift our gaze from the lower middle class when on the look-out for threats to the democratic order or libertarian values. Sanford[12] has reported a finding that in a large ($n=963$) Philadelphia adult sample, high F scale scorers were disproportionately reluctant to engage in political activity. In the USA, authoritarianism has been found not to be related to party choice by Campbell, Converse, Miller and Stokes.[13]

A brief review of the generally thin and inconclusive findings of the research into the relations between authoritarianism and political at-

---

intended as a *mis-en-scène*. The controversy surrounding the subject is considered *in extenso* in Chapter 4 and Appendix E.

[10] H. J. Eysenck, *The Psychology of Politics*, ch. 4.

[11] S. M. Lipset, 'Democracy and Working-class Authoritarianism', *American Sociological Review*, 24 (1959), pp. 482–501; and S. M. Lipset, *Political Man: The Social Bases of Politics* (London, 1960), ch. 4.

[12] F. H. Sanford, *Authoritarianism and Leadership* (Philadelphia, 1950), p. 168.

[13] A. Campbell, P. E. Converse, W. E. Miller and D. E. Stokes, *The American Voter* (New York, 1960), ch. 8.

titudes has been provided by Kirscht and Dillehay.[14] Their book provides a comprehensive, although not very critical, review of the more general literature on authoritarianism.

3.4. Authoritarianism, anomia and ethnocentrism

An early work with an F measure in Australia has been a survey of a sample of schoolchildren conducted by Knöpfelmacher and Armstrong.[15] They found that correlations between F and ethnocentrism scales were not invariant with respect to religious denomination. Significant correlations were obtained between F and E scales in Protestant and Jewish schools, but the correlation dropped below the level required for statistical significance in a Catholic school. This finding is not of great importance, since the Catholic sample was quite small ($n=47$), the correlation was in the expected direction although non-significant, and the *difference* between the correlation in the Catholic sample and the averaged correlation for the other groups was not itself statistically significant. On the other hand, the results obtained with a rather different measure of attitudes to outgroups, the Bogardus scale, which measures 'social distance' from out-groups, but not necessarily hostility to them, indicated that the Catholic sample differed significantly from the other groups in that the usual correlation between the F and the Bogardus scales was in the Catholic case uniquely reversed. Thus it seems that institutional influences may in certain circumstances act as a solvent of the usually reliable connection between authoritarianism and prejudice.

However, the study had two methodological flaws. Firstly, the F and E scales employed were all-positive, and therefore contaminated by agreement tendency to an unknown extent; secondly, the Bogardus measure did not refer exclusively to groups distinctly alien to all the sub-samples, but included British and Italians. It is therefore difficult to say how far scores on the Bogardus scale reflected rejection of out-groups. The data of this survey are accordingly ambiguous.

A chain of research initiated by Srole[16] had also suggested a need for caution in predicting from F scale scores to ethnocentrism. In a

[14] J. P. Kirscht and R. C. Dillehay, *Dimensions of Authoritarianism: A Review of Research and Theory* (Lexington, 1967), esp. pp. 57–69.

[15] F. Knöpfelmacher and D. B. Armstrong, 'The Relation between Authoritarianism, Ethnocentrism and Religious Denomination among Australian Adolescents', *American Catholic Sociological Review*, 24 (1963), pp. 99–114

[16] L. Srole, 'Social Integration and Certain Corollaries'.

large ($n=401$) adult sample in Springfield, Massachusetts, a significant first-order correlation between an F scale and a measure of ethnocentrism was substantially reduced when 'anomia' was held constant. This last term was used to refer to a breakdown in the individual's sense of attachment to society, expressed as a feeling of meaninglessness, social isolation, and powerlessness to achieve life goals, a conception approximating to some meanings of 'alienation'. Since the correlation between his anomia scale and ethnocentrism was not much affected when authoritarianism was in turn held constant. Srole concluded that F scale scores do not stand in close relation to ethnocentrism independently of the anomia factor. This suggested that the magnitude of the correlations between F and E measures found in previous research might be accounted for in large part by their common variance with alienation. Srole's work was naturally regarded as menacing to the view that rejection of minority groups was mainly a function of personality structure, which had until then appeared well supported by the empirical evidence. The position was indeed even more confused than it appeared. Srole's F and anomia scales were very short (five items in each) and all-positive. The measure of ethnocentrism was a mixture of scores on an all-positive five-item scale and 'spontaneous comments' elicited by projective-type pictorial stimuli, and therefore subject to some contamination from agreement tendency. The meaning of the pattern of intercorrelations between these three scales is quite obscure. It may be that Srole's study merely showed that the correlation between two oblique indices of agreement tendency will be reduced if a third index of agreement tendency is held constant, a finding difficult to interpret and perhaps scarcely worth the trouble.

The Springfield survey provoked replications by Roberts and Rokeach,[17] and McDill,[18] all achieving distinction by their use of short, all-positive scales for the three variables. Both found their F and anomia measures to be related, and reported moderate and statistically significant residual correlations between the F and anomia measures and ethnocentrism, when anomia and F were respectively held constant. Both also drew highly precarious conclusions as to the relative importance of authoritarian orientation and anomia as

[17] A. Roberts and M. Rokeach, 'Anomie, Authoritarianism and Prejudice: A Replication', *American Journal of Sociology*, 61 (1956), pp. 355–8.

[18] E. L. McDill, 'Anomie, Authoritarianism, Prejudice, and Socio-Economic Status: An Attempt at Clarification', *Social Forces*, 39 (1960–1), pp. 239–45.

determinants of ethnocentrism. Like Srole, they found an independent negative relationship between their measures of anomia and social status.

McDill went so far as to perform a factor analysis of responses to all fifteen positive items in his three scales, together with four other positive F scale items and one reversed item. Not surprisingly, his analysis extracted a common factor, which was almost certainly agreement tendency or something inextricably confounded with it. This he labelled 'a *Weltanschauung* which is negative in nature', representing 'a dim world view'. 'Negative *Weltanschauung*' might appear to be a rather inflated term to use for a generalized tendency to agree with questionnaire items.

A study by Dean[19] found correlations between measures of powerlessness to achieve life-goals, normlessness (defined as a sense of social disintegration and conflict in moral values), and social isolation. He combined the three scales to form an alienation measure, and found a weak but significant negative relation between it and occupational status, and a weak positive relation with advancing age. The sample consisted of 384 adults in Columbus, Ohio.

The nature of all twenty-four items in Dean's scale is not reported, but of the six given in illustration, five are positive. There is therefore no assurance that this study avoided the methodological weakness of those described above.

Empirical research on alienation, authoritarianism and ethnocentrism to this point therefore presented a somewhat occluded picture. Many of the correlations obtained between the various scales may well have been the result of common variance with agreement tendency. Moreover, the higher authoritarianism and alienation scores reported for working-class and elderly respondents might be accounted for in the same way. The social geography of agreement tendency has yet to be mapped with clarity.

An urgent need for the construction of paired-alternative or balanced scales was evident. So, too, was the necessity for specifying more exactly the meaning of whatever concept of alienation was embodied in a particular scale.

In 1963, Neal and Rettig,[20] using a large (n=603) urban sample,

[19] D. G. Dean, 'Alienation: Its Meaning and Measurement', *American Sociological Review*, 26 (1961), pp. 753–8.

[20] A. G. Neal and S. Rettig, 'Dimensions of Alienation among Manual and Non-Manual Workers', *American Sociological Review*, 28 (1963), pp. 599–608.

constructed a paired-alternative measure of 'powerlessness' and balanced measures of 'normlessness', all-positive in the political domain, balanced in the economic. A factor analysis, using varimax rotations, suggested that scores on these three scales were governed by three independent factors. 'Normlessness' was here understood as a judgement, by the respondent, that immorality and fraud were rife. The content of the items was strictly confined to the polity and the macro-society, and did not enter the field of personal relations.

No significant relationship was found between any of these components and Srole's measure of anomia nor with a 'mobility-commitment' scale (which registered a *penchant* for unscrupulous social climbing).

In 1965 McClosky and Schaar[21] presented a nine-item 'anomy' scale of satisfactory reliability, together with data on correlations with personality characteristics for a large but unrepresentative sample. Unhappily, the scale is all-positive, the items somewhat vague in meaning, and the personality tests not adequately described.

This research was sharply attacked by Srole,[22] mainly on the grounds of sampling and interviewing deficiencies. He adverted briefly to the problem of infection of scores by response-set, but proposed no solution other than careful interviewing.

In a preliminary attempt (published in 1967)[23] to sort out the entangled issues of measurement and interrelation, the present writer constructed and administered three six-item scales, each balanced, and hopefully measuring authoritarianism, alienation and ethnocentrism, to a moderately large and representative Australian urban sample ($n=437$).

The three positive items for the scale to measure authoritarianism were abstracted from the original California scale; the reversed items from the various 'reversed' scales mentioned in Chapter 4. The criteria for inclusion were loose: demonstrably higher discriminatory power; less specificity to 'right-wing' authoritarianism, and avoid-

---

[21] H. McClosky and J. H. Schaar, 'Psychological Dimensions of Anomy', *American Sociological Review*, 30 (1965), pp. 14–40.

[22] L. Srole, 'A Comment on "Anomy"', *American Sociological Review*, 30 (1965), pp. 757–62. Gwynn Nettler offers 'A Further Comment on "Anomy"' in the same issue on p. 762; McClosky and Schaar reply on pp. 763–7.

[23] A. Hughes, 'Authoritarian Orientation, Alienation and Political Attitudes in a Sample of Melbourne Voters', *Australian and New Zealand Journal of Sociology*, 3 (1967), pp. 134–50.

ance of sensitive issues, such as prurience and punishment of six offenders, to attempt to maintain untroubled rapport with interviewees. Judging by the low average inter-item correlation, it was a weak instrument.

The alienation scale was constructed independently of others in the literature, and the items were related to Seeman's[24] review of the sentiments held at different times to relate to alienation: powerlessness, a feeling of meaninglessness, self-estrangement, psychic isolation and normlessness (a sense that the larger society was not governed by moral norms). This measure was clearly more cohesive than that for authoritarianism.

Jews, Italians and Japanese were the designated target groups for the ethnocentrism scale. The items were so phrased as to tap only the negative, outward-looking aspect of ethnocentrism. As the scale was not intended to trap precisely *prejudice* (that is, prejudgements involving derogatory and incorrigible mistake), the items did not need to have a demonstrably *delusional* content. The scale is the most cohesive of the three, but since all three are brief, open to some challenge on their construct validity, and the report of their use lacks standardization data, they must be regarded only as a representing a tentative step forward at that time. Nevertheless, since they are balanced and not all-positive, the outcome is worth noting: the F scale was not correlated significantly with the alienation scale but both correlated significantly with ethnocentrism, authoritarianism in a low degree, alienation moderately.

Twelve political issues (their choice deficient chiefly in omitting those relevant to defence) were also administered and cluster-analysed.[25] Three clusters emerged: the first related to opinions on social services and public ownership of industry, and was labelled the '*Established* Radicalism–Conservatism'; the second to opinions on increased education and defence spending, and the introduction of a 'blanket' capital gains tax and economic planning, the '*New* Radicalism–Conservatism'; and third to opinions on increased economic aid to Asia, relaxation of the White Australia policy, and the abolition of capital punishment, '*Conscience* Radicalism–Conservatism'. Surprisingly, the three clusters were almost unrelated to each other.

[24] M. Seeman, 'On the Meaning of Alienation', *American Sociological Review*, 24 (1959), pp. 783–91.

[25] Using the method proposed by B. Fruchter, *Introduction to Factor Analysis* (New York, 1954), pp. 12–17.

Although no significant correlations were obtained between the three 'psychological' variables and the two economic dimensions, both authoritarianism and ethnocentrism exhibited significant and moderate negative relations with 'conscience' radicalism. Since all three issues in this cluster referred to out-groups (Asians and criminals) the theoretical relations can easily be understood.

3.5. The contemporary situation

The cautionary notes pointing up the inadequacies of the scales used in this study must be emphasized, and the gaping chasms that remained open in both conceptualization and measurement are manifest even in recent publications. An impressive stride forward was accomplished by Rotter in 1966[26] in presenting a twenty-three-item paired-alternative scale, which, although focussed on sentiments of powerlessness, extended also to a sense of normlessness in the governing agencies of society and to perceived personal isolation. Its use has been extensive, and a close evaluation seems to be appropriate here. Sixteen of the items refer to sentiments of powerlessness. Its merits are chiefly the form of the items, which preclude contamination by acquiescence, and satisfactory reliability (test–retest) coefficients, ranging from about 0·50-0·85 in a variety of samples, but generally approximating 0·70.

It is demonstrated to correlate negatively and significantly with social desirability set (a tendency to respond in a manner presenting the interviewee in a favourable light) in varying degrees from sample to sample, ranging from trivial to moderate correlations; but this difficulty may, unhappily, be ineluctable in a scale with implications of inadequacy. To turn to its demerits, there are two quibbles; one is that three items refer to students' problems, implying that the respondent is a student, which to a minor, but irritating extent limits its general usefulness; the second is that many items read much like restatements of others (six refer to 'luck'). More serious are the following three considerations:

(i) Because many (thirteen of the twenty-three) items are phrased as general social or political judgements (omitting words such as 'I' or 'you') it is not possible to tell whether the respondent is projecting his own felt difficulties, i.e. expressing a sense of powerlessness personal to himself, or deploring, from a detached viewpoint, a fault in

---

[26] J. B. Rotter, 'Generalized Expectancies for Internal versus External Control of Reinforcement', *Psychological Monographs*, 80 (1966), no. 1, whole no. 609.

the socio-political system.

This renders an individual's score hard to interpret: is the high-scorer a social critic or low in felt efficacy? Latterly, Certcov[27] has raised a belated cry for the differentiation of the two in the literature surrounding alienation. The unavoidable implication is that a useful measurement scale should lean to the more directly personal expression of felt social estrangement, even if some 'projective' items are employed to 'cushion' its inevitably sharp edge – such scales often suggest personal inadequacy.

(ii) Whether or not those items reflecting isolation, a sense of 'normlessness' in the reigning powers of society, or a felt powerlessness constitute disparate clusters within the scale as a whole, or whether or not they interrelate is a question which remains unanswered by Rotter's data. The question is of considerable importance, and many theorists of alienation, e.g. Israel[28] have adverted directly to the question of whether the five sentiments identified by Seeman are empirically related and, perhaps, form a syndrome. Indeed, Seeman himself, in reviewing empirical work in Sweden, France and the USA in 1971,[29] is inclined to the view that it is a mistake to think to conceptualize 'a unitary package of alienations', and stresses particularly the very low correlations found between 'work alienation' and a sense of powerlessness. (It may be as well, parenthetically, to mention here that the present writer rejects Seeman's view on the evidence presented in Chapters 4 and 5, and Appendix C.)

(iii) Finally, one cannot escape a sense that some of Rotter's items are unrealistically phrased. One of them posits the following alternatives:

(a) As far as world affairs are concerned, most of us are victims of forces we cannot understand nor control.

(b) By taking an active part in political and social affairs the people can control world events.

It takes a power of (optimistic?) imagination to embrace the second view.

The Rotter instrument, therefore, despite its utility in some populations and the merit of its paired-alternative format has

[27] D. Certcov, 'Alienacion Social y Enfermedad Mental', *Acta Psiquiatrica y Psicologica de America Latina*, 17 (1971), pp. 401–9.

[28] J. Israel, *Alienation: From Marx to Modern Sociology* (Boston, 1971), pp. 213–5.

[29] M. Seeman, 'The Urban Alienations: Some Dubious Theses from Marx to Marcuse', *Journal of Personality and Social Psychology*, 19 (1971), pp. 135–43.

serious deficiencies.

Lutterman and Middleton, writing in 1970,[30] having re-analysed data from the three scales used by McDill in the article cited above, found no evidence of a common factor (possibly because in their large (n=1018) sample of college and university students, there was more general alertness to item content and little acquiescence response set contaminated scores) and found that, in their sample, authoritarianism was more important than anomia as a cause of ethnocentrism. They raise the all-too-familiar cry for better measures free of response bias. It may well be that, in an intellectually sophisticated sample, alienation (or anomia) is less likely to have an outcome in irrational hostility (of which ethnocentrism is a sub-category) than amongst others. This is strongly suggested by the data presented in Chapter 5. It is difficult to avoid a feeling of impatience in discovering that, more than ten years after McDill's benighted analysis, these social scientists have expended their energies in re-administering three five-item all-positive scales to a large sample. The same effort might have gone into the construction of those 'satisfactory' scales.

Lest the reader close this book in despair, let me announce that satisfaction, hopefully, is at hand. The next chapter presents an attempt to resolve the inadequacies upon which I have dilated here. Moreover, not only Rotter, but also Aberbach[31] have produced more resilient measuring instruments: in Aberbach's case, paired-alternative measures of interpersonal trust, political trust, sense of personal efficacy and a balanced scale of sense of political efficacy. The intercorrelations between these were found to be trivial. Relevance to political behaviour is suggested, in that, in the course of a careful analysis, political trust is shown to have a relation to voting preference in the US presidential elections of 1964, when those who *lacked* political trust showed a marked preference for Senator Goldwater as against the incumbent President Johnson. Curiously, when the sentiment of political powerlessness was combined with political distrust, 'powerlessness' became an active agent and the effect of this combination of attitudes was to make an anti-Goldwater vote more

[30] K. G. Lutterman and R. Middleton, 'Authoritarianism, Anomia and Prejudice', *Social Forces*, 48 (1970), pp. 485–92.

[31] J. D. Aberbach, 'Alienation and Political Behaviour', *American Political Science Review*, 62 (1969), pp. 86–99; to be found reprinted in S. A. Kirkpatrick and L. K. Pettit, *The Social Psychology of Political Life* (Belmont, California, 1972) on pp. 58–71.

probable. Aberbach's analysis is complex and full justice cannot be done to it here: suffice it to say that it is attentive to the changing political role of different varieties of alienation in different groups of persons, and that the instruments used are clearly well constructed.

This is still far from being the rule. Ray and Sutton[32] in a note on student political attitudes in an Australian university, found that a scale measuring 'general' alienation was correlated with Eysenck's neuroticism scale and to political radicalism; whilst a scale measuring alienation from the university was related to political radicalism but not to neuroticism. Unhappily, the alienation scales used are not described nor exemplified.

It cannot be stressed sufficiently that the weight accorded to empirical research with dispositional scales will always rely heavily on the use of valid and reliable instruments. If these are not used, those who prefer intellectual argument based merely on persuasive conjecture will feel entitled (rightly) to scoff at the social scientists' 'hard' data: it will, in reality, be as 'soft' as they suspect.

[32] J. J. Ray and A. J. Sutton, 'Alienation in an Australian University', *Journal of Social Psychology*, 86 (1972), pp. 319–20.

4 Problems and solutions in measuring psychological dispositions

4.1. Introduction

This chapter examines some difficulties in the measurement of dispositions and develops solutions to them.

The major problem brought to light by the preceding illustrative review of research into two major constructs, authoritarianism and alienation, is the infection of scores on positive scales by acquiescent response set. In the case of alienation scales, there is an *a priori* case, confirmed by data presented in this chapter, that they may be troubled by covariation with anxiety.

The consequential difficulties, it is argued here, are the failure to demonstrate a genotypical basis for authoritarianism; the failure to show that alienation and authoritarianism measures relate in each case to a unitary construct which is phenotypically cohesive; the absence of proof that these two constructs are unique and necessary, and not conceptually uneconomical extensions of other constructs, such as anxiety; and the likelihood that the pattern of research into related constructs has been grossly distorted.

The solutions proposed are the construction of forced-choice paired-alternative scales for the measurement of authoritarianism, alienation and ethnocentrism; the validation of the Authoritarianism Scale against its own internal consistency, and, item by item, against the ethnocentrism measure; the use of a conceptual referent for each alienation item, and an examination of the internal consistency of the putative Alienation Scale when the covariance of each set of items with an anxiety measure is removed; that is, to test whether they are bonded together merely by a 'glue' of anxiety. A use is made of factor analysis (described in detail in Appendix C) to examine the empirical discreteness of each construct. The application of each of these solutions is then described.

4.2. Why measure psychological dispositions at all?

We measure psychological dispositions because they influence social action, or promote attitudes which do so. Authoritarianism and alienation, for example, both predict to prejudice, and are important for historical explanation as well as having contemporary relevance. The range of political action they may influence is not known with precision.

Psychological constructs of interest to the social scientist are often, like those above, complex and multi-dimensional. Scales are used to rank people on these attitudinal continua chiefly because they are highly economical, and avoid the necessity of coaxing out information at great length, which may involve time and skills not available to an interviewer. But the business of ranking people efficiently is a complex one. The items of a scale must be valid indicators, and responses to the items must be shown to go together in a meaningful way. Moreover, the same person must be shown to respond in much the same way on different occasions. In practice, there is heavy reliance on the manifest meaningful content of items; but where their primary function is to predict to attitudes and behaviour, they must be shown to do so. Anxiety scales should predict to psychiatrists ratings of anxiety in the patient; scale items purporting to indicate the personality dynamics of the prejudiced should predict to measures of prejudice. This requirement is more difficult to meet for such constructs as alienation: here, various confessed sentiments of alienation should be shown to predict to each other and high scale scores should be expected from 'criterion' groups, such as convicts. For the sake of parsimony, attitudinal constructs should be shown to be unitary, unique and separable. Extraneous response tendencies, such as a systematic tendency to agree with any item proposed by the interviewer, must be rigorously excluded from influence; otherwise they will corrupt research.

The advantages of administering attitude scales to groups rather than persons lie in the discovery of what functions attitudinal constructs perform. Their generality of function is never absolute. Psychology, sociology and political studies are sciences built on tendency statements. They cannot escape some idiographic bias. Attitudinal constructs can vary in structure from group to group and also be various in function. Group studies are therefore necessary both to provide nomothetic information and to define its limitations. They provide the social scientist with a *repertoire* of explanatory mechanisms for behaviour. The identification of processes general within groups is therefore methodologically prior to a closer understanding of social action in a personal way. For example, if young Albert confesses feelings of powerlessness in a depth interview in the course of a study involving a small number of subjects, and so does little Jenny; and if Albert sees this state as a challenge and plunges into action, whilst Jenny ruminates, becomes depressive, and is hard to entice out of her room, then the social enquirer is left with a conundrum. To be sure, he may wish to assert that both courses of action are consequential upon feeling powerlessness. But are both reactions so characteristic as to be found in about equal numbers of cases? Or is one deviant – or are both deviant? Nomothetic data, revealing the generality or otherwise of social processes based on studies of large groups, therefore provide the appropriate stage lighting, so to speak, for the individual case or process.

The purpose of this chapter (along with the more technical Appendix C) is to elucidate problems in the measurement of psychological disposition, especially two major constructs, authoritarianism and alienation, to propose solutions, and to report their application. Three dispositional scales, measuring authoritarianism, alienation and ethnocentrism, are presented for research use. Standardization data can be found in Appendix C.

4.3. The relation between a construct and its measure

The relation between an attitudinal or personality construct and its measure is commonly reciprocal. The entity to be measured may at first be inductively defined by inference from systematic observation; a questionnaire measure is then devised which taps some of its chief characteristics, identified by reference to criterion groups and the measure's own internal consistency; and the measure is then put to empirical use in order to clarify peripheral, and sometimes central features of the construct. Empirical investigation results in a slow accretion of information about the entity to be measured, and sometimes, after the information has been ordered in a systematic fashion, there may be a modification of the measuring instrument. The procedure is a familiar one in the natural sciences. 'Electricity' is a concept which now has a precise meaning in common usage, but one brought to birth by an empirical procedure: 'Abnormal condition of the atoms or molecules of a body usually due to an excess or deficiency of electrons; *various kinds were formerly distinguished by the methods of production.' (Oxford English Dictionary,* italics added.)

However, the process frequently differs in an important respect from its analogue in the natural sciences, where precise measures of at least the *manifestations* of a construct are usually available. In the social sciences, the principal measuring instrument often ostensively defines some of the chief features of the construct under investigation, and not a *manifestation of an effect specific to a given set of experimental conditions.* Researchers are therefore occasionally in the odd position of having to devise a measuring instrument whilst initially not knowing quite what it is they wish to measure. A systematic defect in the measuring instrument may thus not only corrupt research into the correlates of a construct, but also introduce, or reinforce, misconceptions of central features of the construct itself, i.e. of the 'pure' construct as a functional reality. An imperfect measure may, so to speak, abort a concept. The measure of a construct therefore often has a greater epistemological significance in the social sciences than in the natural sciences.

4.4. The corruption of research on the authoritarian personality

In the case of loose and rambling constructs, such as that of the 'authoritarian personality',[1] defects in the measurement scales can be peculiarly destructive. A very extensive literature bears on the defects of instruments used to measure 'right-wing' authoritarian personality orientation, and in particular the contamination of the California F scale[2] by acquiescent response set; but it had not yet arrived at a consensus. The most recent review of the literature on authoritarianism[3] notes the very general concern with contamination by response biases, but concludes only that 'studies to date do not determine the degree to which these biases independently affect F scale scores . . .' Other reviews have come to conclusions strikingly in conflict. Rorer,[4] after an exceptionally comprehensive account of methodological studies of the F scale, remarks that 'it seems safe to conclude that even if these studies are interpreted unequivocally as showing the effects of acquiescence, they show that effect to be small'. On the other hand, Peabody[5] contends that the best evidence

---

[1] T. W. Adorno *et al.*, *The Authoritarian Personality*.

[2] *Ibid.*, pp. 255–7.

[3] J. P. Kirscht and R. C. Dillehay, *Dimensions of Authoritarianism*, p. 13; see also pp. 14–29.

[4] L. G. Rorer, 'The Great Response-Style Myth', *Psychological Bulletin*, 63 (1965), pp. 129–56.

[5] D. Peabody, 'Authoritarianism Scores and Response Bias', *Psychological Bulletin*, 65 (1966), pp. 11–23.

supports the view that response bias is generally a major factor in determining F scale scores, and, in a sweeping attack on the general use of attitudinal scales of this kind, asserts: 'The ignorant and simple-minded have been taken for fanatical true believers and fascists.' Some evaluation of the strength of each position is required as a basis for the assessment of the great body of work on the psychological and political correlates of authoritarianism as determined by the commonly employed measurement scales. If the principal measure has such a major defect, then the authoritarian individual has been persistently mis-identified, and research on the nature and correlates of the construct systematically distorted.

Having assessed the great body of empirical research on aquiescent response set, and, in particular, work like that of Zuckerman and Norton[6] which suggests that agreement tendency is a *necessary* construct, because the same people appear to be influenced by it *over more than one measurement scale*, I have tentatively adopted the view[7] that Rorer's argument is brilliant but mistaken.

The best view seems to be as follows:

(i) That there is a persuasive, but not conclusive case that the all-positive F scale, and several other standard measures of authoritarianism, are extensively contaminated by acquiescent response set.

(ii) That a satisfactory acquiescence-free measure of authoritarianism is not yet available.

(iii) That the circumstance (i) has rendered uncertain many research findings, and in particular the supposed positive relation with anxiety.

The exploration of the relation with anxiety is of central significance to the clarification of the F syndrome. Although the personality organization of the authoritarian individual is only discursively elaborated in the original work, the *dicta* of the authors indicate that

---

[6] M. Zuckerman and J. Norton, 'Response Set and Content Factors in the California F Scale and the Parental Attitude Research Instrument', *Journal of Social Psychology*, 53 (1961), pp. 199–210.

[7] For a compressed review of the literature on the acquiesence controversy, see A. Hughes, 'Problems and Solutions in the Measurement of Psychological Dispositions', in *Australian Unesco Seminar: Mathematics in the Social Sciences in Australia*, *University of Sydney, May 1968* (Canberra, 1972), esp. pp. 467–72. This was an early and very technical forerunner to this chapter; a more extensive review is to be found in A. Hughes, *Psychological Dispositions and Political Attitudes*, unpublished doctoral dissertation, Australian National University (Canberra, 1971), on pp. 181–216.

a high degree of repressed anxiety is central to the hypothesized personality structure of the highly ethnocentric subject, ethnocentrism being the criterion of the authoritarian. Frenkel-Brunswik[8] found empirical confirmation of a relation between ethnocentrism, a weak ego and a rigid, externalized superego in a clinically evaluated group of eighty subjects. Diffuse anxiety is generated by the inadequacy of the ego in coping with the severe internal conflict between a strong, thrusting id and an externalized superego, and repressed by recourse to the defence mechanisms of anti-intraception, stereotypy and projectivity, which displace hostility on to out-groups perceived as threatening.

Whilst it is true that many low F scorers are described as 'worriers', their anxiety is characterized as being more superficial and situation-specific than that of high scorers, amongst whom it is typically 'vague and diffuse'.[9] The deep-seated anxiety of the high scorer, although repressed,[10] is kept in check only by frail mechanisms of defence which distort external reality and are readily broken down. 'The repressed, unsublimated and unmodified tendencies are ready to break through and flood the tenuously maintained social superstructure.'[11] The authoritarian is thus seen as prone to bouts of acute manifest anxiety. For confirmation of this portrait of the central personality dynamics of the high F scorer, evidence of correlation between satisfactory measures of authoritarianism and anxiety is thus desirable.

Commonly, the syndrome is characterized *phenotypically* by reference to its more superficial features, which constitute the subscales of the chief measure: conventionalism; authoritarian submission; authoritarian aggression; anti-intraception; superstition and stereotypy; emphasis on power and 'toughness'; destructiveness and cynicism; projectivity; and exaggerated concern with sex. But a *genotypical* characterization, in terms of its hypothesized central dynamics, which revolve around a theme of latent anxiety, is also to be found both in the original work and in later research.

The maintenance of a genotypical characterization of the authoritarian must rely on the empirical demonstration of a consistent positive relation between the standard measures of authoritarianism

[8] T. W. Adorno *et al.*, *op. cit.*, p. 447.

[9] *Ibid.*, pp. 412–13.

[10] *Ibid.*, p. 485.

[11] *Ibid.*, p. 455.

47

and indices of at least latent and preferably manifest anxiety over a variety of human groups. The scanty evidence on this point fails, since the relevant studies have been conducted with authoritarianism scales contaminated by acquiescent response set, which itself has a demonstrable covariance with anxiety. The covariance is strong enough to generate an apparent positive relation between authoritarianism and anxiety as an artifact of the defect in measurement.

Therefore, defects in the chief measuring instruments require a cautious assessment of research into the central as well as the peripheral features of the authoritarian construct; a 'purified' measure is required; and pending sufficient evidence of a positive relation with anxiety, authoritarianism is best characterized phenotypically, i.e. as an actually manifested construct which can be ostensively defined by its principal manifest features, without implication as to its psychodynamic basis.

4.5. Other measures of authoritarianism: are they satisfactory?

In arriving at an adequate measure, the positive F scale is a dubious criterion instrument, since it is likely to infect the derived scale with acquiescent response set (hereafter ARS) or indicate the personality correlates of ARS. The use of balanced scales, employing the various reversals together with a version of the positive scale, has several disadvantages:

(i) The positive and reversed items will be individually influenced by ARS, and it is unlikely that this will be precisely 'balanced out'. Apart from the hazards of the balancing procedure, there is a systematic reason for this. Variance on the positive scale is influenced by one component, the interaction between set and content, which is unlikely to have a counterpart on the reversed version, because these two elements are there in conflict.

(ii) Respondents with extreme yeasaying or naysaying tendencies will tend to score at the means of the distributions. This might well produce low, but spurious correlations with other balanced measures where the individual items might be susceptible to ARS, e.g. ethnocentrism and alienation scales.

(iii) A single statement, with which the respondent is asked to agree or disagree, is not always a clear guide to the nature of the item continuum on which the respondent has to place himself. Respondents may reject items because of verbal quibbles which have little to do with the statement's main tendency. Some of the reversed F Scale items are puzzling when standing alone, since they are constructed as ripostes to the originals. A forced-choice paired-alternative item is geometrically more complete, since it identifies a continuum by two positions, not one. It thus clarifies the item for the respondent and the response for the analyst.

The most satisfactory measure of authoritarianism so far presented seems to be that of Berkowitz and Wolkon.[12] They paired twenty-five original F scale items with the reversals of Bass[13] and Christie *et al*.[14] in order to constitute two forced-choice F scales, FCB and FCC respectively. The positive F scale was used as a validating criterion.

Whilst these scales have the advantage of preserving a relation to the sophisticated psychodynamic theory underlying the all-positive F scale, some imperfections in the method of constructing these forced-choice instruments are evident. The Bass reversals are merely semantic reversals of the originals, frequently inserting simple negations, and so often leave an anti-authoritarian position something of a mystery for the respondent: whilst the Christie *et al*. reversals were deliberately phrased to impart a probabilistic, guarded and cautious item tone, which has been shown[15] to provoke the yeasayer to his rare disagreements. The two halves of the FCC items may thus attract ARS differentially: those with high ARS may tend to agree more with the positive halves, which are more crisp and exclamatory, and frequently incorporate familiar sayings. There is a strong case for tightly constructed and substantive reversals, which put an exclamatory gloss on probabilistic content, where this seems desirable. A more eclectic approach to the selection of reversed items from available reversed scales, or their construction *ad hoc*, could be justified in these terms.

Berkowitz and Wolkon do not report item characteristics. This seems necessary in order to demonstrate that items representing *all* sub-scales are related to the construct. A forced-choice ethnocen-

[12] N. H. Berkowitz and G. H. Wolkon, 'A Forced-Choice Form of the F Scale – Free of Acquiescent Response Set', *Sociometry*, 27 (1964), pp. 54–65.

[13] B. M. Bass, 'Authoritarianism or Acquiescence?', *Journal of Abnormal and Social Psychology*, 51 (1955), pp. 616–23.

[14] R. Christie, J. Havel and B. Seidenberg, 'Is the F Scale Irreversible?', *Journal of Abnormal and Social Psychology*, 56 (1958), pp. 143–59..

[15] A. Couch and K. Keniston, 'Yeasayers and Naysayers: Agreeing Response Set as a Personality Variable', *Journal of Abnormal and Social Psychology'*, 60 (1960), pp. 151–74.

trism scale would be a more satisfactory criterion measure than the all-positive F scale.

4.6. The requirements of an adequate measure of a dispositional construct

Research into dispositional constructs, especially complex and multidimensional ones which are of use in clarifying types of social interaction, can be extensively corrupted by their measuring instruments if adequate precautions are not taken in building the measure. It is therefore necessary, on occasion, to interrupt the superficial continuity of social research by reconstituting or modifying the original measures, if these prove to be clearly unsatisfactory. The history of research into the authoritarian personality construct suggests that the following precautions are amongst those desirable in building, or rebuilding, measurement scales:

(i) The influence of response sets should be demonstrably negligible

Forced-choice paired-alternative scales have the advantage of escaping contamination by acquiescent response set, if the two halves of each item are generally matched for 'tone'.

If responses are dichotomized, that is, respondents are directed to make a choice between the two halves of each item *without* indicating gradations of agreement, then the score will not be infected by extreme response set. Peabody[16] has demonstrated that dichotomization of response categories does not appreciably affect results on the F scale. The successful construction of forced-choice measures will be facilitated if items attracting an 'undecided' response on a permissive pilot run can be omitted.

It is possible that a positional response set (e.g. a set to choose the first half-item of each pair) may be influential on paired-alternative measures. Berkowitz and Wolkon[17] have foreshadowed a concern with this, but its possible influence has not, as yet, been explored in the literature. The 'ends' of the scale can be purified by random alternation of the item halves, thus forcing those under a strong set to score in the middle range. Respondents who appear to display a strong positional response set can be extracted from the sample.

Contamination of a paired-alternative measure by social desirability set is possible if the construct dictates a stance on each item

[16] D. Peabody, 'Two Components in Bi-Polar Scales: Direction and Extremeness', *Psychological Review*, 69 (1962), pp. 65–73.

[17] N. B. Berkowitz and G. H. Wolkon, *op. cit.*

50

which is markedly socially attractive or unattractive. This is difficult to offset, but can be done by matching half-items for social desirability, i.e. by forcing the respondent to choose between two equally attractive or unattractive half-items. This may demand considerable ingenuity on the part of the test-builder, particularly since the concept of what is socially desirable or undesirable may vary from group to group or person to person.[18]

(ii) Items, and sets of items, should have a coherent hypothetical relation to the structure of the construct

This consideration applies especially if the structure of the construct is merely speculatively defined. The hypothesized relationship should be supported by a detailed empirical item analysis. Criterion measures need not be narrowly conceived: for example, ethnocentrism scales as well as existing measures of authoritarianism may be used in reconstructing an authoritarianism measure. In the case of such constructs as 'alienation', where no universally acceptable criterion groups are available, sets of items should be capable of representing the various dispositions regarded in the theoretical literature as aspects of the generic term.

(iii) The construct to be measured should be shown to have an identity separate from that of other constructs

If this condition is not met, researchers may find that they are needlessly multiplying supposed constructs, and sometimes reifying entities not distinct from ones previously explored.

Two techniques may be useful here. Firstly, the method of partial correlations can be incorporated in an item or sub-scale analysis. For example, in order to show that a scale designed to measure alienation does not cohere merely because its items are all oblique indicators of anxiety, the relationships of each item, or sub-scale, with anxiety should be partialled out in examining their relations with each other and the construct as a whole. Secondly, factor analysis can be employed. Responses to items supposed to represent a disparate construct may be factor-analysed in the company of responses to an assembly of other items representing other related constructs. The factor loadings should turn out to be grouped in such a way as to show that scales, or candidate scales, under examination are measur-

---

[18] See N. Wiggins, 'Individual Viewpoints of Social Desirability', *Psychological Bulletin*, 66 (1966), pp. 68–77.

ing entitles demonstrably distinct from each other. The employment of varimax procedures, stipulating orthogonal (unrelated) factors is a strong test of this.

(iv) The scales should be standardized on variegated, if not representative, samples of normals

The application of scales to moderately large samples of this kind may provide norms against which deviant samples can properly be evaluated.

4.7. Alienation: an uncertain construct

The career of attitudinal research into 'alienation' proclaims other kinds of problems in identifying a construct than those encountered in the exploration of authoritarianism.

One problem is unavoidable: attitudinal research can tell only half the story, since alienation is understood as a situation of the individual, defined by objective social conditions, as well as an array of sentiments arising out of this situation. In the nature of things, a dispositional scale can indicate only whether the respondent feels alienated, not whether he is alienated. A full-scale analysis therefore requires an investigation of the respondent's environments of work, leisure and creative activity, as well as measurement of his sentiments. Researchers into alienation or satisfaction in the work situation have not been inclined to the use of dispositional scales, but have sometimes employed extensive questionnaires to gauge workers' attitudes. These survey instruments are often discursive in character (e.g. Blauner,[19] and Goldthorpe).[20]

The main point at which rigorous attitudinal scales can presently make a contribution to knowledge in the field is in clarifying the degree to which the various subjective sentiments of 'alienation' are empirically associated with each other; that is, in the discovery of whether or not 'alienation', in so far as the term refers to subjective sentiments, is a unitary dispositional construct, or merely a cover term for a variety of unconnected dispositions.

Subjective sentiments, consciously felt in some way by the individual, play a large part in the philosophical literature of alienation, but it is not assumed that he sees them as connected, or that he is

[19]   R. Blauner, *Alienation and Freedom* (Chicago, 1964).

[20]   J. H. Goldthorpe, 'Attitudes and Behaviour of Car Assembly Workers: A Deviant Case and a Theoretical Critique', *British Journal of Sociology*, 17 (1966), pp. 227–44.

aware of his total situation; rather the reverse.

The principal authorities are agreed that a *tenacious sense of estrangement from society* is central to the concept, arising variously from social breakdown, malfunction or disintegration, systematic tyranny in the social system or the individual's blameworthy incompetence. Marx[21] is concerned with the proletarians' experience of powerlessness in a tyrannical and inefficient social system, the separation of the worker from the product of his work by complex divisions of labour, an associated but not identical loss of 'charm' in the work to be done, and the replacement of personal bonds by the cash nexus. Men are seen in various postures of despair and discontent, as the creatures of their own putative creatures. This conception follows that of Feuerbach and Hegel, who characterized man as the captive of tyrannical religious and social ideas which he himself has created and continues to sustain.[22] Durkheim, Merton and Parsons[23] explored the psychological impact of rapid social changes which are held to sweep away the basis of traditional values and to leave individuals with a sense of social deregulation, or 'anomia', strangers in an unstructured universe, which offers both more and less than they do or do not have a right to expect. 'Anomia' is seen as a particular condition central to the wider concept of 'alienation'.

These appraisals of the nature of social changes and the concurrent individual malaise which, it is suggested, will accompany them, thus incorporate predictions about the likely *attitudes* of persons and groups which invite empirical endorsement. It is worth remark that none of the authorities confines his analysis only to attitudes *immediate* to changes in the social system, that is, to mere judgements by the individual as to whether the system is functioning well or badly. They all pursue notions of the psychological consequences of social tyranny or deregulation, and discuss them as of the same *genus* as partial awareness of an actual change in the social system. Earlier writers followed the same habits. Vico,[24] a philosopher of history of the mid-eighteenth century, remarked of the people in those new cities which could acquire no coherent civil order

[21] Cf. L. A. Coser and B. Rosenberg, *Sociological Theory* (New York, 1964), pp. 521–5.

[22] Cf. E. Kamenka, *The Ethical Foundations of Marxism* (London, 1962), p. 60.

[23] L. A. Coser and B. Rosenberg, *op. cit.*, pp. 539–61.

[24] T. G. Bergin and M. H. Fisch, *The New Science of Giambattista Vico* (New York, 1948), p. 381.

53

' . . . in the midst of their greatest festivities, though physically thronging together, they live like wild beasts in a deep solitude of spirit and will, scarcely any two being able to agree since each follows his own pleasure or caprice . . . through obstinate factions and desperate civil wars, they shall turn their cities into forests and the forests into dens and lairs of men'.

Seeman[25] has presented an analysis of the philosophical literature of alienation which is useful as a starting point for the construction of items related to alienated sentiments. He proposes five logically distinguishable usages of the term, each of which he restates, somewhat awkwardly, in the language of learning theory. These are given below, along with a critical appreciation:

(i) Powerlessness

'The expectancy or probability held by the individual that his own behaviour cannot determine the occurrence of the outcomes, or reinforcements, which he seeks.'

Concern with this aspect of alienation is regarded as stemming from Marx's conception of the wage worker as being 'separated' from the means of production, a conception extended by Weber to other individuals in a modern industrial society, who become functionaries rather than creative agents.

Seeman opines that this meaning need have no normative implication, nor, as a definitional matter, an implication that the individual actually feels frustrated. But this latter interpretation seems untenable. Obviously individuals rarely expect their behaviour to encompass *all* that they hope for. This meaning can only escape a description of universal disappointments if it is addressed to the frustration of what can in some way be regarded, by the actor or observer, in the given society, as at least approximate to *legitimate* aspirations.

This aspect of alienation will therefore be construed as a sentiment of the individual that his *legitimate aspirations are being frustrated* by an exploiting class, or just a spooky 'They', some sort of *personal agency*; or to a sentiment of being frustrated by social conditions, perhaps obscurely perceived, i.e. by *impersonal agency*.

(ii) Meaninglessness

'Low expectancy that satisfactory predictions about future outcomes

[25] M. Seeman, 'On the Meaning of Alienation'.

of behaviour can be made.'

The language of learning theory is here itself unclear. Seeman proposes also that 'meaninglessness' can be defined as a situation where 'The individual is unclear as to what he ought to believe – when the individual's minimal standards for clarity in decision making are not met.' Mannheim is cited as the chief commentator on this condition, and it is clear that it comprehends moral as much as intellectual confusion.

(iii) Normlessness

'High expectancy that socially unapproved behaviours are required to achieve given goals.'

The chief commentators cited here are Merton and Goffman; Marx might well have been added. The sentiment is close to that of 'meaninglessness' and indeed can be seen as an outcome of a social condition which engenders feelings of 'powerlessness' and 'meaninglessness'. 'Normlessness' thus represents a hostility to a purely instrumental attitude to means of achieving social goals, which is seen to be widespread but not formally endorsed by the accepted moral code. This formulation of 'normlessness', like Seeman's conception of 'powerlessness', is very broad, and perhaps could be usefully constrained by emphasis on the Marxian view that meaningful human links are under threat from the development of the cash nexus in society, the replacement of *Gemeinschaft* by *Gesellschaft*.

(iv) Isolation

The alienated 'assign low reward value to goals or beliefs that are typically highly valued in the given society'.

Here Seeman suggests that isolation should be confined to hostility or dissent from the reigning values of society as a whole. This follows from his general view that alienation should be seen in relation only to the macro-society, which has certain difficulties. Firstly, it fails to differentiate adequately his conceptions of 'normlessness' and 'isolation'. Secondly, simple folk commonly perceive *an isolation arising out of a lack of common outlook* (the core of this sentiment of alienation) as an aspect of their immediate social environment, and are incapable of making sophisticated judgements about the macro-society; indeed, if subjective alienation is a unitary construct, then a sense of meaninglessness may well prevent this.

This sentiment will therefore be extended to isolation from the smaller social group where this arises out of social distrust or a lack of identification with group norms.

(v) Self-estrangement

Alienation in this aspect is defined by Seeman as 'the degree of dependence of the given behaviour upon anticipated future rewards', meaning that an individual may do things not for their own sake. Fromm is quoted as defining the condition as 'a mode of experience in which the person experiences himself as an alien'. What is implied in this somewhat cryptic term is a sense that the individual cannot develop and display an integrated personality which commands his own respect, and is socially driven to a form of role-playing which he privately despises.

Seeman's categories of meaning for the subjective sense of alienation, as modified in the light of this critique, served as a basis for the construction of scale items for each sentiment.

Empirical research using measures of subjective alienation and anomia has not yet determined whether or not the five sentiments of alienation discussed above are part of a unitary and unique attitudinal construct. There are two main reasons for this.

(i) With a few exceptions they have employed all-positive, or nearly all-positive scales and sub-scales, which might be expected to exhibit a spurious unity because of covariance with ARS.

The empirical research of Neal and Rettig[26] has been discussed in Chapter 3. Whilst their measures are an advance on many others, they are not capable of yielding satisfactory findings.

In a later discussion[27] of their processing of these data and subsequent empirical work, they appear to reach an ambivalent conclusion: the use of different factorial techniques may issue in different outcomes, namely empirically ordered views of 'alienation' as either a multi-dimensional *or* a unitary construct. They aver, however, that these different outcomes are not as mutually exclusive as they appear at first blush: to put the pith of their argument, a building is made of many components. How 'unitary' the building is, or may appear, is left an open question. Their difficulty lies fundamentally in the fact that their items and scales swing too wildly from

[26] A. G. Neal and S. Rettig, 'Dimensions of Alienation amongst Manual and Non-Manual Workers', *American Sociological Review*, 28 (1963), pp. 599–608.

[27] A. G. Neal and S. Rettig, 'On the Multidimensionality of Alienation', *American Sociological Review*, 32 (1967), pp. 54–64.

the respondent as a pessimist *for himself* (a 'retreatist') to the respondent as a dispassionate *critic* of social and political structures (an 'activist'), precisely the ambiguity (or confusion) which has been pointed up by Certcov.[28]

This objection cannot be sustained when raised against the scales designed to measure interpersonal and political trust, and personal and political efficacy designed by Aberbach,[29] and accordingly his report that their inter-correlations are trivial in a large and (impliedly but not specifically) US nationwide sample ($n=1006$) is disturbing to the view of alienation as a unitary construct. However, since the statistical characteristics of both his items and scales are not presented, nor even the type of correlation between the scales precisely specified, one cannot draw firm conclusions about the cohesiveness of alienation from his data. Some types of correlation coefficients have surprisingly low maxima when used with short scales.

A lack of essential detail in Seeman's later work discussed above[30] (the 'industrial alienation' measures are not described) makes his central thesis (the divorce of the sentiments of the alienated worker from those of felt powerlessness) likewise impossible to evaluate.

The construction of paired-alternative items for the five sentiments, and an examination of their interrelations, is thus indicated for the clarification of the nature of the concept.

(ii) Most of the sentiments of alienation are related to anxiety (see below, Table 4.1). It is thus possible for responses to alienation items to covary with each other for this reason alone. Furthermore, this makes questionable the conception of alienation as a disparate construct, since it could be objected that it may better be regarded as a social modality of anxiety.

The solution to this problem lies in the examination of the relation between measures of alienated sentiments when their covariance with anxiety is removed. This can be done by the method of partial correlations. If the residual correlations between the sub-scales are statistically significant and non-trivial, then the construct can be said to be unitary. Another useful general exercise is the factor analysis of a large number of items designed to measure authoritarianism, alienation, anxiety and ethnocentrism, specifying orthogonal (indepen-

[28] D. Certcov, 'Alienacion Social y Enfermedad Mental'.

[29] J. D. Aberbach, 'Alienation and Political Behaviour'.

[30] M. Seeman, 'The Urban Alienations: Some Dubious Theses from Marx to Marcuse'.

dent) relations, to see whether the factor loadings of the items suggest that these constructs are, in fact, empirically disparate. This can be found in Appendix C.

4.8. Ethnocentrism in the Australian context

Scales constructed overseas for the measurement of ethnocentrism often require extensive adaptation for Australian use, and it seemed better to begin at the beginning. The 'target' minority groups selected were Greeks, Italians and Jews. Japanese were also included, but failed to attract sufficient hostility. Paired-alternative items were invented to relate to social distance from, and intolerance and derogatory misconception of each target group. Only the last of these sentiments is strictly 'prejudice'.

English and English[31] define ethnocentrism, in its stricter sense, as 'a hypothesized syndrome of underlying attitudes that involve the following: division of the social world into in-groups with which one identifies and to which one submits and out-groups to which one is hostile; positive stereotypy of the former and negative stereotypy of the latter; and the arrangement of the in-groups and out-groups into an evaluative hierarchy in which the former are always dominant and the latter always subordinate'. It should be noted that such a syndrome can only be *inferred* from the scale score, since the scale does not range over *all* the attitudes spelt out in the above definition; for example, positive stereotypy of the in-group was not included. The intent was to focus the scale content on hostility to, and negative stereotypy of named out-groups.

Not all unfavourable conceptions of identifiable minority groups are untrue. An attempt was made, in constructing item halves which reflected derogatory misconception (stemming, hypothetically, from negative stereotypy) to offer statements with a certain currency, but which were, as far as possible, demonstrably false. These items require some detailed discussion (to be found in Appendix C, Section 4). A general reference should be made to the works by Medding[32] and Price[33], for portraits of the Southern European and Jewish com-

---

[31] H. B. English and A. C. English, *A Comprehensive Dictionary of Psychological and Psychoanalytical Terms* (New York, 1958), p. 189.

[32] P. Y. Medding, *From Assimilation to Group Survival* (Melbourne, 1968).

[33] C. A. Price, *Jewish Settlers in Australia* (Canberra, 1964) and C. A. Price, *Southern Europeans in Australia* (Melbourne, 1963).

munities. Jupp[34] has a good general discussion of the position of migrants in Australia.

The Alienation, Authoritarianism, and Ethnocentrism Scales are to be found below (as Exhibits 4.1, 4.2 and 4.3). These are the definitive outcome of the general analysis made heretofore and the method described in Appendix C. The standardization data, also in Appendix C, makes it possible (*inter alia*) for the self-curious reader to determine whether or not he or she scores high or low in relation to the 1966 Australian urban sample. A note on the method of scoring precedes them.

4.9. Anxiety

Here the measure used was a modification of the forty-item balanced Anxiety Scale constructed by Cattell.[35] Twenty items were extracted from it under the constraint of preserving the contribution made by each of the sub-scales to the original measure. Cattell's scale has the attractions of good criterion group validation, diversity of item content and the relatively 'covert' character of the items themselves: the sentiment that is being measured is not overly clear to the respondent. As the scale is available only to members of a recognized association of psychologists the items cannot be published in this book but standardization data for the modified scale as they emerged in this study are displayed in Table C.10. In a general measure of this kind, the anxiety tapped is diffuse and non-specific: it is the general level of anxiety in the personality structure which is chiefly responsible for governing scores. (Of course, an anxiety-provoking episode or circumstances conducive to calm will also have an influence over the subject's responses.)

4.10. A note on administration of the scales

The best form of administration is face-to-face, with the interviewee (if literate) holding cards on which the items appear in sequence. The interviewer should read each pair of statements in turn, from a questionnaire which he holds, after the introductory remarks which appear above each scale. 'Can't decide' is a permissible, although undesirable, response, and should be included in the questionnaire

---

[34] J. Jupp, *Arrivals and Departures* (Melbourne, 1966), esp. pp. 64–82.

[35] R. B. Cattell, *IPAT Self-Analysis Form* (Melbourne, 1957). Published by the Australian Council for Educational Research by arrangement with the Institute for Personality and Ability Testing, Champaign, Illinois, USA.

only, NOT on the cards. Scoring should be 2 for starred alternatives, 1 for 'can't decide' and 0 for unstarred alternatives. The stars should not, of course, appear either on the cards or the questionnaire. The scales should be given only non-committal titles such as Questionnaires 1, 2 and 3; *not* 'Alienation', etc.

4.11. Exhibits of scale items

EXHIBIT 4.1   *The Alienation Scale* (Questionnaire 1)

Now on this card, you will find pairs of statements about social opinions. Would you choose the statement out of each pair which expresses your own feelings *better*? Just say (A) or (B).

Even if you find it hard to choose, just say which statement better expresses whatever slight preference you have.

1. (A) Our community is an easy and pleasant place to live in.
   (B) Our community is a difficult place to live in.*

2. (A) In this society, people seem to get to the top mainly by chance or good fortune.*
   (B) In this society, the better people mostly get to the top.

3. (A) Mostly, people are fair in their dealings with me.
   (B) I often feel I am not fairly treated.*

4. (A) Nowadays, a person has to live pretty much for today and let tomorrow take care of itself.*
   (B) It is quite possible to plan one's life ahead with confidence.

5. (A) In this society, most people can find contentment.
   (B) For most people, the society we live in breeds discontent.*

6. (A) Often, people don't appreciate it when you do good work.*
   (B) People usually appreciate it when you do good work.

7. (A) I sometimes feel my life is being pushed in directions where I don't want to go.*
   (B) Usually, I can control what happens in my own life.

8. (A) My work is of real benefit to me.
   (B) In my work, I feel exploited by other people.*

9. (A) I often feel I am only a cog in a big machine.*
   (B) In lots of important matters, my decision can affect what happens.

10. (A) It's easy to find a job worth doing.
    (B) It's hard to find a job worth doing.*

11. (A) I can normally do what I want to do in today's set-up.
    (B) In today's set-up, I often feel frustrated and prevented from doing what I want to do.*

12. (A) In getting ahead in life, it's not what you know that counts, it's who you know.*
    (B) What counts in getting ahead is hard work and talent.

13. (A) In this society, money will get you anywhere.*
    (B) In this society, people's respect for your character will get you a long way.

14. (A) Most members of parliament and city councillors are sympathetic people and do a good job.
    (B) Most politicians and city councillors are only in politics for what they can get out of it, and are not much good.*

15. (A) For most people these days it is more important to make money than to make friends.*
    (B) For most people, it is more important to make friends than to make money.

16. (A) The individual these days has a good chance of finding sensible moral standards to live by.
    (B) There is a lot of confusion about moral standards these days.*

17. (A) Life seems to be rather meaningless.*
    (B) On the whole, life makes good sense to me.

18. (A) Life has a clear purpose.
    (B) There is no clear purpose in life.*

19. (A) You have to be careful otherwise people will take advantage of you.*
    (B) Most people are quite trustworthy.

20. (A) Most people are willing to help someone in need.
    (B) In this society people often don't care what happens to others.*

21. (A) These days, a person doesn't really know who he can count on.*
    (B) You can usually be sure who you can count on.

22. (A) I seldom feel lonely.
    (B) I often feel lonely.*

23. (A) People usually accept and welcome you just as you really are.
    (B) With most people, you have to put on a bit of an act.*

24. (A) I don't really feel at home in any group of people.*
    (B) I really feel at home with the people I mix with.

EXHIBIT 4.2 *The Authoritarianism Scale* (Questionnaire 2)

Here are pairs of statements on other social issues. Would you do the same thing as before, say which statement you prefer, out of each pair?

Just say (A) or (B). Just choose whichever statement better expresses your own feelings.

1. (A) Obedience and respect for authority are the most important virtues children should learn.*
   (B) Obedience and respect for authority are not the most important things to teach children.

2. (A) If people spent more time talking about ideas just for the fun of it, everybody would be better off.

61

(B) If people would talk less and work more, everybody would be better off.*

3. (A) The artist and the professor are much more important to society than the businessman and the manufacturer.

(B) The businessman and the manufacturer are much more important to society than the artist and the professor.*

4. (A) The findings of science may some day show that many of our most cherished beliefs are wrong.

(B) Science has its place, but there are many important things that can never possibly be understood by the human mind.*

5. (A) Young people sometimes get rebellious ideas, but as they grow up they ought to get over them and settle down.*

(B) If it weren't for the rebellious ideas of youth there would be less progress in the world.

6. (A) No sane, normal, decent person could ever think of hurting a close friend or relative.*

(B) A sane, normal, decent person might have to hurt a close friend or relative.

7. (A) What the young people really need most is freedom to find themselves, to be creative and sensitive and happy, instead of drudging or learning military discipline.

(B) What the youth needs is strict discipline, rugged determination, and the will to work and fight for family and country.*

8. (A) People who commit sex crimes, such as rape and attacks on children, should be considered mentally ill instead of being severely punished.

(B) Sex crimes, such as rape and attacks on children, deserve more than mere imprisonment; such criminals ought to be publicly whipped, or worse.*

9. (A) There is hardly anything lower than a person who does not feel a great love, gratitude, and respect for his parents.*

(B) Honest people must admit to themselves that they have sometimes hated their parents.

10. (A) Most problems in the society we live in could be reduced by more education.

(B) Most of our social problems would be solved if we could somehow get rid of the immoral, crooked, and feeble-minded people.*

11. (A) Homosexuals are hardly better than criminals and ought to be severely punished.*

(B) It's nobody's business if someone is a homosexual as long as he doesn't harm other people.

12. (A) It's all right for people to raise questions about even the most sacred matters.

(B) Every person should have complete faith in some supernatural power whose decisions he obeys without question.*

13. (A) Nowadays more and more people are prying into matters that should remain personal and private.*
    (B) Study and discussion of what used to be thought personal and private matters is a good thing.

EXHIBIT 4.3   *The Ethnocentrism Scale* (Questionnaire 3)

This card has pairs of statements about various nationalities and groups of people in Australia. Would you choose from each pair the statement which expresses your own feelings BETTER? Again, just say (A) or (B).

If you find it hard to decide, just make a snap choice.

1. (A) On the whole, the intake of a large number of migrants from Southern Europe has been a good thing for this country.
   (B) The intake of a large number of emigrants from Southern Europe has not been so good for this country.*

2. (A) It is a bad thing that the Italians keep to their own neighbourhoods, and do not live like most Australians.*
   (B) It is a good thing that the Italians can keep their own customs in this country.

3. (A) When Italian people move into a district, they often spoil it for others.*
   (B) Italian people should be welcome in any district.

4. (A) I wouldn't mind if an Italian married into my own family.
   (B) I wouldn't want an Italian to marry into my own family.*

5. (A) Italian migrants are more likely to start street brawls than Australians.*
   (B) Italians are not more likely to start street brawls than Australians.

6. (A) The Italian communities have made the districts they live in brighter and more pleasant places.
   (B) Italians mostly turn the districts they live in into slums.*

7. (A) Italians admire elegance and good manners.
   (B) Italians don't seem to place much importance on good manners and careful dressing.*

8. (A) When Greek people move into a district, they often spoil it for others.*
   (B) Greek people should be welcome in any district.

9. (A) It is a bad thing that the Greeks keep to their own neighbourhoods, and do not live like most Australians.*
   (B) It is a good thing that the Greeks can keep their own customs in this country.

10. (A) I wouldn't mind if a Greek married into my own family.
    (B) I wouldn't want a Greek to marry into my own family.*

11. (A) Greeks mostly try to improve their standard of living.

(B) Greeks seem to be content with a lower standard of living than most Australians.*

12. (A) Australians had better look out, or they will find that the Southern Europeans will take over the country.*
    (B) Migrants from Southern Europe have added much of value to this country.

13. (A) When Jewish people move into a district, they often spoil it for others.*
    (B) Jewish people should be welcome in any district.

14. (A) I wouldn't mind if a Jew married into my own family.
    (B) I wouldn't want a Jew to marry into my own family.*

15. (A) Jewish people have too much power and influence in this country.*
    (B) The Jews do not have too much power and influence in this country.

16. (A) Many Jewish people place great value on education and culture.
    (B) If Jewish people are interested in education, it is probably so they can use it to make more money.*

17. (A) The Jews are as valuable, honest and public spirited citizens as any other group.
    (B) The Jews are less honest and public spirited than most.*

18. (A) Jewish people seem to keep their money for their own charities.*
    (B) Jewish people give generously to other charities beside their own.

4.12. Standardization data:

Standardization data for the scales, as well as item characteristics, are to be found in Appendix C.

4.13. Some results: alienation

The Alienation Scale items are depicted in Exhibit 4.1. Five sub-scales of the Alienation Scale were defined by a five-factor varimax analysis of the twenty-four alienation items alone. Each factor was taken to represent a sub-scale of alienation and items were allotted to the various sub-scales on the basis of their highest factor loading. The sub-scales were constituted as in Table 4.1. Their principal conceptual referent is indicated on the basis of those elements in each sub-scale most closely bearing on their *a priori* classification. The correlations of each sub-scale with the anxiety and E measures are also given.

The relations between the Alienation Sub-scales are exhibited in Table 4.2.

The residual relations between the Alienation Sub-scales when their mutual correlations with the Anxiety Scale are partialled out are given in Table 4.3.

TABLE 4.1 *The Alienation Sub-scales: conceptual referents, and correlations with Anxiety and E Scales*

Sub-scale no.	Item nos.	Conceptual referent	Relation with anxiety (Product-moment correlations)	Relation with ethnocentrism (Product-moment correlations)
1	1, 3, 7, 10, 11, 16, 22	Powerlessness (impersonal agency)	0.43**	0.28**
2	13, 14, 15	Normlessness	0·13*	0·22**
3	5, 17, 18, 23, 24	Meaninglessness and self-estrangement	0·38**	0.23**
4	19, 20, 21	Isolation	0·24**	0·27**
5	2, 4, 6, 8, 9, 12	Powerlessness (personal agency)	0·26**	0·27**

For a sample of this size (*n* = 355), all correlations at or above 0·11 are significant at the 5 per cent level and denoted by one asterisk. Those significant at the 1 per cent level (at or above 0·14) are denoted by two asterisks. (This one–two asterisk convention holds throughout this book.)

TABLE 4.2 *Relations between the Alienation Sub-scales (Product-moment correlations)*

	1	2	3	4	5
1	1·00	0·31**	0·43**	0·38**	0·41**
2		1.00	0·37**	0·36**	0·39**
3			1.00	0·38**	0·37**
4				1·00	0·38**
5					1·00

TABLE 4.3 *Partial correlations between the Alienation Sub-scales (covariance with anxiety withdrawn) (Product-moment)*

	1	2	3	4	5
1	1·00	0·28**	0·32**	0·36**	0·34**
2		1·00	0·38**	0·36**	0·37**
3			1·00	0·30**	0·30**
4				1·00	0·34**
5					1·00

4.14. The heart of the matter

Correlations between all four substantive scales are given in Table 4.4.

TABLE 4.4 *Correlations between four psychological dispositions* (*Product-moment*)

	Alienation	Authoritarianism	Anxiety	Ethnocentrism
Alienation	1·00	0·08	0·41**	0·36**
Authoritarianism		1·00	−0·08	0·40**
Anxiety			1·00	0·17**
Ethnocentrism				1·00

4.15. Discussion

This must relate partly to the technological exercise described in Appendix C. The factor loadings depicted in Table C.2 are in fact 'bunched' within domains located by the putative scale items; there is little cross-loading. These data support the view that four disparate constructs corresponding to those ostensively defined by the candidate scale items are being measured. The hypothesis central to much of the research in this book, that four *disparate* structures are measured thereby survives a violent empirical attack. The scales were purified by the exclusion of those items (five) which were shown to be ambivalent by a further principal components analysis.

Although the perception of the grouping of the alienation items by respondents differed somewhat from that advanced *a priori*, the subscales defined by a separate factor analysis of these seemed meaningful and related to the sentiments of alienation considered in the philosophical literature. However, the few 'self-estrangement' items tended to be lost through unevenness of response split, or a covariance attributable only to a common relation with anxiety.

When the moderate relations between all five sub-scales are assaulted by withdrawing covariance attributable to the common relation with anxiety, they retain relations of about the same order. This emphasizes that the empirical cohesiveness of the construct of 'subjective alienation' cannot be caused by a common loading of alienated sentiments with anxiety, except perhaps for 'self-estrangement'.

The clear and unequivocal implication of this research, therefore, is that subjective alienation is a unitary construct: a number of connected sentiments, which, although separable, appear typically as related to each other as a syndrome. It will be noted that the phrasing of the items of this scale, leans heavily towards a questioning of the *respondent's* characterization of his place in the larger society (to be exact, fourteen of the twenty-four mention 'I' or 'you'). The colour thus imparted to the scale as a whole is thus less that of gauging the viewpoint of the detached sceptic and more that of assessing the respondent in his own relation to the macro-system. Even when the respondent is intellectually sophisticated, he is nonetheless asked to construe his position as *un philosophe engagé*. The immediacy of the items to the interviewee is intentional.

The fact that the sentiments of alienation do not cohere because they are all oblique indicators of anxiety, but remained related when covariance from that source is withdrawn – anxiety is thus *not* a 'glue' holding the scales together – is a further test of the cohesiveness of the construct. One function of all sentiments associated with alienation is production of ethnocentrism.

The significant but statistically trivial correlations between the three indices of positional response set (see Appendix C) indicate that it is of negligible importance in influencing scores on any of the three forced-choice scales tested on this sample.

The overall relations between the four psychological constructs suggest that both authoritarianism and alienation predict to ethnocentrism and that alienation is heavily laden with anxiety. There is no significant relation between authoritarianism and anxiety. This failure to demonstrate an implication of the hypothesized genotypical basis for authoritarianism suggests that the defence mechanisms of the high F scorer may be quite as efficient in reducing internal conflicts capable of generating anxiety as those of the low F scorer.

The absence of a significant correlation between the F and Alienation Scales suggests that the relation observed in previous research may have been an artifact of response set infection of the scales.

The reliabilities of the Alienation and Ethnocentrism Scales are satisfactory. The reliability of the F Scale is only moderate, and further research will be required in expanding it for general use. As it stands, it may be a useful 'core' instrument. Eleven of the thirteen items of this F Scale predict significantly to the E Scale.

The purpose of this empirical exercise has been to illustrate the application of various devices for overcoming difficulties in measuring psychological dispositions speculatively considered. The three scales developed by their application are intended for research use.

5 Dispositions and their correlates

5.1. Introduction

The preceding chapter has advanced the argument of this work by describing the development of adequate measurement scales for the psychological constructs with which we are concerned. It is now possible to proceed with greater confidence in charting the social incidence of these dispositional constructs, their interrelations, and, after the structure of political opinion has been explored in Chapter 6, to investigate their relation to the various dimensions of political attitudes, to perceptions of politically relevant subjects, to voting choice and reasons for voting choice. The concern of this chapter is to pause, before doing so, to analyse the dispositional constructs in more detail, and, in particular, to discuss alienation in a more discursive way.

It will be argued that alienation (as estrangement), ethnocentrism and anxiety can be usefully viewed as a 'triptych' of dispositions in which alienation is causally dominant. In interaction, these three dispositions constitute a system which will be named after its prime motor: it will be called the 'alienation triptych'. As an analytical device, it provides a useful summation and a partial explanation of the dispositions found in 'cultures of poverty', for example.

This chapter will also explore variations in the inter-correlations of dispositions between different social groups.[1]

[1] A note might conveniently be offered here on the various statistical devices employed in analysing the data and the presentation of findings. Where possible, product-moment correlations have been computed; but, since a large number of correlations have had to be computed by calculator, it has often been found more convenient to use the tetrachoric coefficient, estimated always by the use of Davidoff and Goheen's table (as reprinted in Edwards, *Statistical Methods for the Behavioural Sciences*, p. 510), and corrected for unevenness of marginal split, where necessary, by Jenkins' method (described in *Psychometrika*, 20 (1955), pp. 233–8). The level set for statistical significance throughout this research is 0·05. Where a correlation is significant at this level, a single asterisk accompanies it; when the probability is less than 0·01, two asterisks do so.

A problem arises in assessing the probability of the tetrachoric coefficient. On the

5.2. Ethnocentrism and anxiety: the partial correlation

Covariance between the alienation and anxiety scales is substantial enough to give rise to a non-independent correlation between anxiety and ethnocentrism (displayed in Table 4.4). However, when covariance with alienation is withdrawn by the method of partial correlations, anxiety has no relation to ethnocentrism. The residual correlation is only 0·03. The commonly held notion that insecurity gives rise to aggressive behaviour thus finds no confirmation here,

one hand, Guilford (in *Fundamental Statistics in Psychology and Education*, third ed., pp. 305ff.) notes that 'under the appropriate conditions, it gives a coefficient that is numerically equivalent to a Pearson *r* and may be regarded as an approximation to it'. One of the appropriate conditions, a roughly median split for both variables, is met in most cases of its use in this thesis, or when this is not so, its absence is compensated by Jenkins' correction. Another, that the sample be relatively large, is not met with the same satisfaction, but in nearly all cases the sample exceeds 100. It therefore seems not unreasonable to attach to the tetrachoric the same probability values as for the product-moment correlation, as given in Fisher's table as reprinted in Edwards (*op. cit.*, p. 502), provided that these are treated with reserve, and that Guilford's cautionary note on the greater variability of the standard error of the tetrachoric is borne in mind: 'The tetrachoric *r* is less reliable than the Pearson *r*, being at least 50 per cent more variable . . . to attain the same degree of reliability as the Pearson *r*, *one needs twice the number of cases in a sample*' (my emphasis). In an investigation of the type of this thesis, which involves the exploration of much untrodden ground, particularly in looking for variations in correlation, a generous estimate of significance seems appropriate, and so, with the above reservations, the levels of significance for the product-moment correlation have been assigned to the tetrachoric coefficient.

On the other hand, considerable uncertainty arises in its use when, for example, the *difference* between two tetrachoric coefficients from two independent samples is tested by Fisher's z_r transformation (see G. A. Ferguson, *Statistical Analysis in Psychology and Education*, pp. 153–4). In all such cases, when both coefficients have, in the first instance, differed significantly from zero, the significance of the difference between the two groups has been retested by a more rigorous procedure. The frequencies displayed in the two four-cell tables for each of two groups have been collapsed in the following manner:

Method of collapsing data from two four-cell tables to one

Group 1	High on both variables and Low on both variables	High on one variable and Low on the other
Group 2	High on both variables and Low on both variables	High on one variable and Low on the other

'High' and 'low' mean above and below the median of the *total* sample. Frequencies, are, of course, entered in the four cells.

This permits testing of the significance of the difference by chi-square.

These procedures seem to preserve the generosity desirable in assigning significance in an exploratory work of this kind, whilst maintaining the appropriate degree of rigour. They are directed towards the avoidance of both Type I errors (rejecting the null hypothesis when it is true) and Type II errors (accepting the null hypothesis when it is false), but with greater emphasis on the avoidance of Type II, i.e. (usually) overlooking a real variation in the data.

however true it might be in some circumstances.

5.3. The principal components analyses

The result of the four-factor varimax analysis of the eighty scale items administered to the Melbourne–Sydney sample is set out in Appendix C. Further principal components analyses were carried out, extracting at first six components, and then ten. There are two reasons for describing briefly the outcome of these analyses here. The first is that in their use to develop sub-scales, they make possible a more detailed picture of the relations of the elements of the major constructs.

There is no special virtue residing in the numbers six and ten; although, of course, there was a special significance in at first extracting four orthogonal factors, and using varimax procedures, rotating to simple structure, since this was a strong test of the initial hypothesis that four disparate constructs were measured by the items. The absence of much cross-loading and the 'bunching' of factor loadings within their appropriate domains was consistent with the initial hypothesis. The purpose of pursuing the investigation with principal components analyses was simply to penetrate the data further with the powerful techniques available.

Principal components analysis, as opposed to factor analysis, attempts to explain total variance, and not merely common variance. It is attractive in that it permits variety in the data to exhibit itself more fully; 'warts and all', so to speak.[2] The pattern of the component loadings in each analysis suggested that the best imaginative conception of the unfolding picture was a *branching-out* of the original four constructs, which in turn sprang from and disclosed their internal structure. Thus, ethnocentrism 'branched out' into groups of items which reflected (a) social distance from, and distrust of, Greeks and Italians, (b) fear and distrust of Jews and (c) an assimilationist attitude (as opposed to one favouring integration) towards Southern Europeans. The candidate authoritarianism items displayed two major groupings, one emphasizing respect and obedience (conventionalism) the other anti-intellectualism and a punitive tendency, which could be dubbed 'ego-defensiveness'. The branching of the alienation and anxiety items was more complex. If one conceives the

[2] For a technical discussion of varimax procedures and the measurement of principal components, see H. H. Harman, *Modern Factor Analysis*, revised ed. (Chicago and London, 1967), pp. 304–13 and 348–50.

process of stipulating more and more components as one which increases pressure on a construct to 'branch out', then alienation must be considered resilient and resistant to pressure: most items remained loaded on the first principal component (these reflecting powerlessness and isolation). The anxiety items drawn from Cattell's IPAT anxiety measure formed three groups: one where the respondent expressed personal inadequacies and confessed to small faults, seeming to reflect an intra-punitive tendency; one where the items chiefly consisted of physiological symptoms of anxiety, such as insomnia; and ones where the items in some way depreciated other people or expressed lack of engagement with a supportive social environment, seeming to express an extra-punitive tendency.

Conventionalism and ego-defensiveness are related negatively to 'intra-punitive anxiety', and positively to 'extra-punitive anxiety'. Thus it seems that those low and high on authoritarianism have their own *social modalities* of anxiety: the liberals finding the fault in themselves, the authoritarians in others, in keeping with their generally hostile tendency. The overall zero relation between authoritarianism and anxiety conceals this contrapuntal relation.

The difficulty with the genotypical psychoanalytical account of authoritarianism remains, since the magnitude of the positive relation with 'extra-punitive' anxiety shows no hint of difference to that with 'intra-punitive' anxiety. However, consider the following hypothesis. To confess anxiety seems weak; the authoritarian avoids it, preferring to appear tough; but is caught unawares by the 'extra-punitive' items, where the confession of anxiety involves no self-depreciation. This hypothesis implies that the 'intra-punitive' and 'physiological' sub-scales are infected negatively with social desirability set from the special viewpoint of the authoritarian, and therefore only the 'extra-punitive' anxiety scale gives a true indication of the relation with anxiety. This conjecture seems plausible, but requires additional data on the influence of response sets, and the use of an extended anxiety scale of the right kind for substantiation. It is clearly an alternative, emphasizing response set considerations, to the 'contrapuntal' hypothesis advanced in the preceding paragraph.

A third possibility is that the defence mechanisms of the high scorers are more efficient than the original authors of the 'authoritarian personality' concluded, in the context of the Australian urban culture, which has many pockets tolerant of 'us–them' attitudes, and involves the high F scorer in no special difficulties in a variety of social settings, ranging from informal fraternities of 'one-eyed' football-club followers to war veterans' associations. Universities and school-teachers' common rooms, on the other hand, are liable to be intensely intolerant of ethnocentrism. On the whole, therefore, the genotypical characterization of authoritarianism, based as it is on in-depth studies of individuals, whilst not specifically supported here, can hardly be dismissed.

The three sub-scales of ethnocentrism are also related to 'extra-punitive' anxiety, in greater strength than could be accounted for simply by their common variance with alienation. It may be that the response-set considerations discussed above also apply here.

5.4. Mechanisms connecting dispositions

5.4.1. Authoritarianism and ethnocentrism

The relation of these dispositions has been considered previously in Chapters 3 and 4; at this point a systematic review of the mechanisms possibly connecting them is appropriate.

(a) We must first consider whether the shared surface content of the F and E Scales is itself enough to generate a correlation of the magnitude obtained, but of trivial significance, in the non-statistical sense. The evidence for this appears to be negative. Table C.7, in Appendix C, indicates that eleven of the thirteen F items predict to ethnocentrism, whilst only three F items (Nos. 8, 10 and 11) have a manifest punitive content. None of these is in the 'conventionalism' group, which predicts to both anti-Southern European sentiment and anti-Semitism. This explanation is therefore contradicted by the data, but the desirability of developing an authoritarianism measure consisting of items more central to personality structure, rather than secondary attitude structures, which at some points directly bear on social issues, is quite obvious. The paired-alternative F Scale developed in this thesis is capable of being used as a 'core' instrument which may serve as a starting point not cursed by contamination by acquiescence.

(b) The psychoanalytical portrait of the generation of authoritarianism and its relation to ethnocentrism,[3] resting as it does on analyses of individuals in depth, emerges with considerable force,

---

[3] This has been described at the beginning of Chapter 3. In addition to its elaboration in T. W. Adorno, *et al.*, *The Authoritarian Personality*, *passim*, a more concise account can be found in R. N. Sanford, 'The Approach of the Authoritarian Personality', in J. L. McCary (ed.), *Psychology of Personality: Six Modern Approaches* (New York, 1956), pp. 261–82.

albeit in a residual way (in this research) through the elimination of a more superficial alternative. It is not the business of this analysis to offer a critique of the depth studies, but merely to acknowledge their apparent persuasiveness in the absence of other general explanation.

5.4.2. *Alienation and anxiety*

(a) It may well be that these covary, in part, because of their common association with threatening social situations; but, as will be made clear later in this chapter, alienation is not a trivial appendage of, say, financial deprivation, and has an independent and tenacious character, with demonstrable personality correlates (in two groups of university students) apart from anxiety. It will be argued that it cannot be considered to be, for example, a social modality of anxiety. Given its disparate ontological status, it is reasonable to suppose it to be an independent *cause* of anxiety, which in the highly alienated is liable to be diffuse and to arise from a core of deep-seated social uncertainty. (See Table 4.1, where the positive relation of anxiety to lack of perceived structure in the environment is suggested by the data.)

(b) At the same time, it should be pointed out that the alienation–anxiety relation is likely to be reciprocal. High levels of diffuse anxiety are disabling and thus adversely affect the individual's capacity to cope with threatening social situations. An actual social failure would reinforce alienation.

5.4.3. *Alienation and ethnocentrism*

In adducing, by external argument, the mechanisms connecting alienation to ethnocentrism, the following four seem most persuasive:

(a) There may be a *generalization* of some sentiments intrinsic to alienation: notably social pessimism and mistrust. If these are felt in immediate personal relations and of the larger society, they may be gratuitously extended to out-groups and minorities, about whom, after all, less is known, and little to be hoped for. This hypothesis views ethnocentrism as *incidental* to alienation.

(b) An individual may negate his confessed distrust of his own society by identifying with a glorified conception of it, as a *reaction-formation* to social despair. Such an identification might be an *ersatz* affair, where the individual joins an *imagined* in-group, in a process entailing no actual change in his social relationships. Alternatively, the alienated individual may join an actual group, perhaps an ethnocentric one, as, it is often suggested, alienated sections of the German lower middle class joined the *Sturmabteilungen* in the late 1920s and early 1930s.[4] In this last case, there may be a kind of double resolution of alienation, resulting in its actual reduction with the discovery of a supportive in-group, and a satisfactory discharge of aggressive behaviour, directed towards real and illusory opponents perceived as threatening.

(c) A fairly simple frustration–aggression hypothesis is also quite viable.[5] The individual develops aggressive activity directed at first toward the real obstacles between himself and his goals. Finding these intractable, as they may well be in many circumstances, such as a large-scale economic depression, he may withdraw and retreat, often into isolation, with reduced hopes, and/or work off his aggressive drives in punitive activity, perhaps merely verbal, directed at minority groups, especially innocuous ones unlikely to retaliate.

(d) Another mechanism which may connect alienation with ethnocentrism is the possible function of ethnocentrism as an 'answer-system'.[6] Where the individual is trapped within a social situation which is confused and de-regulated, or suffers an inexplicable loss of status or income, then a 'grey area' of incomprehensibility may grow around him. In such a situation, paranoid conspiracy systems may be seen as an explanation of why things have 'gone wrong'. Thus anti-Semitism, linking 'the Jew' with international finance and international communism, may 'explain' social ruin. These, of course, will entail the construction of ideological belief-systems which will seem bizarre to strangers and objective observers.

However, two pre-conditions for this kind of mechanism to operate efficiently are (i) that the vilified and, of course, stereotyped outgroup should be capable of sustaining the weight of an 'answer-system' which must be broad in scope. The Jews are admirable candidates for such an out-group, because of their international dis-

---

[4] See, for example, Z. A. B. Zeman, *Nazi Propaganda* (London, 1964), pp. 76–103.

[5] A summary of the literature of the frustration–aggression hypothesis has been provided by H. T. Himmelweit, 'Frustration and Aggression: A Review of Recent Experimental Work', in T. H. Pear (ed.), *The Psychological Factors of Peace and War* (London, 1950), pp. 159–91.

[6] For another discussion of this mechanism, see T. W. Adorno *et al., op. cit.,* pp. 618ff.

persion, intellectual and social energy, and their actual connection with merchant banking and left-wing movements. Of course, these activities are not co-ordinated in the fashion that anti-Semites suggest. I wish merely to say that what is known as 'Jew-spotting' in these fields may bring handsome rewards to the bigot. Jews are, therefore, in the required 'big-league' as contenders for the status of manipulators of international conspiracies. (Since they are few in number, their influence must be ascribed by the bigot to conspiracy, to *devious* means: they cannot win by numerical majorities.)

By contrast, an Italian or Greek world conspiracy has not a blush of plausibility.

A second requirement (ii) is this: the person beset by anomic sentiment, who finds in such 'sophisticated' ethnocentrism an 'answer-system', must operate on at least a constrained, even if not a primitive cognitive level: the anti-Semitic 'answer-system', although it has a lengthy intellectual history, will not bear close analysis. Removal from social information centres, such as metropolitan cities, will help: the large country town is, perhaps, the ideal *milieu* for it.

Since this type of ethnocentrism *reifies* the out-group in an extraordinary mode, i.e. involves mental constructs ('the International Jew') often vastly removed from immediate experience, it is less corrigible by experience, than for example, anti-Southern European sentiment, which may well involve closer personal contact. It follows that fraternal association with individual Jews remains possible, since *they* may not be aware of what their more powerful brethren are 'up to'. On the other hand, it may even assist those actively persecuting Jews to justify their actions to themselves. In the case of Nazi Germany, when the SS were actually involved in murderous operations from day to day, their victims being often patently non-conspiratorial (many were women and children) their active destruction could be seen as a means to a *higher end*: an 'idealistic' SS man was enabled to imagine that in extinguishing the lives of innocents, he was nevertheless ridding the world of the 'cancer of nations'; the Jews at hand being merely *latent* in their demonic quality.

It follows also, that when the state-system which supported the SS fraternity was destroyed, the ideological idea of the 'cancerous Jews' was no longer vigorously propagated, and the SS man, together with everybody else, returned to the ordinary (but difficult) business of daily living and of more sober object-appraisal, the anti-Semitic

75

construct may have melted away quite quickly, as in waking from a dream. A turning from anti-Semitism to philo-Semitism, such as seems to have occurred in West Germany in the last twenty years, may take place. It is no very difficult thing, especially for those not involved in the killing process: it merely involves a *mental* switch, not a painful and difficult rebuilding of one's actual social relations.

This is not true, of course, of the remaking of direct contact with Israel and world Jewry, where the pain of reconstructing good relations has been severe and protracted.

I have been speaking, thus far, of an ideological ethnocentric 'answer-system' (reliant in large part upon one of the most common human pathologies, paranoia) capable of functioning so as to resolve macro-problems of 'unknowing'. It should, perhaps, be added that 'lesser' ethnocentrisms, such as anti-Southern European sentiment, can perform much the same function for relatively minor irritations, like a food price rise.

The mechanisms connecting alienation with ethnocentrism suggested above are not incompatible with each other, but, on the contrary, may be mutually reinforcing. Generalization of distrust and the discharge of aggressive drives seem to me equally attractive as explanations of the relation; the data of this research do not indicate which may be the dominant mechanism. It seems plausible to suggest that they are complementary.

The least likely explanation of the connection seems to lie in the alienation–anxiety relation, in view of the lack of a clear independent correlation between anxiety and ethnocentrism. However, moderate to high levels of anxiety may well be a force motivating the alienated individual to *some* activity, at least to an analysis of his situation, perhaps to a self-preoccupation, realistic or otherwise.

In conclusion, to postulate alienation as the prime motor in the triptych of alienation, anxiety, ethnocentrism, seems theoretically sound. It is not imperative, of course, to group these dispositions alone. Authoritarianism is also a cause of ethnocentrism; and anxiety may have many other causes apart from alienation as estrangement. However, if we stand back to contemplate only the four dispositions considered in this research, the most obvious feature of their interrelations is the systematic clustering of these three, with alienation, within the cluster, acting as the *primus auctor*. The argument for the usefulness of the alienation triptych is pursued below, accompanied by some ontological house-cleaning.

5.5. The ontology of alienation: an illustration

For something to be considered different from something else, that is, to have a separate ontological status as a thing, in its own right, two criteria are required in common usage. One is that there should be a disparate manifestation of it, so that it is apparently distinguished from its surroundings. The other is that it should have disparate function. Thus the weary traveller, asking in a strange place for a 'bed', would be dissatisfied with an area of the floor; even if it could be slept on, he would not consider he had been offered a 'bed'. Even a mat, disparate as it would seem, might satisfy him, if it were suitable for sleeping on. The bed should have the function of accommodating the would-be sleeper for sleep. Therefore everything from a soft mat, preferably with a blanket, to a fourposter, is unquestionably a bed, if it can be used for sleeping on.

If these two canons of disparate ontological status are accepted, then alienation, on the evidence so far presented, is not the same thing as social anxiety. Firstly, it has a disparate manifestation of a sophisticated kind: it is factorially distinct from anxiety. In order to make this clear, Figure 5.1 is presented, which displays the alienation and anxiety items located in a two-dimensional space by their factor loadings on the orthogonal factors I and III of Table C.2 of Appendix C. It can be seen that the two groups of items form two distinct clouds adjacent to the lines defining the factors. If one were to draw a line at 45 degrees to the point of origin, only two anxiety items and one alienation item would transgress it, out of forty-four items.

Secondly, alienation has a function which distinguishes it from anxiety. Alienation generates ethnocentrism, whilst anxiety does not. The relation of anxiety to ethnocentrism is non-independent, as the partial correlation demonstrates.

We may conclude that alienation is not a form of anxiety, but has a separate ontological status.

One further objection might be raised. Even if alienation is not a form of anxiety, might it not be a trivial attitudinal epiphenomenon of a social condition, such as financial frustration? If this were so, then the alienation scores would be a close associate of income level, for example. As we shall see, there is an association, but not a close one. Moreover, when education is held constant, the relation between alienation and income (of the householder) is trivial, although significant at the middle and higher educated levels. Nor does the

77

income level perform the *function* of alienation. At every level of education, the relation between income and ethnocentrism is trivial.

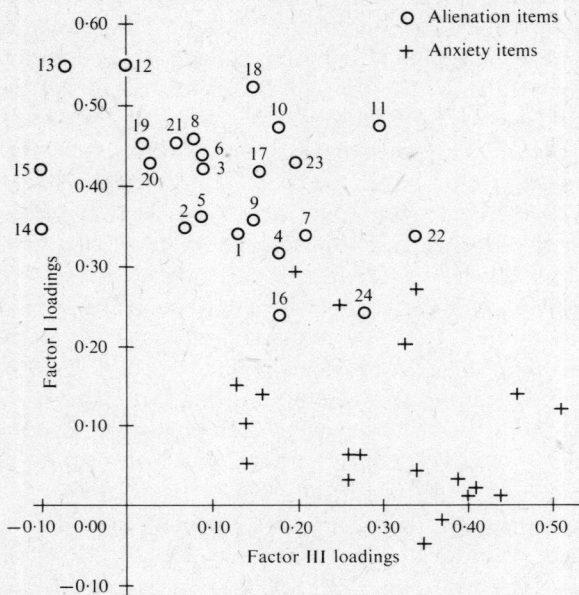

Figure 5.1. Relations between the items of the Alienation and Anxiety Scales

The purpose of discussing the empirical evidence surrounding alienation in this section at such length is to emphasize that alienation, considered as social estrangement, is a dispositional construct with disparate ontological status, and is not identical with, although related to anxiety, as well as other personality attributes which locate it as a deep level in the individual's attitudes. It may be encountered at all levels of society, and is not a simple derivative of the characteristic social experience at the lower level. To show clearly its importance in forming attitudes, two illustrative studies will now be presented. They are both drawn from interviews conducted during a survey of poverty in Melbourne in 1969, conceived and directed by the present writer. Both studies are of men, whom we shall name 'John' and 'Patrick'. Both are subject to extremely frustrating social circumstances, the first very high in alienation, the second low.[7]

[7] I must thank here Mr Gabriel Lafitte who interviewed 'John'. The interview

John is a metal press operator, aged twenty-seven, married, with two children. He earns $70 per week, and was in fact interviewed in error, in the belief his income was lower. He is a lapsed Catholic, and a Mason. He lives with his wife in Fitzroy, a very poor inner industrial area, in a single room, with a shared kitchen (refrigerator in the hall). The room was untidy and fairly cluttered. Few decorations, bare painted brick walls, poor light. His wife was present throughout the interview but made no comment. Although the interview took place in August, Christmas cards still hung on the wall.

The scales administered were those described in Chapter 4. His scores suggest that he is very high in alienation and anxiety and low in ethnocentrism. He nevertheless often lapses into ethnocentric patter, and his conversation teems with symptoms of irrational hostility.

John is quoted verbatim. Two dots indicate a pause. He began hesitantly, but quickly became garrulous. The sentiments of alienation will be noted as he voiced them. The first to emerge were feelings of isolation and powerlessness.

(Question: If you could choose JUST ONE matter for MORE GOVERNMENT ATTENTION . . . which ONE would you choose?)

It's hard to say . . . to be honest I really wouldn't know . . . to be able to choose it'd be OK but you're not able to choose . . . This is supposed to be a free country but they never ask the average bloke, you've got to do what the man with the big collar tells you to do. I don't reckon anyone could give you any answer, matey, except the hypocrites. Nobody ever asks the ordinary man.

There followed perspicacity and violent hostility, with isolation and normlessness in close company.

(Question: Would you like to see any CHANGES in SOCIAL WELFARE ARRANGEMENTS for the citizens of this state?)

Yes.

(Question: What changes would you like to see?)

I would like to see a reform . . I mean people that go for these things and it's a cold air like a business. It's like they're giving you something and they ain't. I mean it all comes out of your taxation and when you get on your feet you pay it all back. It's this stiff-necked attitude by these welfare mongrels – you can't talk to them, the ordinary man in the street. You want to talk to a person, you talk to them properly, they think you're shit – it's Commo tactics, they can shove their charity up their ring.

---

would have been impossible without his capability for writing in shorthand, as well as his quick ear.

He always votes for the ALP, and is asked why. In the following flood of words, note his habit of not getting things quite right, preoccupation with images of violence, ethnocentric patter (not confirmed by his E Scale score, when he considered his attitudes more carefully) and tendency to use the cliches of racial bigotry as pejorative epithets to be stuck on to politicians or institutions which he sees as oppressive. 'Normlessness' and irrational hostility are manifest.

(Question: What are your MAIN REASONS for voting for the party of your choice at this election?)

'Cause I believe . . this country's been in two Great Wars, federal parliament shit themselves both times and Labor's the only party that can run it. When we got a war Labor did a good job. Bolte's[8] a Jew mongrel. I've got nothing against Jews but he's money happy like all of federal parliament. I'd say 75 per cent of Labor is Commo but the other 15 per cent get things done, or 35 per cent. This bloody Gorton government's[9] ruined this country, doing this, doing that, lickin' the Yank's arse. The federal government is nothing more than a glorified Com party anyway – the pensioners are struggling to live and they got more dagos here than fucking white Australians. I reckon two out of three people you see here are dagos. They come here, sponge the money dry and piss off home. The Yanks own this joint. They sit up there in Canberra on their big fat butts doing frigging nothing and getting their corn each year just flappin' their mouths. You get a shovel in their hands and see what they're good for. This Gorton, he's a prick – he's lickin' everybody's arse, including his own, taxes on this, taxes on that like he owns the place. You see him on TV and he doesn't know what he's talking about. Menzies[10] was good, I really admired him. We need a Labor government while we're in the war.[11] The man in the street has got Buckley's.[12] Unless you live in Toorak.[13] A change is as good as a feed to what we got now. Gorton I reckon is too young to run this country. Kennedy of America, he was different, he was young but he had an old mind, that's why they killed him. I liked Menzies, Pigiron I called him because of the Japanese. Gorton is too young, he hasn't got the experience, not like Menzies, he may have been a bastard but he knew what to do. We shouldn't have our boys getting their guts shot out – the Yanks are getting out now with Nixon, where are our troops being pulled out – our head goes in every time, soon as there's trouble we have to be in it, what about *this* country?

[8] Then the State Premier (not Jewish).

[9] The federal government (then a coalition of Liberal and Country Parties). Mr Gorton was Prime Minister.

[10] Sir Robert Menzies, the Liberal Prime Minister 1939–40 (then of the United Australia Party) and 1949–65. In the earlier period he permitted sales of scrap metal to Japan, hence 'pig-iron Bob'.

[11] In Vietnam.

[12] 'Buckley's chance', a very slim one.

[13] Melbourne's élite suburb.

In all this, two themes seem to be dominant. The first, motivated apparently by anxiety and hostility, is a drive to assume mastery of a situation and emotional catharsis by emotive explication, talking it out. His sharp insight into the realities of social welfare arrangements – 'When you get on your feet you pay it all back' – which owes much to his hostility, is in contrast to this fantasy-laden outburst. The second is a barely concealed plea for acceptance into the in-group, as one Aussie to another. *Ersatz* identification, the generalization of social distrust and the aggressive discharge of the tensions of frustration are all suggested here. There are overtones, too, of authoritarian sentiment for a strong leader – 'he may have been a bastard but he knew what to do.' Unfortunately, no F scale was administered.

John was also asked about his day dreams.

(Question: Everybody daydreams sometimes. If you had to name your favourite daydream, what would it be? When you are just sitting back and letting your thoughts drift, what do you LIKE thinking about?)

There is a poignant response. He gropes awkwardly for a phrase to express self-estrangement. He returns quickly to a mood of outspoken protest.

Well, I'd like to go to sea, like, you know, just to see the world. I'd always come home, I mean Australia's me home. I mean you're working in a factory – I mean I'm not gratified in myself, but on a cargo boat, you're doing something worthwhile, taking goods where they're needed. I mean I'd be in Vietnam right now – just look at the marbles ballot[14] they whack your number out of the barrel and you've had it – there's no justice.

(Question: If you had to name the BEST thing about your life at the present time, what would it be?)

My wife. [no elaboration]

The most oppressive features of his social situation now emerge.

(Question: If you had to name the WORST thing about your life at the present time, what would it be?)

Er – when I had to give up me kids – the social welfare people took them away.

(Why?)

Well, an unfit father.

(Why did they say that?)

Because I've got a police record and because I drink. I was upset, but it upsets the old woman more than me. But it only makes me drink more.

[14] Conscription for military service in Vietnam was selective and by lot. Marbles were drawn from a rotated barrel which denoted the birthdays of those to be conscripted.

> That's why I've got an affliction against the rules. I don't like a man in uniform. I obey the rules, but you don't have to like them, matey.

For this tragic man, of less than thirty, alienation has been reached by paths made fairly clear by the interview. Even *in extremis*, as here, it is a situation-relevant disposition, with consequences for personality functioning, but not a personality syndrome. But it is not an inevitable concomitant of objectively frustrating conditions.

We turn to Patrick, a homeless man of about fifty, jobless, interviewed by the writer after he had spent a night in Melbourne's only free hostel for homeless men. Accommodation is limited, and it is difficult to spend two nights there. Preference is given to strangers in the afternoon line-up, where tickets for the night are distributed. A high proportion of those sheltering there are handicapped accident victims or alcoholics. Patrick is a church-going Catholic, born in Ireland. His last job was as a storeman-clerk. His income is literally nil, since he has not applied for unemployment benefit. ('I know it's silly, but I just haven't been near them.') He is separated from his wife, who has one young child. His scale scores suggest that he is low in alienation, very low in ethnocentrism and rather high in anxiety. The interview took place in the echoing dining-room of the hostel about midday. No natural light – only fluorescent light.

In contrast to John, who is self-preoccupied, Patrick's sympathetic imagination dwells on the unfortunate, although his pride does not permit him to instance his own case. Noticing the interviewer writing in long-hand, he slows his remarks to dictation pace.

(Question; . . . JUST ONE matter for MORE GOVERNMENT ATTENTION . . . Which ONE would you choose?)

> Oh, education.

(Probe)

> Yes, 'course I'm . . at the present time an ordinary working man can't give his children the education they should get. Even if they are intelligent enough to win scholarships, in a working family, when they come of working age, to help their parents financially they have to go to work. And this is a handicap to their children and the country.

(Question: . . . CHANGES in SOCIAL WELFARE ARRANGEMENTS?)

> I'd like to see elderly people and all pensioners getting a better deal from the state – nothing to do with the Commonwealth.

(Probe)

> Yes, well they already get a small pension from the Commonwealth, this is not sufficient, so the state should be able to help by providing cheaper accommodation and free meals. They already have free medical attention,

don't they? [Looks enquiringly]

(Yes)

Ah.

In Patrick's imaginative world, there is a good deal of basic trust. People are 'helped', or will be. Something is being done, but improvements are possible. He spells out general issues calmly. He always votes DLP, and is asked why.

> In my book, they have the right attitude towards defence, and family allowances, national development. That's about all, I suppose; that covers everything – of course, foreign policy, too.

When asked about his daydreams, he becomes a little more agitated and confesses small faults.

> One time I knew what I used to think about. What I'd do if I won Tatts.[15]

(What?)

> Well, it varies . . sometimes I'd like to go for a world trip, sometimes I'd like to just tour Australia and settle down here, other times I'd like to go home and stay at home, in Ireland. Occasionally, I'd like to think I'd give it all to charity, more to make a big fellow of myself than anything else. That's about it, I suppose.

(Question: . . . BEST thing about your life?)

> Oh, I'd say peace of mind. The last six months have been an emotional and mental strain. But in the last few weeks I seem to have come to grips with myself and things don't seem at all too bad. It's a domestic and financial thing, I don't know if I could elaborate on it much.

(Family troubles?)

> Family, yes, it's anonymous,[16] so what difference does it make?

Patrick adheres to polite, almost courtly conventions, which allow him to keep some distance from the interviewer whilst maintaining rapport. Although destitute, he is socially poised, not pleading for admittance to a fraternal social world. He considers himself, *despite his destitution*, to be in one, and *in fact is so*. Even consideration of the worst thing in his life provokes anxiety, but not despair.

> The worst . . oh, I don't know, I don't think I'd be capable of holding a job at the moment, though I don't know. If I could get a suitable job I could hold it. I'm not capable of manual, I'm kind of . . . [makes an unclear gesture with his hands] I used to do clerical work before, storeman for the . . [pauses] If I had a job in that suitable environment I'd jump at it.

[15] A lottery.

[16] The interview.

(Why couldn't you hold down a job?)

I feel restless. I feel I want to go walkabout.

Patrick has no enemies. In his view, his difficult social position is self-inflicted, and the resolution of it lies within himself, assisted by a helpful chance, quite likely to crop up. He is clear-sighted, if not perspicacious. He has a 'home', in Ireland, and no doubt the Catholic faith. Considered as a foil to John, he is constructive in the face of social difficulty. John is pessimistic and lives in a world peopled by vengeful enemies, *seemingly sought for*: 'I don't like a man in uniform.' John's hectic exposition of the perilous situation which confronts the whole nation, although at times insightful and intelligently contrived to evoke a sympathetic response, has no happy ending, only a desperate 'patriotic' plea: 'What about *this* country?' In his personal life, he expects things to get worse: '. . . it only makes me drink more'.

One salient fact hardly needs emphasis: in broad terms, the objective social situation of Patrick is much worse than that of John. He has no income, no wife, no family. John has a good income and his wife's support. The distance between them, and it is a long one, is created by John's alienation.

5.6. Some characteristics of alienation considered as social estrangement

'Since the meanings of alienation are so diverse, the entire literature on deviance, psychopathology, political rebellion, withdrawal, and criminality, in addition to much writing on personal misery and unhappiness, is often considered relevant to the understanding of alienation.' So writes Keniston in guiding the reader to the massive literature of alienation.[17] Bell[18] has distinguished two broad *genres* of alienation: 'estrangement' (*feeling* alienated) and 'reification' (*being* alienated). The latter concept owes much to Marx, but the normative overtones of Marx's position lead him to speculate on the nature of the sense of estrangement. The conception of alienation explored empirically in this book is of a tenacious sense of social estrangement, and the outcome of this exploration is the proposal of the concept of the alienation triptych, based on the general empirical

[17] K. Keniston, *The Uncommitted: Alienated Youth in American Society* (New York, 1960), p. 492.

[18] D. Bell, 'The Rediscovery of Alienation: Some Notes along the Quest for the Historical Marx', *Journal of Philosophy*, 56 (1959), pp. 933–54.

relation with anxiety and ethnocentrism, which suggests a broader relation to irrational hostility. The argument is that the alienation is a cause of these. Although a situation-relevant disposition, and not primarily a personality construct, it has consequences for the mode of personality functioning.

It has been noted that there are many paths to alienation, i.e. that it may arise out of a variety of social circumstances. One of these may be the circumstance of being reared in a family of poverty. In such a case, alienation is not so much a deviant as a characteristically maladaptive disposition. Keniston's remark that 'the concept of alienation in every variation suggests the loss or absence of a *previous* or desirable relationship' and his question: 'What replaces the *old relationship?*'[19] (my italics) may be considered tendentious. There may well be a mode of *socialization into alienation* amongst the very poor, such that the individual never *loses* anything, but is accustomed to social distrust, frustration, uncertainty, and anxiety as 'natural' features of social experience. One might conjecture[20] the following six agents of alienation for the children of the poor:

1. An unstable family structure, with the father often absent.
2. Intense sibling rivalry.
3. Maternal deprivation.
4. An uncertain pattern of discipline.
5. Pervasive anxiety in the parent(s).
6. Frustration and humiliation at school.

When the disposition of alienation arises out of such conditions, which would conduce to the development of a weak ego structure and the lack of internalized values, which would in turn conduce to a customary social failure, there is no *depletion*, as there never grew anything to be lost. In such a case, the alienation triptych would be situation-relevant in a much more remote sense, than, for example, in men thrown out of work during an economic depression. Amongst the poor, therefore, we might expect it to move closer, as it were, to the core of personality functioning. Many features of Lewis's concept of the culture of poverty, as they relate to the attitudes and values of people in a slum community, such as fear, suspicion and apathy, lack of trust, fatalism, helplessness, dependence and a sense of inferiority, strongly suggest that they may be given a theoretical

[19] K. Keniston, *op. cit.*, p. 454.

[20] For suggestions of these characteristics among some 'cultures of poverty', see Oscar Lewis, *La Vida* (London, 1967), pp. xxxixff.

summation in the concept of the alienation triptych. This is true also of the attitudes of the poor in some *traditionally* poor communities, such as that described by Banfield in a Southern Italian village.[21] There, many themes of the alienation triptych, such as social anxiety, *preoccupazione* ('mingled worry, fear, anxiety and foreboding'), pervasive social distrust, uncertainty and hostility, often expressed as 'jealousy', are to be found.

Having established the notion of alienation as a functioning entity which characteristically invokes other dispositional constructs, we may speculate on its implications for man in his role as a social analyst, or an interpretative observer of social situations. In his recent analysis of alienated university youth, Bettelheim[22] attributes sentiments of estrangement and hostility to the prolongation of adolescence, more particularly when the individual is taught speculative habits rather than a craft, a technique for producing finished work with special skills. He quotes with approval Herman Melville's intuitive grasp of the connection between social frustration and irrational hostility.

> Whenever I find myself growing grim about the month; whenever it is a damp drizzly November in my soul; whenever I find myself involuntarily pausing before coffin warehouses, and bringing up the rear of every funeral I meet; and especially whenever my hypos get an upper hand of me, that it requires a strong moral principle to prevent me from deliberately stepping into the street and methodically knocking people's hats off – then, I account it high time to go to sea. This is my substitute for pistol and ball.

In broad terms, if one contemplates the relationships between alienation, anxiety and ethnocentrism in the mass sample, it seems reasonable to expect the alienated observer to be imperfect in his judgement. His anxiety will seek catharsis through 'insights' rather than sustained analysis, particularly when many elements in a historical situation have to be weighted. He is therefore prone to simplistic constructions. He will also tend to seek out *culprits*, blameworthy persons, classes or institutions. In sum, the alienated social analyst, or the non-expert social observer, although likely to be penetrating, as Otto Rank[23] suggests, will tend to be a destructive agent, unusually given to paranoid misconstruction. The case of

[21] E. C. Banfield, *The Moral Basis of a Backward Society* (New York, 1958), esp. pp. 103–22.

[22] B. Bettelheim, 'Obsolete Youth', *Encounter*, 33 (1969), no. 3, pp. 29–42.

[23] O. Rank, *The Myth of the Birth of the Hero* (New York, 1959), pp. 184–210.

John provides a striking example of this. A deviant case, a person high in alienation but low in hostility and anxiety, would seem the most promising for constructive analysis, which requires both a drive for mastery and good judgement. Fortunately, this type may be more frequent at the higher educational levels (see Table 5.7) where the alienation triptych is much less cohesive and the personality correlates of alienation may be muted. But where the social analyst is a marginal intellectual, without assured status and working with 'soft' data requiring careful interpretation, the alienation triptych may be more cohesive, high levels of anxiety and hostility more common, and the analysis may be prone to mistake. Consider the following dictum of Marx, himself perhaps a case in point, speaking, as it happens, of social conditions engendering alienation. Here the Marxist characterization of alienation spills over into speculation about the attitudinal concomitants of estrangement. He is speaking of capitalism in its developed phase.

Constant revolutionising of production, uninterrupted disturbance of all social conditions, everlasting uncertainty and agitation distinguish the bourgeois epoch from all earlier ones. All fixed, fast, frozen relations . . . are swept away. All new-formed ones become antiquated before they can ossify. All that is solid melts into air, all that is holy is profaned, and *man is at last compelled to face with sober sense his real conditions of life and his relations with his kind* (my stress).[24]

TABLE 5.1 *The EPI Scales and alienation in a sample of Sydney students (Product-moment correlations)*

	L	N	E	A
L	1·00	−0·28**	−0·12	−0·19
N		1·00	−0·07	0·50**
E			1·00	−0·21*
A				1·00

Sometimes, as we now know, rapid industrialization disturbs 'all social conditions'; sometimes not. Where, and if it does, and social dislocation disorients the working class and produces a condition of social estrangement, nothing could be more mistaken than the expectation of *sober* assessment expressed above. On the contrary, it would be more reasonable to expect the kind of outlook exemplified in the account of John, namely, a wildly hostile mood of despair,

[24] K. Marx, *The Communist Manifesto*, in H. J. Laski, *Communist Manifesto: Socialist Landmark* (London, 1948), p. 124.

caricaturing the 'conditions of life' and striving for *unreal* 'relations with his kind'. Information-saving individuals, whose synthetic capacities are enhanced by good judgement are *not* likely to be commonly found under such social conditions. However, perspicacity of an incomplete kind can often be expected.

5.7. Alienation amongst university students

Much could be written of this;[25] the purpose of this section is merely to present data which suggest an occasional constancy of function of alienation in generating ethnocentrism and some indication of relation to anxiety in élite educational groups. The data presented here also suggest that the disposition has important personality correlates, although the samples are of limited relevance. Mr B. Sheil[26] administered the Alienation Scale together with the scales of the Eysenck Personality Inventory;[27] that is, the Neuroticism (N), Extraversion (E) and Lie (L) Scales, to a sample of ninety-eight male students from the first year psychology course at the University of Sydney in 1968. All subjects filled out Form B of the EPI. Results are given in Table 5.1.

In June 1969, the Alienation, Authoritarianism and Ethnocen-

TABLE 5.2 *Alienation, ethnocentrism and personality indices in a sample of Melbourne students (Product-moment correlations)*

	L	N	E	A	Eth	Angst
L	1·00	0·13	−0·08	0·06	−0·08	−0·07
N		1·00	−0·18	0·18	0·36*	0·58**
E			1·00	−0·47**	−0·30*	−0·34*
A				1·00	0·47**	0·27
Eth					1·00	0·24
Angst						1·00

For the purposes of this table L, N and E refer to the above mentioned sub-scales of the EPI, A and Eth to the alienation and ethnocentrism measures developed in this research; and Angst to the second-order anxiety from the Cattell 16 PF.

[25] For what is perhaps the most complete discussion of it see K. Keniston, *op. cit.*, esp. pp. 273–310.

[26] With whose permission these data are reproduced. They are drawn from personal communications of 9 July 1969, and 11 November 1969. At these times Mr Sheil, who is a psychologist, was on the staff of the Psychology Department, University of Melbourne.

[27] H. J. Eysenck and S. B. G. Eysenck, *Manual of the Eysenck Personality Inventory* (London, University of London Press, 1964).

trism Scales together with the EPI, and the Cattell 16 PF Test Pro-file,[28] were administered by Sheil to a sample of second-year psychology students of mixed sex (n=47) at the University of Melbourne. The sample was sophisticated, most subjects being Honours students. Some results are set out in Table 5.2.

The most surprising feature of Table 5.2 is the correlation between alienation and ethnocentrism in relatively sophisticated groups at a high educational level. Table 5.3 indicates that both groups exhibit high levels of alienation; but the Melbourne student sample was low on ethnocentrism in relation to the representative voter sample. The correlation has to be understood within this context, but remains remarkable when one considers the constriction of the variance on ethnocentrism.

TABLE 5.3   *Alienation and ethnocentrism in two student samples*

	Alienation		Ethnocentrism	
	Mean	Standard deviation	Mean	Standard deviation
Students (Sydney)	17·59	9·59	–	–
Students (Melbourne)	17·57	8·72	5·02	5·18
Representative voter sample	12·35	8·79	11·58	7·74

The Ethnocentrism Scale was not administered to the Sydney student sample.

Neuroticism and the anxiety scores are closely related in the Melbourne student sample. Alienation predicts significantly to neuroticism in the larger Sydney student sample, but to neither neuroticism nor anxiety in the smaller Melbourne one. The absence of evidence of a relation between alienation and Eysenck's Lie Scale, which consists of items which reflect a tendency to try to 'fake good', suggests that the Alienation Scale may (mercifully) not be negatively infected by social desirability set. Alienation shows a marked negative relation to extraversion in both samples and it would appear that the highly

[28] R. B. Cattell, D. R. Saunders and G. Stice, *Handbook of the 16 Personality Factor Questionnaire* (Institute for Personality and Abilities Testing, Champaign, Illinois, 1967).

alienated student is located in the 'melancholic' quadrant of the EPI.

Sheil also found a significant correlation in the Melbourne student sample between the Alienation Scale and three sub-scales of the Cattell 16 PF, displayed in Table 5.4. These are A (Schizothymia –Cyclothymia: aloof, cold–warm, sociable), H (Threctia–Parmia: timid, shy–adventurous, 'thickskinned') and Q4 (Low Ergic Tension–High Ergic Tension: phlegmatic, composed–tense, excitable). The alienated student in this sample is thus cold, shy and tense, as well as introverted and tending to a deviant, though mild ethnocentrism. The general picture is of a withdrawn, slightly hostile individual. It will be noted that the three sub-scales of the 16 PF are more closely related to alienation than to each other. Although not a personality syndrome, therefore, alienation gives indications of relations with a number of personality correlates. Whilst it may be reached by a *chosen* path at the higher educational level, rather than one *imposed* by constricting social circumstances in a working-class environment, it seems nevertheless to involve the alienated individual in more than a pose. Rather, it leads to variations in personality functioning which may not easily be shed.

TABLE 5.4 *Alienation and the 16 PF Sub-scales in a sample of Melbourne students* (*Product-moment correlations*)

	Aln	A	H	Q4
Aln	1·00	−0·42**	−0·39**	0·35*
A		1·00	0·35*	0.20
H			1·00	−0·06
Q4				1·00

Aln here means alienation, A the sub-scale of the 16 PF.

5.8. The social incidence of dispositions

5.8.1. *Authoritarianism*

The social correlates of each disposition which have been examined are self-identified social class, education level, income of the head of the householder, and the age, sex and religious affiliation of the respondent.[29]

[29] (a) More respondents placed themselves in the 'middle class' category than in the 'working class', probably because 'average middle' (apparently a very persuasive self-description for an Australian) was offered as a self-designation, as well as 'lower

Authoritarianism is significantly and markedly higher in those identifying themselves as 'working class' (65 per cent of these are above the median score), significantly and even more strongly and negatively related to degree of education, less strongly but significantly to householder's income. There is no relation to sex, but a weak, positive (but significant) relation to greater age. Older age groups are less educated (see Appendix A) and have had their outlooks formed in times when higher education was more uncommon and child-rearing methods more autocratic. It is therefore hazardous to suppose that the cross-tabulation indicates that one grows more authoritarian as one ages; it seems more likely that it reflects a generational difference.

On pp. 30–1, 46–8 and 70–3, the personality structure of the authoritarian type has been discussed, both in its genetics and its outcome. The 'in-depth' studies which are referred to there suggest that it is chiefly a production of a family constellation, experienced in infancy, dominated by a punitive and cold patriarch, more common in the working class than in the middle class. Although the differences by social class, education and income are commonly regarded as being generated in this way, another explanation is possible.

The lower reaches of our society do not provide a secure environment. In the working class, skills for the mastery of social and work relations are not effectively taught, and the individual must cling to simple rules of conduct to ensure a minimum of personal security. An aggressive attitude is therefore adopted toward 'rule-breakers', rebels who challenge the prescriptions which constitute the few certainties, where certainties are scarce. This kind of stance would lead the subject directly to a high score on the F scale employed here.

middle class' and 'upper middle class'.

(b) In this account of the social incidence of dispositions, 'low' and 'high' refer to those below and above the medians for the whole sample, set out in the standardization data in Appendix C.

(c) It will be remembered that the probability values refer to chi-square tests on four-cell tables of frequencies split as near as possible to the median, i.e. at *below* 'middle' on education and *above* 'middle' on income level.

(d) The educational categories were those which follow: 'higher' refers to Leaving Certificate or above (including university education); i.e. about ten years' education or above, 'middle' to Intermediate Certificate and/or a Tradesman's Certificate (the Intermediate Examination was then taken about age 15, after nine years' education); 'lower' to less than Intermediate. The three groups are roughly equivalent in size.

(e) Income levels were as follows: 'higher' refers to a *householder's* income of more than $3000 p.a., i.e. more than $60 per week; 'middle' to a householder's income of between $45 and $60 per week; 'lower' to a householder's income less than $45 per week. Again, the three groups are roughly numerically equal.

There is a pronounced difference in measured authoritarianism between Protestants and Catholics; 67 per cent of the latter are above the median. This difference is not matched by denominational differences in ethnocentrism. It follows that the correlation in the Catholic sample is depressed, and this is in fact so, although the *difference* in correlation between Catholics and others is not significant. This finding is therefore partially consistent with the Knöpfelmacher –Armstrong hypothesis discussed in Chapter 3, although not supportive of it, since the correlation remains significant and not greatly different. The theme of the explanation for the difference in correlation, indeed the *dissolution* of the authoritarianism–ethnocentrism correlation, advanced by Knöpfelmacher and Armstrong[30] is that the more authoritarian of the Catholics acculturate more closely to the liberal values of the Catholic church on racial matters. Another viable hypothesis is that the scale is not a very good measure of what was intended, i.e. the personality dynamics of the prejudiced person, amongst Australian Catholics. The Irish Catholic tradition is the dominant one, and there is amongst them a strong emphasis on sexual Puritanism and a devotion to the church. The exaggerated emphasis on familial virtues and 'uprightness', in the 'conventionalism' items in particular, are therefore not, amongst Catholics, mildly neurotic *individual* symptoms; they are the badges of the Irish Catholic sub-culture. Of course, the function of the F items is not entirely vitiated by this fact, since they do predict to ethnocentrism within the Catholic sub-sample, and, of course, it is true that authoritarianism may be culturally transmitted. The point is that the items do not function quite as they were intended, and the case for a genuine 'personality' measure of F is reinforced.

5.8.2. *Alienation*

Alienation is not significantly related to social class identification, nor to education; but its negative relation to income is marked and significant. Of the upper third of the sample by income, 30 per cent are below the median; 53 per cent of the middle third, and 58 per cent of the upper third.

A negative relation between alienation and status indices is imperfectly reflected here, being in the expected direction but not significant, in the case of education and class, but highly significant for income. It should be noted (see Appendix A) that the relation be-

[30] F. Knöpfelmacher and D. B. Armstrong, 'Australian Adolescents'.

tween these three 'status' indices stops far short of identity. Of the three variables, income offers the most direct opportunities for *control* of the social situation, and so the reduction of socially frustrating circumstances: hence its reliable relation with alienation.

Whilst the general negative relation between status and alienation is by no means a misleading one, it is wrong to over-emphasize it, and it is clear that there may be many paths to alienation.

There is no significant overall relation to age or sex. However, the data do suggest that the youngest age group (21–25) is more alienated than their immediate elders (26–45), but this difference merely approaches significance.

The apparent contrast between these groups may be related to marriage, job-promotion and 'settling down'. There is no significant relation to religious denomination.

The relationship of alienation to membership of organizations might be expected to be negative. The data of this survey show no relation between alienation level and membership of trade unions or professional organizations, which is not surprising, since membership of these will, in many instances, be purely nominal. More surprising is the lack of relation between alienation and membership of what was broadly described, in the relevant question as 'any sort of social club'. However, organizational involvement implying a celebration of shared values, as in membership of church clubs and attendance at religious ceremonies, shows the expected negative relations of some magnitude, approaching significance in the case of church attendance, and significant for church clubs' membership.

Here again there is the suggestion of the depth at which alienation inhabits, as it were, the personality and outlook of the individual.

5.8.3. *Ethnocentrism*

Ethnocentrism is weakly but significantly related to low income, more strongly to working class identification, and most strongly to low educational level.

These data follow the pattern of the dispositional antecedents of ethnocentrism. Even a little education, it seems, is not a dangerous thing, in this regard. Ethnocentrism also shows a slight but significant relation to greater age.

What has been said earlier of the educational background of older age groups is relevant here. So, too, is their experience of the Second

World War and the Depression. Neither experience would have reduced suspiciousness and hostility, although how long these might 'stick' is a matter for conjecture.

Ethnocentrism is unrelated to religious denomination.

5.8.4. *Anxiety*

The pattern here is interesting in that the relations of anxiety with income and class, although negative, as might be expected, are weak and not significant, whereas the negative relation with education is marked and significant. These data reinforce the suggestion, made above, that anxiety is related to lack of perceived structure in the environment. Education is likely to assist intellectual comprehension of the environment and reduces anxiety. Income lends a *potential* for control of the environment, but does not, to the same extent, make it *knowable*. There is a pronounced and significant tendency for women to be more anxious than men (42 per cent of the latter are below the median).

The data by sex follow the pattern determined by R. B. Cattell for samples in other countries,[31] although the relation of anxiety to sex is more marked than expected. It may be based primarily on the greater physical vulnerability of women and the normative circumscription of their opportunities for overt initiatives and environmental control in the Australian culture. The sample is rather too small to confirm the curvilinear relation to age described by Cattell, where the very young (about twenty) are most anxious, the level of anxiety falling in a gentle gradient thereafter. The sub-samples do, however, suggest that those in the youngest group in this sample are more anxious than their immediate elders.·

TABLE 5.5   *Anxiety by age (sub-groups) (frequencies)*

	Low	High	
Less than 25	19	30	$n = 49$
26–45	91	68	$n = 159$

($p < 0.05$)

[31] R. B. Cattell, *Handbook for the IPAT Anxiety Scale (Self Analysis Form)* (The Australian Council for Educational Research, Melbourne, 1957), esp. pp. 13 and 14.

These data follow those for alienation, and the reasons may be much the same: i.e. ones chiefly related to increasing control of the environment in the transition from youth to early middle age.

No differences in anxiety are apparent by religious denomination.

5.9. Variations in correlations between dispositions

Table 5.6 exhibits variations in the correlations between the four major dispositions at each social class level.

TABLE 5.6 *Correlations between four psychological dispositions within social classes (Tetrachoric correlations)*

	A	F	E	Angst
Middle class (n = 214)				
A	1·00	0·22**	0·36**	0·45**
F		1·00	0·31**	−0·12
E			1·00	0·14*
Angst				1.00
Working class (n = 108)				
A	1·00	−0·01	0·34**	0·31**
F		1·00	0·55**	0·11
E			1·00	0·19*
Angst				1·00

A, F and E refer to the Alienation, Authoritarianism and Ethnocentrism scales; Angst to the adapted IPAT Anxiety Scale.

There are no marked differences in the relation of alienation to anxiety by class, nor in the alienation–ethnocentrism relation by class. In other respects, there are class variations. Whilst no relation is shown between authoritarianism and alienation in the working class, the relation between these two dispositions is significant in the middle-class group. As we have observed, authoritarianism and ethnocentrism are mildly deviant amongst the middle class, where, moreover, opportunities and occasions for 'mixing freely' are likely to be more common. The authoritarian is not a 'good mixer' outside his own group. In the more fluid middle-class situation, it is not therefore surprising to find him mildly frustrated and uncertain of himself; and the (low) authoritarianism–alienation relation is to be expected. Likewise, 'free-mixing' in the higher social class level may dampen the overt expression of ethnocentrism, and even perhaps reduce its actual incidence amongst 'conventionalist' and 'ego-defensive' persons. The significant reduction in the authoritarianism–ethnocentrism relation is in accord with this hypothesis. It must, however, be recognized that this variation in the correlation is weaker. Its failure to be matched when education is held constant (Table 5.7) throws some doubt on it. In an exploratory work, variations in correlation of this status cannot be totally ignored, nor accepted without reservation. An explanatory hypothesis is therefore tentatively afforded to each one.

Table 5.7 exhibits variations in correlation at each educational level.

TABLE 5.7 *Correlations between four psychological dispositions within educational groups (Tetrachoric correlations)*

Education	A	F	E	Angst
Higher (n = 105)				
A	1·00	0·37**	0·15	0·20*
F		1·00	0·43**	−0·17
E			1·00	−0·06
Angst				1·00
Middle (n = 118)				
A	1·00	0·08	0·54**	0·37**
F		1·00	0·38**	−0·12
E			1·00	0·20*
Angst				1·00
Lower (n = 127)				
A	1·00	−0·05	0·23**	0.57**
F		1·00	0·32**	−0.02
E			1·00	0·17*
Angst				1·00

Here the authoritarianism–ethnocentrism relations are roughly constant at each educational level. Authoritarianism is related to alienation at the higher educational level. The same hypothesis as for class is suggested. Ethnocentrism exhibits a trivial and probably non-independent relation with anxiety at the lower and mid-levels. The two features of chief interest are, firstly, the apparent reduction of the relation between alienation and anxiety as the educational level rises, and secondly, the apparently higher relation between alienation and ethnocentrism at the middle educational levels, compared with both the higher and lower levels.

The first variation is significant but not very pronounced. We may hold in reserve, as it were, a hypothesis that the emotional management of frustration is made easier by higher education.

The second apparent variation is more important and better supported, being significant beyond the 1 per cent level. An explanation is thus required. The variation is a curious one. A reduction of the correlation by education could have been expected, since the more educated might employ their intellectual resources to control their aggressive drives. This hypothesis is persuasive but not sufficient for the *curvilinear* relation. The correlation is also depressed amongst the *less* educated.

Two statistical hypotheses can be considered and discarded. The first is that there might be attenuation of the variances of both scales at the lower level. An inspection of the frequencies in each quartirange suggests the reverse. The second is that the reliabilities of both scales might be lower in the less educated group because the items might be less well understood. This hypothesis is not plausible in view of the constancy of the authoritarianism–ethnocentrism relation, and the strong alienation–anxiety relation in the less educated group.

A sociological hypothesis is more persuasive: that social frustration at the mid-level of education is more productive of ethnocentrism. The data of the survey indicate that there is a greater range of income in the middle-educated group than in the lower, and therefore a greater variability in financial frustration. Financial frustration is more the norm in the less educated group, where a high degree of frustration is not deviant from their educational peer group. There is a common norm of 'managing'. At the middle level, however, one can 'go far', 'do well', 'get on'. Frustration at this level seems more likely to lead to aggressive behaviour than at the lower level, where retreat is more probable. The special position of the middle-educated group, which seems conscious of its 'middling' position, will emerge when eccentricities in correlations between the dispositional constructs and political attitudes are examined in Chapter 7.

Ethnocentrism is demonstrably stronger amongst the working class, the less educated and those with lower income in this sample – findings which, if generally true in Western societies, seem to undermine the thesis that the lower middle class is the seed-bed of ethnocentric mass movements. But the very much greater relation of alienation to ethnocentrism amongst the middle-educated suggests that there is much greater volatility in this group in times of stress, of such a kind as to support the views of Ranulf and Gusfield.[32] Consider that these data were collected in a period of social stability and improvement in economic conditions. The shared variance of alienation with ethnocentrism is not determinate amongst the upper educated, but cannot exceed a figure approximate to 3 per cent; amongst the middle third in the sample, it is about 30 per cent; amongst the lower third, by education, the shared variance is only about 5 per cent. If all three groups were subjected to such social stress as to double their average scores on alienation, the commensurate leap in ethnocentrism would be trifling in the upper and lower sectors, but, if the shared variances remained constant, relatively great in the *middle* third, bringing it, at a bound, to a level approximating to that of the less educated. Thus if ethnocentrism follows swiftly on the heels of a rise in felt alienation, the explosive potential is located amongst those in the middle third by education. This group, unlike those 'below' it, is less likely to have political affiliations with socialist parties led by a liberal intelligentsia who may dampen the expression of ethnocentrism; on the contrary, they may well be seeking a leader who will give their sudden growth in resentments violent expression.

A cautionary note: Table 5.6 gives no hint of this inconstancy, but this is, perhaps, because the measure of status location is broader and more crude.

A depression in the authoritarianism–ethnocentrism relation amongst Catholics is anticipated and discussed above. The correlations are, to be exact, 0·35 for Catholics in the sample, as against 0·47 for all others; the difference is not, however, significant.

5.10. Conclusion

This chapter has considered in more detail the relations between the dispositional constructs given in broad outline in Chapter 4, both as they emerge from the examination of sub-scales of the constructs,

---

[32] See, for example, S. Ranulf, *Moral Indignation and Middle Class Psychology* (New York, 1964), esp. pp. 8–12, where Geiger, Schuman and Lasswell are acknowledged as subscribers to this view; and also J. R. Gusfield, *Symbolic Crusade: Status Politics and the American Temperance Movement* (Chicago, 1963), where the 'temperance' and 'prohibition' movements are characterized as examples of 'expressive' politics of the lower middle class of America following 1840. It is argued that these movements had as their chief purpose the 'distancing' of the Protestant middle class from Irish and German working-class immigrants, by deploring their devotion to alcohol and so enhancing lower-middle-class respectability. The point is that moderation in liquor was not the real aim of the movement: its *authentic* function was to punish and repel those threatening to penetrate to higher levels of social status.

and as variations in the magnitude of the intercorrelations of the major scales in different social groups. An attention to detail, both in their internal complexity and in their social context, is clearly necessary for a comprehension of their interrelations and mode of function. Particular attention has been given to alienation, which is perhaps the most various in nature and function, as well as the least well explored. It has been conceived as an estrangement from the macro-society as well as more immediate social groups, since its component sentiments seem to be diffused over both the larger and smaller imagined social worlds. Whilst disparate from anxiety, it seems to be a cause of it, as of ethnocentrism, the three constructs together constituting a tripartite system of dispositions of considerable analytical utility.

In its most extreme degree, where the subject evidences social despair and uncertainty, along with diffuse anxiety, symptoms of an unreal conception of external reality and intense and misguided hostility, it must be considered a pathological disposition. If *central* to personality functioning, it would indicate paranoid schizophrenia, with a prognosis of deterioration in the personality structure. However, this seems to be rare, both because its social incidence is low and because the disposition, although it has correlates in personality functioning, usually has a contemporary relevance to the subject's social situation. Despite this, the possibility of socialization into alienation cannot be excluded, especially amongst the poorest sections of the community. In its lesser degree, alienation, especially when not accompanied by irrational hostility or a high level of anxiety, as seems more often to be the case amongst the more educated, is a potential motive force for creative social analysis.

6 The structure of political attitudes

6.1 General structure

There is a deep confusion as to what is 'left' and 'right' in Australian politics, which keeps company both with a dissatisfaction with these *terms* and their facile use by both academic commentators and journalists.[1] The basic difficulty arises because of a persistence in the use of one continuum. This is not a viable procedure, since policy questions are grouped in clusters and to generalize from, say, a radical opinion on the issues in one cluster to those in another is hazardous, or, plainly, improper.

A factor analysis of policy opinions seemed desirable for the data of the 1966 survey, partly to delineate a more complete structure, partly to test the stability of the structure discovered in 1963. Table 6.1 sets out the policy questions asked in 1966, the response splits obtained, in the sequence in which they were asked. This was intended to be a 'global' inventory of policy questions, i.e. to raise as many questions as time would permit in an interview in which the psychological scales were also administered (there being a grand total of 167 questions). Questions concerning civil liberties, and questions concerning judgements or perceptions of political situations, are discussed separately.

TABLE 6.1 *Policy questions and responses, 1966 (percentages)* (*n*=395)

1. Do you think that government spending on education should remain about the *same* as it is now, or be *moderately* increased . . .   38%
or
do you think it should be *greatly* increased?*   60%
Undecided   2%
= 100%

[1] For a striking example of this, see T. Truman, *Ideological Groups in The Australian Labor Party and Their Attitudes* (Brisbane, 1965), University of Queensland Papers, Department of History and Political Science, Vol. 1, no. 2. The initial distinction between 'left' and 'right' is made on the *sole* ground of attitude to nationalization (see pp. 49–50).

TABLE 6.1 (*continued*)

2. Do you think that the government should help finance *church schools . . .**   55%

or

should the government spend its money on *state schools only*?   42%

    Undecided   3%

    = 100%

3. Do you think Australia should increase its spending on defence . . .   54%

or

does Australia spend *enough* on defence already?*   42%

    Undecided   4%

    = 100%

4. *Apart* from the *conscription* issue, do you support the *sending of Australian troops* to South Vietnam . . .   70%

or

do you feel it would have been better *not* to send Australian troops to South Vietnam?*   26%

    Undecided   4%

    = 100%

5. On *conscription*, do you oppose sending *national servicemen*, that is, *conscripts*, to *Vietnam . . .**   59%

or

do you support sending *national servicemen*, that is, *conscripts*, to *Vietnam*?   37%

    Undecided   4%

    = 100%

6. If Australia were in danger of *attack*, would you be *against* conscription for overseas military service . . .*   16%

or

would you *support* conscription for overseas service *at such a time*?   84%

    Undecided   0%

    = 100%

7. Should Australia seek *closer defence ties* with the USA through treaties . . .   30%

or

keep defence ties with the USA the *same as they are now . . .**   57%

or

have looser defence ties with the USA than at present?*   12%

    Undecided   1%

    = 100%

TABLE 6.1 (*continued*)

8. Do you think that Australia should set about getting *atomic weapons* for defence *now* . . .   46%

or

do you think we should *avoid* getting atomic weapons at the present time?*   52%

Undecided   2%

= 100%

9. Australia now gives *equipment to some Asian countries* to help them develop . . .

do you think this *economic aid* should be *increased* . . .*   46%

or

kept about the *same* as it is now?   51%

Undecided   3%

= 100%

10. Do you think the *White Australia policy* should be *kept as it is now* . . .   46%

or

should the policy be *relaxed*, to allow *more Asians to settle* in this country?*   52%

Undecided   2%

= 100%

11. There has recently been a change in government in Indonesia. Should Australia offer *special aid and* co-operation to the new Indonesian Government . . .*   36%

or

should Australia be wary of too much aid and co-operation at the present time?   57%

Undecided   7%

= 100%

12. On *New Guinea*

Should Australia spend a lot *more* on New Guinea development . . .*   59%

or

should Australia spend about the *same* as it does *now*?   36%

Undecided   5%

= 100%

13. Now on political topics here *in Australia*, should the Commonwealth government start up *new business enterprises* of its own . . .*   43%

or

should it *keep out* of new business ventures?   50%

Undecided   7%

= 100%

TABLE 6.1 (*continued*)

14. Should the government avoid *nationalization* and promote private enterprise . . .   56%
or
should it *nationalize* some business monopolies?*   37%
Undecided   7%

= 100%

15. There has been much American *investment* in Australian *industry* in the last few years . . .
do you think that the Australian government should put special controls on American investment in this country . . .*   55%
or
should the government use the *same* controls as for Australian business?   42%
Undecided   3%

= 100%

16. On *economic planning*, should the government use *controls to guide business development* more closely . . .*   39%
or
should the government use only *present controls* and *not interfere* with business development . . .   54%
Undecided   7%

= 100%

17. Suppose the government *does* introduce detailed economic planning. Do you think it should use *strict* controls to *force* businessmen to do what is best for the country . . .*   17%
or
use *mild* controls and *discuss* its plans with business and union leaders?
80%
Undecided   3%

= 100%

18. If a man owns *stocks and shares* and makes some money from *increases* in their *value*, should such gains be left *free of tax* . . .   47%
or
should the gains be *taxed*?*   50%
Undecided   3%

= 100%

19. Do you think there should be a *death penalty* for murder . . .   49%
or
do you think there should be *no death penalty*?*   44%
Undecided   7%

= 100%

TABLE 6.1 (*continued*)

20. Do you think that *child endowment* should be increased . . .*   70%

or

kept about the *same* as it is now?   29%

          Undecided   1%

= 100%

21. Should age pensions be kept the same, or *moderately* increased . . .   41%

or

do you think they should be *greatly* increased?*   59%

          Undecided   0%

= 100%

22. Do you think that Australia should be a *republic*, with a *president* as head . . .*   32%

or

should it remain a *monarchy*, with the *Queen* as head of state?   62%

          Undecided   6%

= 100%

Note: There is an intrinsic interest in these response splits, and a note on their approximate standard error for a *random* sample (which this is not) of this size may be useful. For response splits of the order 70/30, the sampling error is about 6·5 per cent, i.e. the probability that the value estimated will be 6·5 per cent above or below the sample figure is 0·95.[2]

An asterisk denotes those responses dubbed, for convenience, 'radical' or 'left'. There can obviously be argument with the procedure for Q. 7, where support of the *status quo* as well as one sort of change is dubbed 'left'. This was done because the two latter categories were collapsed for the purposes of computing a scale score, and the best (i.e. nearest median) split was obtained by dividing the first response from those which follow.

The response splits may well have changed somewhat since 1966. They are spelt out here as a rough guide to opinion.

How many dimensions of radicalism are there in Australian political opinion? The technical exercise, incorporating factor analyses, is described in Appendix D. This suggested that the intercorrelations, or groupings of issues, were governed by three almost independent factors.

The first factor is related to various socio-economic issues in dom-

[2] See L. Kish, *Survey Sampling* (New York, 1965), p. 576.

estic politics, and also to the question of a change to a republic. It is clearly the factor most nearly representing the 'established' radicalism identified in the article reported in Chapter 3, but has annexed, as it were, the issues of economic planning and educational finance, two of the four issues of the 'new' radicalism. What has happened to the 'new' radicalism, no trace of which seems to remain? The main connections within it were those between education spending and the introduction of economic planning, and between education spending and a capital gains tax. When 'don't know' and 'other opinion' respondents were excluded, there was a significant connection also between education and defence spending, and between economic planning and a gains tax. What has happened to these four relationships? A comparison of the 1963 and 1966 indices make it clear that the correlations *dissolved*, and that a substantive change took place in the structure of attitudes. This was probably due to three things:

(i) The changed complexion of defence spending. In 1963 it was seen in the context of 'defence neglect'. In 1966 it appeared directly related to the war in Vietnam, and hence lost its connection with those issues which represented a concern with under-spending in the public sector of the economy.

(ii) In 1966, the stock market was recovering from a 'bearish' triennium, and there had been less talk of a capital gains tax. Indeed, the issue of a capital gains tax hung in a limbo, not noticeably related to any of the three factors.

(iii) The 1963 question on economic planning was probably construed loosely as management of the economy to provide full employment without inflation, and seen in the light of the badly mismanaged 'credit squeeze' of 1960–1. The change in phrasing of the question with the reference to *additional* government controls made it clear that what was spoken of went beyond a broad management of the economy, and there was less enthusiasm for it. It became more firmly identified as a *socialist* proposal.

In short, the death of 'new' radicalism was partly a result of neglect. The ALP did not exploit and nourish the *connections* between the issues but instead permitted them to wither, whilst the party focussed attention on external policy.

The sentiment governing this dimension of political attitudes will be called the 'established socio-economic radicalism', or, for brevity, ER.

The second factor clearly represents the 'conscience' radicalism of 1963. The stability of the cohesion of this group of issues and its disparateness from others is manifest. It is related to the new questions posed about increased spending on development in New Guinea and special 'aid' to and 'co-operation' with the new régime in Indonesia. Its central themes appear to be nurturance and sympathetic identification with the 'other'. The items associated with it do not cross-load extensively on factor III, nor do items associated with factor III cross-load much on it. This is surprising in the case of conscription for Vietnam or even, perhaps, the whole issue of participation in the Vietnam war. The moral argument about the war was still in its initial stages, and it was by no means clear that Australian non-involvement would benefit any group of clearly identifiable victims. Indeed, the contrary could have been argued: that Australians were *defending* a civilian population. The case of conscription for Vietnam is a more difficult one, for the conscript is a potential symbol of a victim. However, the conscript *as rescuer* is also a possible mental portrait. It should be remembered that these groups of issues do not assemble themselves in patterns in the outlook of a totally *unguided* public, but, as has been suggested, their assemblies are plastic and susceptible to a degree of influence by opinion-forming agencies, such as political parties. In the case of the symbol of the conscript, the ALP, on the one hand, and the DLP and Government parties on the other, were rivals, the latter describing him as a 'national serviceman'. The DLP, in the field of external policy, had been a champion of the radical position on the 'conscience' issues, and this may help to explain why the question of state aid to church schools is loaded on factor II; the suggestion is that this dimension of radicalism is supported as a cohesive set of issues by a section of Catholic lay opinion which also supports aid to church schools. Of course, it is also possible that since 'state aid' is probably seen by the mass public as aid primarily to the vast network of poor Catholic schools, Protestant schools being few and rich by comparison, sympathetic Protestants are identifying with the needs of their Separated Brethren. The meaning of the factor loading on this item is thus unclear. Since opinions on the item seem to be more clearly dependent on immediate self interest (the data show that Catholics are overwhelmingly in favour of 'state aid') it was not included in the scale measuring 'conscience' radicalism (CR for brevity).

Factor III represents the left–right ('dove'–'hawk') dimension in foreign policy. It is related to the most obvious issues of defence and the American alliance. Its firm embrace of the question of the acquisition of nuclear weapons is surprising, since this question had not been the subject of much popular debate. The issue of special controls over US investment is loaded most heavily on this factor. This suggests that the issue was seen as one of relations with US rather than of economic policy, and its placement in the scale measuring 'defence leftism' (the name is awkward, but clear: DL for brevity) seems appropriate.

The factor loadings can thus form the basis for the construction of three indices measuring established domestic radicalism (ER), conscience radicalism (CR), and defence leftism (DL), each named after the radical end of the three continua. A 'radical' or 'left' response on each item contributed a score of 2; 'undecided' 1, and a conservative choice 0. The item numbers, possible ranges, medians, quartiles, and split-half reliabilities of the three indices are exhibited in Tables D.2, D.3 and D.4 of Appendix D.

Armed with these three indices, which measure the major dimensions of radicalism as they are to be discerned in the mass public, we can now gauge the extent to which the three dimensions converge. The correlations between the three scales are displayed in Table 6.2.

TABLE 6.2 *Correlations between the political indices ER, CR and DL (Product-moment)* (n = 395)

	ER	CR	DL
ER	1·00	0·07	0·18**
CR		1·00	0·18**
DL			1·00

These are low, and in only two cases significant. It follows that the three groups of issues, as *measured by these indices*, are almost independent. This is illustrated by Figures 6.1, 6.2 and 6.3, each of which shows the relationship of two groups of items in two indices, located in each case in a two-dimensional space by their factor loadings. Figure 6.1 displays the relations of the items of ER and CR items. Education spending can be seen to be the socio-economic issue with the closest relation to CR. Increased spending on New Guinea shows

107

some relation to ER. But what is most striking is the lack of cross-relations.

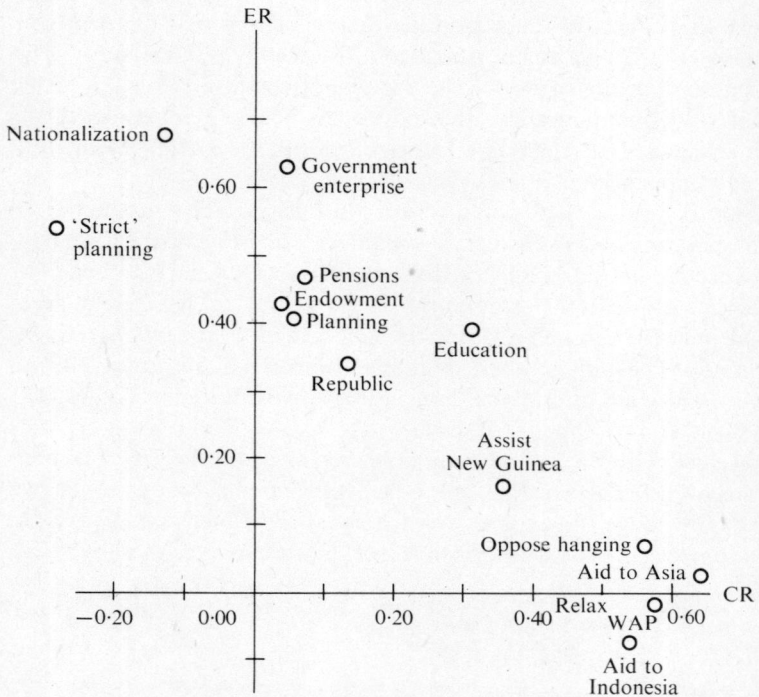

Figure 6.1. Relations between ER and CR items

There are more cross-relations evident in Figure 6.2. Economic planning is repugnant to 'hawks' and attractive to 'doves', although more closely related to ER; both domestic radicals and 'hawks' tend to favour a change to a republic; conscription for Vietnam and participation in the Vietnam war are inimical to those radical on domestic issues.

Cross-relations in Figure 6.3 are evident also. Both 'hawks' and conscience radicals would spend more on New Guinea. 'Doves' are anti-hanging, and support further relaxation of the White Australia policy. The acquisition of atomic weapons is repugnant to conscience radicals. Those 'doves' who would oppose conscription even if Australia were in danger of attack tend to be conscience radicals.

It is therefore convenient to think in terms of a three-dimensional space defined by the three factors, not a unidimensional continuum, when describing what is 'right' and what is 'left' in Australian poli-

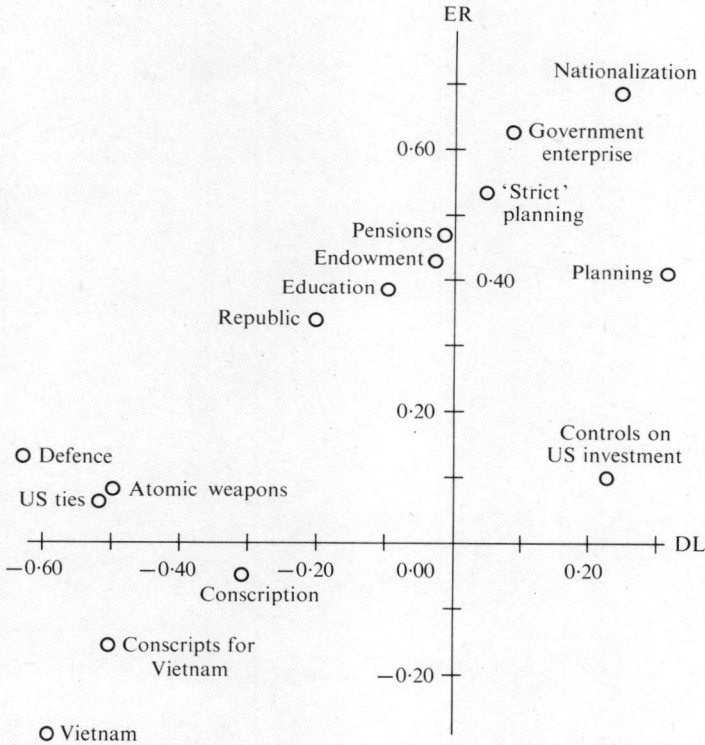

Figure 6.2.   Relations between ER and DL items

tics; and not merely convenient, but, if the twenty-two items were to be regarded as exhaustive, *mandatory*. The three-factor solution was compelled by the data.

Two qualifications should be made here. The first is that, since the twenty-two policy questions are not, of course, identical with the universe of all possible content, there are other possible questions. Amongst these are ones concerning civil liberties, which represent a set of minor issues within an important but restricted field. Since they do not have an identity with conscience radicalism, they are treated as separate. Whether or not they should be regarded as representing a *dimension of radicalism* is a matter for judgement; I would prefer to say that, in view of their lesser status in public debate compared with the issues of the three dimensions identified, these items, shortly to be

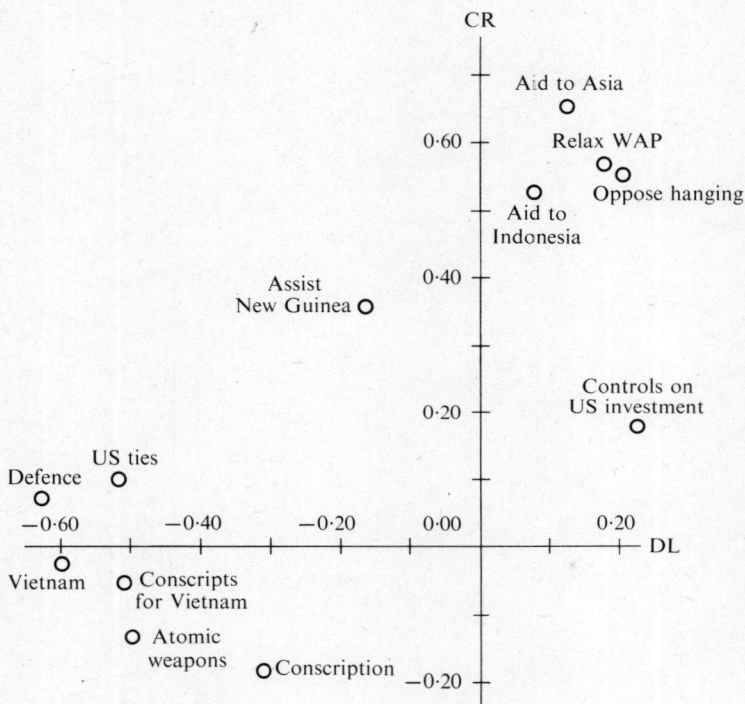

Figure 6.3. Relations between CR and DL items

introduced, represent opinions on issues within a distinct field, but have a *lesser* status (as a 'sentiment') than the major issues, which, each of considerable moment, constitute the three dimensions of radicalism. Others may judge otherwise.

The second qualification is that, although the indices of the three dimensions of radicalism display only trivial intercorrelations, it does not follow that we are justified in regarding the three axes of our three-dimensional spaces as being nearly orthogonal. This is because the indices are most imperfect as measures of *the sentiment governing* scores on each dimension of radicalism, as is clear from their very modest reliability coefficients. If we 'correct for attenuation' a procedure which assumes each measure to be 'perfect', i.e. having a reliability of $+1\cdot00$, then the relationships obtained are those in Table 6.3.

TABLE 6.3   *Correlations between the political indices ER, CR and DL, corrected for attenuation (Product-moment correlations) (n = 395)*

	ER	CR	DL
ER	1·00	0·17**	0·41**
CR		1·00	0·45**
DL			1·00

This procedure elevates the correlations considerably, but even the highest (between CR and DL) indicates a shared variance between the two sentiments of only 20 per cent. We must nevertheless consider the axes of the three-dimensional space to be oblique, indicating a low to moderate covariance between the sentiments governing the three dimensions.

6.2   Libertarianism

Six questions (put in the form of a choice between paired statements) intended to tap libertarian sentiment were administered to the sample. They are displayed in Table 6.4, along with their response splits.

TABLE 6.4   *Libertarianism items and responses (Percentages)*
            (n = 352)

An asterisk denotes the 'libertarian' alternative.
An attempt was made to force a choice between the two substantive alternatives.

The approximate standard error for a random sample of this size is 7 per cent for response splits of the order 70/30.

1. (A) The Communist Party should be banned		52%
(B) The Communist Party should *not* be banned*		47%
	Can't decide	1%
		= 100%

TABLE 6.4 (*continued*)

2. (A) The powers of the Commonwealth Security Police should be *restricted* to safeguard civil liberties*   34%

(B) The powers of the Commonwealth Security Police should be *strengthened* so that they can fight effectively the enemies of this country
64%

Can't decide   2%

———

= 100%

3. (A) Homosexual acts between consenting adults *should be punished* by law   45%

(B) Homosexual acts between consenting adults shou:d *not* be punishable by law*
50%

Can't decide   5%

———

= 100%

4. (A) Long-haired beatnik types *are a nuisance* and ought to be brought into line with community standards   37%

(B) Long-haired beatnik types *are all right on the whole* and should not be interfered with*
62%

Can't decide   1%

———

= 100%

5. (A) Powers of censorship over books, magazines and films should be used *much less* than at present*   43%

(B) Powers of censorship over books, magazines and films should continue to be used the same as they are now
56%

Can't decide   1%

———

= 100%

6. (A) Nazi and fascist organizations *should* be banned   73%

(B) Nazi and fascist organizations should *not* be banned*   25%

Can't decide   2%

———

= 100%

The public seems more tolerant on social than on political issues, where they are less tolerant than the legal norm: neither Communist nor Fascist parties are banned in Australia. Homosexual acts between consenting male adults carry a gaol sentence, but the legislation is erratically policed. The responses to these questions are sufficiently cohesive for it to serve as an index of libertarianism (LIB for brevity). Standardization data are set out in Appendix D, Table

D.5. Libertarian responses contribute 2 to the total score, 'can't decide' 1, anti-libertarian responses 0.

6.3 Political perceptions

Respondents were asked five questions having to do with their judgement or perception of political situations: one related to the domestic issue of poverty, the other four in the area of external relations. These are depicted, with responses, in Table 6.5.

TABLE 6.5 *Political perceptions (n=395)*

1. Do you think there is enough *real* poverty in Australia to require *special government action* . . .   43%

   or

   do you think that poverty is a *minor problem* which will come right *without* special government action?   53%

   Undecided   4%

   = 100%

2. Do you think that *Communism* in Asia is

   a *great* danger to Australia's security . . .   62%

   a *minor* danger to Australia's security . . .   26%

   or

   no danger to Australia's security?   11%

   Undecided   1%

   = 100%

3. Do you think Australia may be in *grave danger of attack* at some time in the next *ten* years . . .   34%

   or

   do you think there is *little danger* of an *attack* on Australia in the next ten years?   59%

   Undecided   7%

   = 100%

4. Do you think that *Britain* might let us down in an emergency if *they* were in any danger themselves . . .   46%

   or

   do you think they would *help* us, *even* at some risk to themselves?   51%

   Undecided   3%

   = 100%

5. Do you think that the *USA* might let us down in an emergency if *they* were in any danger themselves . . .   15%

   or

TABLE 6.5 (*continued*)

do you think they would *help* us, *even* at some risk to themselves?

	84%
Undecided	1%
	= 100%

Asian Communism was thus seen by most as a 'great threat', and there is some apprehension of 'grave danger of attack'. Overwhelmingly, the USA was seen as Australia's most reliable ally, opinion being divided on Great Britain. This survey was, of course, taken before the British decision to withdraw forces East of Suez.

The perception items were treated as continua in the same fashion as the policy items have been, and their relationship to the political indices tested by the tetrachoric coefficient.

Those who perceived poverty in Australia as a problem requiring special government action were markedly and significantly higher on the index ER, but no other. There was a slight tendency for conscience radicals to assess Communism in Asia as less threatening than those conservative on this index, and strong tendencies for 'hawks' and anti-libertarians to see Asian Communism as more threatening. Only one item of six in the libertarianism index has to do directly with Communism. The item on the Security Police is also relevant in substance. But the correlation here, as below, with the LIB index seems greater than could be accounted for by these items alone. Libertarian sentiment is, in a low degree, at odds with 'hawkish' sentiment. It may be that libertarian sentiment is dependent in a diffuse way on feelings of security.

'Hawks', as might be expected, were significantly more apprehensive of external attack, whilst 'doves', one might almost say, were prone to a sense of security. The same might be said of anti-libertarians and libertarians, the proportions being very similar; those 'high' on LIB were (significantly) apt to dismiss the danger of external attack.

'Trust in Britain' was not significantly related to the ER, CR or LIB indices. In its relation to defence leftism, it was the 'hawks' who were significantly more distrustful of Britain. 'Doves' were curiously old-fashioned.

Most people trusted the Americans, but 'doves' significantly less so than 'hawks', and libertarians significantly less than anti-libertarians. 'Doves' and libertarians are much less prone to perceive threat or apprehend danger of attack, that is, do not live in an apparently threatening world, peopled by allies and enemies. They may therefore have a margin for scepticism about our greater ally.

The realities of Australia's external situation, although they cannot be debated here, may justify a quite *realistic* perception of threat and danger, and it would be unwise to see 'hawks' or those who perceive 'danger' or 'threat' as being irrational. There is little to justify speculation on an unreal 'siege mentality'. There is *ex hypothesi* a good deal of room for stereotypical thinking about the outside world, with which very few people have first-hand acquaintance. However, defence leftism and perceptions of threat have rather weak psychological correlates. Cues from political leaders seem to play a much more decisive role than psychological dispositions in forming conceptions of the external world. However, libertarianism has strong psychological correlates. Thus it is not the area of the *unknown* in which policies are structured by dispositions; rather *one* area of the *known* world, where aggressive and punitive traits are important in forming attitudes to outgroups perceived as *familiar*.

6.4. The social and political correlates of political opinion opinion

6.4.1. *Established socio-economic radicalism*

The established radicalism is much stronger in those identifying as 'working class' (about 70 per cent are high). The difference is also pronounced by education, those at higher levels scoring lower. In both cases, the differences are highly significant. However, there is a curvilinear relation of ER to income: those on middle incomes appeared more radical than those on higher or lower pay.

The negative relation of ER to class and education level is explicable in terms of the conventional wisdom: the higher levels would have their assets diminished, or their businesses regulated, if the proposals constituting the ER index were implemented. There is a minor paradox in the income levels in that the lowest level seemed less radical than the middle level; but the difference is not reliable, and the overall negative relation of ER to householder's income significant. It might be noted that the discrepancies exhibited here, although significant, are not very great.

ER had no significant relations with age, sex or a tendency to talk politics. It was strongly related to vote. Amongst Liberal voters, about 35 per cent were high, as against about 75 per cent of Labor voters. (The difference is highly reliable.) But it is evident that many voters are strikingly deviant from the party norm in their views on policy. *All* the proposals of the ER index were in opposition to the policy of the government parties. However, few voters are oriented to policy.

This finding strikes a blow at economic determinism, since it shows a stronger relation between political allegiance and policy opinion than is apparent between any sociological variable and policy opinion. Political views are obviously *not* epiphenomena of sociological variables, and the data leave a very large space to accommodate detached consideration and intention.

An examination of the detailed pattern of the relation of ER with social indices reveals the openings for a forward strategy for the proponent of established socio-economic radicalism. Hostility from higher income and class levels is concentrated on the 'old' issues, the nationalization and income redistribution proposals. Proposals for increased spending on education are popular generally but more so amongst political talkers and women.

6.4.2. *Conscience radicalism*

The story here is a relatively simple one to tell. The CR index has no overall significant relation to householder's income, social class, age, sex and vote. There are trivial and non-significant disproportionalities which suggest it may be slightly more common at the higher levels in income, amongst political talkers and in the middle class, but no reliance can be placed on them. If the whole sample is dichotomized, the difference even by education is not significant, but the 'higher' group is significantly more conscience radical than the 'lower' group, when the 'middle' group is excluded.

Chi-square tests of the relation of all background variables to all CR items disclosed only these significant relations:

(i) The educated are more radical than others on 'aid to Asia'.

(ii) Those higher in income, and political talkers, presumably partly because of their alertness, were more in favour than others of aid to the new regime in Indonesia.

(iii) ALP voters were more in favour than others of developmental spending in New Guinea.

(iv) Women are more opposed to the death penalty for murder than men.

The slight, almost absent, sociological relations of the CR items are in marked contrast with their strong psychological correlates. In fact, CR issues, and also libertarian sentiment, constitute the great arena within which psychological dispositions are dominant in assembling the opposing forces.

6.4.3. Defence leftism

Here again, sociological correlates are few. The DL index has no significant relations with householder's income, class, age or tendency to talk politics. The same weak but significant relation which CR has with education obtains: the 'higher' educated being 'dovish' and the 'lower' 'hawkish'. By vote, however, differences are significant and very marked: amongst those intending a Labor vote, about 70 per cent were 'high' on DL; whilst those with Liberal intentions had only 30 per cent 'high'.

Of the handful of DLP voters ($n=17$), 12 are low, 5 high.

A detailed scrutiny, by chi-square tests, of every issue by every background variable shows ALP voters to be more radical than LCP voters on most of the seven issues of the index, at a high level of confidence. They differ less on defence spending and the acquisition of atomic weapons (although significantly so) but not at all on the question of controls on US investment. Social correlates are as rare as for the CR issues, but anomalous: despite the weak positive overall relation of education to DL, it reaches significance on only one issue: defence spending, where the educated were more 'dovish'. Other 'status' variables play an *opposite* role. Those at the higher income level were significantly more in favour than others of sending troops to Vietnam, as were the middle class. Political talkers were significantly less in favour than others of acquiring atomic weapons and significantly more in favour of imposing controls on US investment.

We shall shortly see that this sentiment has few psychological correlates. In view of this, and the sparseness of sociological correlates, taken with its strong relation to vote, political opinion on the left –right dimension in foreign and defence policy may be regarded as a political phenomenon *sui generis*. There seems no general class conditioning; little influence by dispositional variables. If we assume that the mass public, especially those less interested in politics, is not very well informed and does not 'make up its own mind' on these

117

issues – a very reasonable assumption – then leadership by opinion forming agencies such as the political parties and the press may play a very big role indeed. One is reminded of the picture of the old and retired mariner pointing out to sea and telling the small boy of the world. The portraits of the overseas world painted by political leaders seems to be accepted largely on trust, and not even, in any marked degree, selectively accepted or rejected by those with differing dispositions. This applies also to defensive activity: the public are told by their rival leaders what is required and adjust their attitudes accordingly to party loyalties. The issue of foreign and defence policy was *rated* high in importance by relatively few. Where a group of issues is lacking in salience, the responsibilities of political opinion leaders are great.

6.4.4. *Libertarianism*

Whilst scores on the index LIB are strongly influenced by dispositions, its relation with the sociological variables is also marked. However, the LIB index bears no relation to party allegiance. It is in these respects the precise inverse of the index DL. The 'middle class' group is significantly, but only in a slight degree, higher in libertarianism than those 'working class'. The 'higher' group by income is much higher than those in the 'middle' or 'lower' groups, who each contain about the same number of those low in libertarianism. However, the positive overall relation with income achieves significance. The strongest significant relation between libertarianism and a sociological variable is that with education. Amongst the 'higher' group, 75 per cent are high; amongst the 'middle' group, about 50 per cent amongst the 'lower', 30 per cent.

Libertarianism is more common amongst the middle class, the well off, and emphatically amongst those with higher education. Five of the six items of the index refer to groups not 'reputable': Communists, Fascists, 'long-haired beatnik types', homosexuals, and least 'respectable' of all, 'the enemies of this country'. It is true that the more educated are more directly concerned with censorship and the operation of the Security Police (officially, the Australian Security and Intelligence Organization, ASIO), which screens applicants for senior public service positions and has a watching brief on political demonstrations. But obviously, being libertarian at the higher status levels, in the terms defined by the index, in most instances requires an imaginative leap into the shoes of an uncommon and *different kind* of person. The central mechanism involved in being, or becoming libertarian seems likely to be the same as that for conscience radicalism: sympathetic identification with the *other*. The data also suggest that since libertarianism is more common at the higher status levels, it is in accordance with the reigning values of Australian society: it is 'a free country'. But at the lower status levels, normative considerations are overwhelmed by punitive and aggressive traits. The *outré* groups named are alien and yet at the same time familiar at these social levels also, but their existence is deplored. This may be partly a function of aspiration to social respectability, since intolerance of a disreputable group at least distances the respondent from it: 'I'm not one of them.' But psychological dispositions are also important in influencing attitudes of this kind.

No reliable difference in libertarianism is apparent by age. Men, perhaps because they are more involved in worldly affairs and usually have a greater range of social experience than women, are significantly more libertarian.

Libertarian sentiment, although not by any means absent, is deviant amongst Catholics, at a high level of significance, and to a degree which cannot be accounted for merely by their disproportionately working-class identification. There is, indeed, a sharp cleavage in the Catholic lay community on libertarian issues, which is reflected in their publications, and which corresponds, at the level of public debate, with the views of the orthodox and oecumenical factions.

Political talkers are much more libertarian than non-talkers at a high level of confidence. We may construe the category 'political talkers' as the 'political public'. This may be taken with the facts that political talk is more common at the higher status levels and that the higher status levels exhibit more libertarianism. In short, we have a liberal intelligentsia, moving as a powerful influence in the social structure to dampen anti-libertarian sentiment and to support public institutions, such as the courts, on occasion, and privately founded institutions, such as councils for civil liberties (which exist in most states) which uphold freedoms.

6.4.5. *Perceptions of a 'problem' of poverty*

All the questions asked about the perception of political situations were related to external affairs, with the sole exception of poverty.

Responses to this question were positively related to the dimension ER. Its social correlates are surprisingly few: it was not significantly related to class, education, householder's income, or age. Nor was it related to a tendency to talk politics. Women, perhaps because of their role as managers of domestic income, are significantly more prone to see poverty as a social problem than men but the difference is slight. There is a distinct and reliable relation with vote, Labor voters perceiving poverty as a problem in 58 per cent of cases, Liberals in only 36 per cent.

6.4.6. *Two residual issues*

The policy issues of 'aid to church schools' and the introduction of a capital gains tax were not placed in any of the political indices. In the case of the former, its low loading on the factor related to the CR issues was ambiguous; in the case of the latter, no factor loadings were apparent. 'State aid' was something of a *fait accompli* in Australian politics, with bipartisan support, when the 1966 survey was taken. It had no sociological correlates apart from religious affiliation, but was significantly better supported by political talkers. The denominational difference on this issue is reliable and very great: 90 per cent of Catholics were in favour of it.

As for a gains tax, speculative gains were taxed, but where shares had been bought for 'investment' purposes, there was no tax on capital gains, even when they were realized. This issue has no sociological correlates except by sex, men being significantly more radical. Why this should be so, especially as there is no difference by vote, strains this writer's speculative powers. Recalling our hypothesis, advanced in relation to the greater libertarianism of men, that males are more wise in worldly affairs, we can extend this to financial dealings. Support for a capital gains tax reflects, seemingly, more 'business sense'. Women may see capital gains as 'windfalls' and taxing them as being akin to taxing Christmas presents. Political talkers are also significantly more radical on this issue than are others. The lack of support for such a tax by the working class and at the lower income level suggests that the same attitude may be pervasive there, or that there is a general apprehensiveness about *any* new tax proposals amongst those on marginal incomes. At the lower status levels, there is likely to be little 'business' knowledge. The meaning of a gains tax proposal, even phrased as simply as this, may well be obscure. The poor may therefore be fearful that its incidence may some-how fall on them.

6.5. Variations in correlations of the political indices

Table 6.6 exhibits variations in the correlations between the four political indices by social class.

TABLE 6.6 *Correlation between the political indices ER, CR, DL and LIB within social classes (Tetrachoric correlations)*

	ER	CR	DL	LIB
Middle class (n = 215)				
ER	1·00	−0·01	0·36**	0·01
CR		1·00	0·15*	0·18**
DL			1·00	0·16*
LIB				1·00
Working class (n = 108)				
ER	1·00	−0·04	−0·10	−0·32**
CR		1·00	0·40**	0·31**
DL			1·00	0·52**
LIB				1·00

There are four variations apparent. The most obvious are firstly, that the tendency for ER to be associated with DL is found only amongst the middle class, and secondly, that the negative relation be-tween the ER and LIB indices is found only amongst the working class. In the first case, since ER represents measures broadly anta-gonistic to middle class interests, those scoring high on this index will be a minority of class rebels, who, if they are policy-consistent in their vote, will tend to class-deviant support of the ALP. It would not be surprising that they should adopt the ALP's 'left' position on foreign policy issues. On the other hand, in the working class, ER represents class interest, at least as it is traditionally conceived. Here we find those associated with support of the interest of the in-group intolerant of dissent and deviance, a theoretically consistent pattern.

The less marked variations are the apparently higher relation be-tween DL and LIB, and also DL and CR, in the working class than in the middle class. Both differences in magnitude are significant.

The second of these apparent variations is difficult to explain. Neither CR nor DL have a significant relationship with social class.

If there is a greater strength in the relation in the working class, it may have to do with the antagonism between authoritarianism and DL, which is significant only in the working class (see Chapter 7). Authoritarianism in both classes is uniformly antagonistic to CR. At this lower class level, therefore, psychological factors play some part in shaping opinions on *both* political dimensions, and their closer relation may therefore be a function of their partly common genetic basis in the psychological disposition of the respondents. At the middle class level, the common psychological genesis is not as apparent.

The basis of the first (and more reliable) variation, the greater magnitude of the DL–LIB correlation in the working class, may lie in the fact that libertarianism is deviant in the working class, and argues either an intellectual sophistication or anti-authoritarian disposition, or both. Either would involve an unusual orientation. The small, deviant libertarian group is likely to have an awareness of police harassment of public demonstrations against the Vietnam war, for example, and to connect freedom to demonstrate, *and* the liberties with which the LIB index is concerned, with 'left' views on foreign policy. This hypothesis is consistent with the higher relation of LIB sentiments amongst political talkers, compared with non-talkers, which is very pronounced.

A priori, political talkers, construed as the 'political public', might be expected to perceive more connection between the different varieties of radicalism, to relate them to each other, and to take up connected positions on the various dimensions. It follows from this hypothesis that the four indices should be more closely correlated amongst political talkers than non-talkers. This is in fact so, as Table 6.7 demonstrates.

The two low but significant correlations, negative in the case of ER–LIB, and positive in the case of CR–LIB, suggest that, in a minor degree, and in the manner the argument above suggests, dispositions form relations between the political indices in the non-political public. However, evidence of an awareness of the connectedness of radical positions is notably absent. By contrast, amongst political talkers, there are no significant *negative* relations between the dimensions of radicalism, and the mean correlation is significant (at $0.23**$).

The variations in correlations amongst the political indices between both political and social groups emphasize the heavy dependence of the nature of political outlooks on the social context in which they are held, on the one hand, and on intention and self-

TABLE 6.7   *Correlations between the political indices ER, CR, DL and LIB by political talk (Tetrachoric correlations)*

	ER	CR	DL	LIB
Political talkers (n = 186)				
ER	1·00	−0·06	0·33**	−0·04
CR		1·00	0·39**	0·24**
DL			1·00	0·53**
LIB				1·00
Non-talkers (n = 165)				
ER	1·00	−0·06	0·04	−0·24**
CR		1·00	0·05	0·23**
DL			1·00	−0·08
LIB				1·00

The mean correlation between the indices amongst non-talkers approximates zero.

orientation on the other. However, this is not to say that the inconstancies in the data overwhelm the constancies. Rather, there is a delicate balance between the two. Moreover, as can be seen, for example, in the explanation for the theoretical consistency in 'interested' groups being anti-libertarian in the working class, some apparent inconstancies merely verify an underlying consistency in the data. Two lessons which can be drawn are firstly, that the interrelations of attitudes and dispositions are very complex and require careful analysis and explication; and secondly, that a reductionist approach which makes simplistic deductions from first causes and attempts to constrain the data thereto is bound to fail. The complementary natures of the idiographic and nomothetic modes of analysis, noted in Chapter 1, are very evident. This will appear with more force in considering variations in the relation of psychological dispositions to political attitudes.

6.6. Future prospects

Any prediction of trends in political opinion must take into account the rising levels of educational attainment and the *embourgeoisement* of the electorate.

The issues connected with the index ER have diverse prognoses. Those involving greater expenditure on public services, such as education, and the introduction of moderate 'socialist' measures, such as competing public corporations in new fields of industry, seem not to be fated to encounter a stiffening class resistance. On the other hand, expropriative proposals, such as nationalization, are very likely to do so. Redistributive measures, such as expenditure on cash social services, are also likely to attract declining support. However, they are presently popular, and the drift in opinion away from them is likely to be slow.

Libertarianism is a sentiment which relies heavily on both sociological and psychological bases. Given rising levels of general education and greater affluence, both its sociological and its psychological bases should be strengthened. We can expect a slow subsidence in authoritarian tendency, if social conditions continue to improve. The climate of opinion will thus become more favourable to individual initiatives in promoting civil liberties, and opinion-forming agencies, such as the press and the political parties, will become increasingly populated by liberals.

Conscience radicalism, where, as we shall see, the influence of psychological dispositions is most dominant, is likely to undergo a gentle accretion in strength, if the tendency to decline in authoritarianism and also alienation develop, as seems probable.

Issues in foreign policy are most heavily dependent upon political leadership. The views of political leaders must, of course, turn on the course of future external events, which are difficult to predict. Of all the political dimensions, the future prospects here are most fluid.

6.7. Conclusion

Having reviewed *in extenso* political opinion in the mass public, and its variations, the most outstanding features of its structure will be now noted, in anticipation of the investigation of its relation to dispositions to be reported in Chapter 7. There are at least three dimensions of radicalism, not one 'left–right' continuum. These are the established socio-economic radicalism (ER), conscience radicalism (CR) and defence leftism (DL). These are not closely related to each other. Libertarian sentiment (LIB) is distinct from these, although significantly related to the DL and CR indices. Of all these political sentiments, CR is most lacking in sociological and political correlates. The LIB index has sociological correlates but no relation to vote. It seems that amongst the politically less interested public, there is little relation between political sentiments. Amongst the 'political public', the dimensions tend to converge.

A further, related argument can be put in the following way: when political leadership is lacking, and class conditioning not apparent (as is the case with the CR issues), then, most of all, will psychological dispositions have a free rein in forming opinion. This we shall see to be the case.

The basic mechanisms of libertarianism are sympathetic identification with the other (the alien) and a concern for personal autonomy. Since 'libertarians' often have an interest in being left alone (as may be the case with censorship), then we may hypothesize a lesser dependence on external authority for guidance, and by implication, less authoritarian tendency. Sympathetic identification may also be the basis of conscience radicalism, but, since the measures proposed by the index go beyond non-interference to assistance, *nurturance* of the *other* may also be involved.

Inconstancies in the data encountered thus far should prepare us for irregular patterns in psychological influence on political opinion, and indeed, there are apparent eccentricities in this. However, an underlying consistency, if we have recourse to theoretical considerations, is often evident. In analysing the interplay of sociological, psychological and political factors, an understanding both of particularities and general tendencies is required. It is plain, moreover, from the data examined so far, that, in general, political opinion is a phenomenon *per se*, and not a simple derivative of psychological disposition or class location.

7 Psychological dispositions and political attitudes

7.1. Introduction

Parts of the domain of this research lie within the wider realms of social psychology, political science, and sociology. This is inevitable, and indeed the central intention of an inter-disciplinary work. But the central *locus* of the concern of this book lies in the area best described as 'political psychology'.

If earlier researchers had produced satisfactory instruments for the measurement of the various constructs in the psychological and political domains, the adaptation of these to the Australian urban *milieu* might have been describable as a dustpan and hand broom task. As things were, it turned out to be one requiring a large research enterprise in itself: a bulldozer and replanting operation, to preserve the analogy. It might be remarked here that the instruments developed in this research for the measurement of psychological constructs are, on the whole, stronger and more dependable than those for the measurement of political attitudes, as the generally higher reliabilities of the former demonstrate. This is partly an outcome of the fact that the psychological dispositions had long been identified, if not always well measured, in previous research, whereas this was not the case with the different varieties of political radicalism: the scales for the measurement of the political dimensions have come to hand in the course of identification, so to speak. Nevertheless, since the overall structure of political attitudes has now been identified, and the reliabilities of the indices of each political sentiment are known, in every case, an attempt can be made to gauge the intrinsic strength of the relationships to be discovered by correcting for attenuation. The 'psychological dispositions' are called by this name because, in the first place, 'disposition' is a term which adequately describes a construct inclining an individual to particular behaviours without the inconvenient connotation that the individual is *aware* of the grounds of his inclination, but it does not *preclude* awareness. It is therefore preferable to 'attitude' (which connotes a greater degree of

126

awareness) particularly in the case of anxiety. This perhaps is best described as a '*condition*' of personality functioning, but one for which 'disposition' is also a possible description. The prefatory term, 'psychological', is not to be taken to mean that we are concerned with the impact on political opinion of only *central* aspects of personality functioning: it is merely intended to remind the reader that personality functioning plays a part in the formation of the dispositions whose influence is being measured. This is a truism in the case of anxiety. As the genetic structure of 'authoritarian personality tendency' *of the 'right'* had been elaborated in the first place in terms of its psychodynamics, the term is also appropriate here. However, since the measurement scale is couched in terms of opinion on minor familial or social issues, it must be remembered that here we are dealing essentially with a secondary, more 'attitudinal' structure. This is more obviously the case with ethnocentrism where the scale is patently concerned with larger social issues, but is supposed to tap an underlying syndrome stemming from central personality dynamics.

In the case of alienation, even when this is considered as social estrangement and not 'reification', the term 'psychological' sits less easily. The primary justification for it lies in the generality with which the construct embraces so large a part of the individual's conception of his relationship to his imagined social world. Whilst in many cases the alienated individual may not be aware of the totality of his disposition, in some he may well be, just as he might regard himself as, for example, an 'anxious' or 'nervy' person. The term 'alienated' is in somewhat restricted use, of course, and the awareness of the disposition may be described differently. In the case of 'John', the alienated person actually coined his own haunting phrase to describe his alienation: 'an affliction against the rules'.

This recapitulation of the terms in which the 'psychological' constructs have been defined leads to an important general consideration. In so far as the dispositions influence opinion, it does not follow that in that degree the subjects' *intentions* are dismissed. For example, 'John', having decided (as he has done) upon an estrangement to which he holds with a conscious tenacity, proceeds immediately to a *seen* implication of it: 'I don't like a man in uniform.'

The alienation, ethnocentrism and authoritarianism scales all involve the respondent in determinations of minor social or familial issues, on every item. *Intention* therefore plays at least a trivial part in the measurement of these 'dispositions', seen from the respondent's point of view, even if the decisions are taken step by step, item by item. However, the low correlations between the items of the psychological scales suggest that most respondents do not see each construct as a totality, a familiar dimension on which they confidently locate themselves in a manner which is self-aware. By contrast, the higher correlations between the items on the dimensions of political radicalism, and libertarian sentiment also, suggest a much higher degree of awareness and guided intention. In short, intention and awareness are probably present to a greater extent in the determination by the subject of his 'political' scores, and to a much lesser extent, although varying from person to person, in the determination of 'psychological' scores.

This chapter will begin with an examination of the relation of psychological dispositions to vote and reason for party choice, where psychological correlates are sparse, and often a function of covariance with class identification. Its main concern, however, is with the relationship of psychological dispositions to opinions on matters of policy. Here, correlations are marked and of substantive significance. We will then progress to an analysis of variations in correlation by class and education. Since we have already seen the variations in the intercorrelations of the dispositional scores, on the one hand, and political policy indices, on the other, occur between different social groups, the complexity of the variations in correlation of the two kinds of measures might be expected to be greater, and this is in fact the case. However, certain marked constancies are also to be found.

7.2. The psychological correlates of party choice

There is no relation between voting choice and the three dispositional constructs authoritarianism, ethnocentrism, and anxiety. However, there is a relation with alienation. The alienated are significantly more likely to opt for the ALP. But this quite pronounced relation remains significant only in the middle class when the data is fractionated. However, the frequencies are small in the working-class sub-sample, and the disproportionality is about the same as in the middle-class sub-sample. These data therefore suggest that the relation of vote to alienation may be a general one. The relation later to be demonstrated between the established socio-economic radicalism (ER) and alienation is consistent with this hypothesis. Of all the psychological dispositions, subjective alienation is most variable in its function. This is, perhaps, intrinsic to its nature. The question must always be asked: alienated from what? There is always the possibility of a supportive in-group attracting the alienated stray, or an alternative position to 'allegiance' to the macro-society being on hand. Support of the ALP and its economic orientation seems to be the 'alternative' to an 'allegiant' orientation in the Australian social environment. The importance of comprehending the *milieu* before comprehending the function of the disposition is once again emphasized. 'Alienation' resembles, mathematically, a non-equation between two terms: the first, the individual's orientation; the second, those of the macro-society and the relevant smaller social groups. Both halves of the equation require special description. We may understand what an 'ethnocentric' disposition may be like in most societies; but the outlook of the alienated person is more opaque before further information is added. Contrast, for example, the outlook of an 'alienated' political prisoner (in a gaol) in a Communist society and that of an alienated intellectual in a Western one. An understanding of the society is a first requirement; an understanding of the nature of the social estrangement and its dispositional and attitudinal correlates is a second. The *alternative* allegiance, if there is one, likewise requires the environment to be sketched in before comprehension is possible.

7.3. Psychological dispositions, the dimensions of radicalism and libertarianism

7.3.1. *A general consideration*

A general presumption is made that, if a causal relationship exists, it will flow from the psychological disposition to the political attitude and not vice versa. This need not be the invariant causal direction, but it is expected to be the general one. It requires some justification. All of the dispositions are inclinations or conditions which are, firstly, of a very general nature, encompassing a large part of the individual's perspective on the social world. Even the possible exception, ethnocentrism, has implications which go well beyond the item content. Secondly, they involve, in some degree, aspects of personality functioning. The political attitudes are the sums of opinion on political issues. It seems unlikely that these would exercise much influence upon personality functioning and the symptoms of one's more general relation with the social world. Rather, it seems likely that the psychological disposition will shape the political attitude, consciously or unconsciously.

7.3.2. *The established socio-economic radicalism*

Table 7.1 displays the relations of each dispositional construct with established socio-economic radicalism (ER).

TABLE 7.1 *ER by four dispositional constructs (Product-moment and tetrachoric correlations) (n = 353)*

A	ER	$r = 0.19^{**}$	$r_t = 0.33^{**}$
F	ER	$r = -0.08$	$r_t = 0.03$
E	ER	$r = -0.01$	$r_t = 0.01$
Angst	ER	$r = 0.06$	$r_t = 0.12^{*}$

A stands for alienation; F for authoritarianism; E for ethnocentrism, Angst for anxiety.

The relation of alienation to the ER index is low but significant. As the introduction to this chapter suggests, allegiance to a well-recognized set of reformist economic policies is a salient alternative to allegiance to the present socio-economic system in the Australian urban context. Corrections for attenuation were calculated on the more reliable basis of the product-moment correlations. These are given in Table 7.2.

TABLE 7.2 *ER by four dispositional constructs (Product-moment correlations corrected for attenuation) (n = 353)*

A	ER	$r = 0.35^{**}$
F	ER	$r = -0.17^{**}$
E	ER	$r = -0.02$
Angst	ER	$r = 0.12^{*}$

Anxiety and authoritarianism have slight relations with ER, the more authoritarian being conservative and those anxious more radical.

It would seem that ER stems in part from social frustration. It seems also that the F–ER relation might stem from a conventionalist apprehensiveness of change.

It may be that a back-reaction is involved in the case of the anxiety –ER relation; that a radical stance is marginally more socially precarious than a conservative one, so that, here, the *opinion* invokes the disposition.

7.3.3. *Conscience radicalism*

Table 7.3 indicates the relations of dispositions with conscience radicalism (CR). The relations here are marked and cannot be

TABLE 7.3 *CR by four dispositional constructs (Product-moment and tetrachoric correlations) ($n = 353$)*

A	CR	$r = 0.17**$	$r_t = 0.26**$
F	CR	$r = -0.39**$	$r_t = -0.36**$
E	CR	$r = -0.33**$	$r_t = -0.41**$
Angst	CR	$r = 0.06$	$r_t = 0.01$

accounted for by covariance with sociological variables, since CR correlates with only one (education) and in that case only weakly.

It seems that, in the case of alienation, social distrust is generalized to that 'other' specified in the political questions (Asians and convicted criminals) and/or aggressive sentiment is discharged upon these, perceived as out-groups. Anxiety plays little or no direct role, although the correlation reaches significance when corrected for attenuation; the mechanism suggested is that for radicalism generally, argued above. The radical, on the other hand, sympathetically identifies with the groups concerned – whether or not they are perceived as *the other* – and exhibits a generous and co-operative sentiment.

It should be noted that whilst the *absence* of alienation, authoritarianism and ethnocentrism, following the theoretical construction placed upon their function, facilitates *identification*, it also encourages a *nurturant* orientation. In our discussion thus far we have concentrated our attention upon the mechanisms *of hate, not of love*. Since the anti-alienated and anti-ethnocentric item halves are in many cases symptomatic of an *affectionate* disposition, and not merely absence of hostility, in these dispositional constructs, and in the case of authoritarianism, the negative poles (anti-alienation, or 'allegiance', and anti-ethnocentrism) imply a capacity for a wide-ranging object cathexis.

When the correlations are corrected for attenuation, the correlations range from low to very high. These are displayed in Table 7.4. It should be remembered that it is the *sentiment* governing opinion on the CR issues which is involved when a correlation is made for attenuation, not opinions on each and every issue. If the latter were the case, near-perfect prediction for the dispositions to opinion each issue would be entailed. What *is* entailed is near-perfect prediction, when *all* dispositions are known, to the *sentiment* CR.

TABLE 7.4   *CR by four dispositional constructs (Product-moment correlations corrected for attenuation) (n = 353)*

A	CR	$r = -0.37$**
F	CR	$r = -0.93$**
E	CR	$r = -0.62$**
Angst	CR	$r = 0.14$**

Psychological dispositions thus play a dominant, indeed unchallengeable, role in influencing opinion on CR issues, accounting for much of the variance on the sum of opinion on the various issues (when the correlations are uncorrected) and sharing nearly all of the variance of the underlying sentiment. In the absence of strong political leadership they therefore play a very major role in creating the 'climate of opinion', which will vary on these issues as the dispositions wax and wane in the mass public. However, the introduction to this chapter makes it clear that to say this is not to take a 'determinist' position. Self-awareness and intention can be accommodated *within* the structure of both dispositions and attitudes.

7.3.4.   Defence leftism

Table 7.5 exhibits the relations of dispositions with defence leftism (DL).

Relations here are thin. Authoritarianism has a low negative relation to 'dovish' sentiment; but 'hawks' are not ethnocentric. The variable role of alienation is notable: we have seen it promote a radical stance on socio-economic domestic issues (ER) and a conservative position on issues of conscience (CR); here it again gives an impetus to radicalism, albeit a small one.

Table 7.6 shows the correlations corrected for attenuation.

That authoritarians should be 'hawkish' is theoretically consistent; but the zero relation between DL and ethnocentrism is puzzling.

TABLE 7.5 *DL by four psychological constructs (Product-moment and tetrachoric correlations) (n = 353)*

A	DL	$r = 0.12*$	$r_t = 0.12*$
F	DL	$r = -0.19**$	$r_t = -0.12*$
E	DL	$r = 0.00$	$r_t = 0.06$
Angst	DL	$r = 0.08$	$r_t = 0.03$

TABLE 7.6 *DL by four dispositional constructs (Product-moment correlations corrected for attenuation) (n = 353)*

A	DL	$r = 0.23**$
F	DL	$r = -0.42**$
E	DL	$r = 0.00$
Angst	DL	$r = 0.17**$

One might have expected bigots to be hostile to the putative 'enemy' to be confronted. But this is not so. There may be two reasons for this, each involving opposed tendencies which, operating together, produce a zero correlation. One may lie in the conception advanced in Chapter 6 of the mechanism by which views on external policy are transmitted: they are 'handed down' to trustful followers by leaders of opinion. No dispositional influence need be adduced for this process to occur, although there seems to be some selection involved, authoritarians 'choosing' hawkish sentiments, the alienated, 'dovish' ones (perhaps because of their slight orientation to the ALP). The second may be as follows. The most adamant proponents of a strong defence and foreign policy posture, the leaders of the DLP and the NCC, are in fact anti-ethnocentric, proposing closer regional co-operation with non-Communist Asian powers and abandonment of the White Australia policy. In so far as these opinions and the sentiment underlying them is received, it will counteract the ethnocentric underlay of the old-fashioned 'hawkishness', which was often associated with a certain disdain for coloured peoples. The zero correlation with ethnocentrism may be the result of this strange confluence.

Radical sentiment is again associated with a low degree of anxiety.

Alienation plays a radical role for the in-group, as we have seen; a conservative role for the out-group, and now, once again, a radical role, although a lesser one, in shaping sentiments on defence policy. It is tempting to suggest that 'meaning' is supplied in external affairs by political leadership; external affairs is argued to be the area of *greatest* suggestibility, and that in other fields, ideas are less liable to be accepted on trust.

7.3.5. *Libertarianism*

The relationship between psychological dispositions and libertarianism (LIB) was tested only by the tetrachoric correlation. The results are set out in Table 7.7.

TABLE 7.7 *LIB by four dispositional constructs* (*Tetrachoric correlations*) (*n* = 352)

A	LIB	$r_t = 0.08$
F	LIB	$r_t = -0.55**$
E	LIB	$r_t = -0.38**$
Angst	LIB	$r_t = 0.07$

The relation with authoritarianism is strong, and with ethnocentrism moderate. This is a wholly consistent pattern theoretically. The authoritarian is expected to be hostile and punitive towards outgroups; the LIB index has to do with punitive attitudes towards outgroups on four items out of six, and in the remaining two refers to the restraint of threatening, sinister forces, by censorship and the Australian Security and Intelligence Organization. There is, in fact, one item specifically referring to punishment of homosexuals in both the F scale and the LIB index. Of all the indices and scales, these are the two with the most shared surface content, although, of course, *most* of the F items are not similar in surface content with those of the LIB index.

However, an objection might be raised at this point that the strong correlation between the authoritarianism scale and the LIB index is not of great substantive significance, and is indeed trivial, because of the degree of shared surface content shared by the two measures. In order to test the strength of this objection, let us, in fact, adopt this view. We will now, for the sake of this argument, regard the LIB index as nothing more than a *restatement* of the F measure, and see what difficulties this position involves.

The first point of discomfort is that five of the six LIB items are stringently political, referring, for example, to the banning of fascist parties. The remaining one, referring to 'long-haired beatnik types' is more loose, but is suggestive of police action. *All* of them refer to punishment, banning or elimination of 'outsider' political or social groups. If we turn to the F Scale, we find that comparatively few items (three out of thirteen) are of this type: the 'outsiders' of the F scale are homosexuals (also mentioned in the LIB index), sex criminals, and 'immoral, crooked or feeble-minded people' who are to be 'got rid of'. There are many times which have no reference at all to out-groups, such as item 3, which weighs the merits of professors as against businessmen, and item 2 ('talk less and work more'). The obscurantist items 4, 12, and 13, and the 'obedience' item 1, have no mention of out-groups, and the items referring to 'young people' and 'youth' (5 and 7) are very generally phrased. Items 6 and 9 refer only to family 'virtues', phrased in a deliberately exaggerated way. In short, the F Scale seems to do what it is supposed to do, that is, to offer items which range in a general way over the individual's perceived relation with the social world, and to deal in such diffuse themes as anti-intellectualism and over-statement of family 'virtues', as well as the punishment of out-groups: it is much more a dispositional scale, even if a far from perfect one, than a political questionnaire.

These difficulties are thus sufficiently troublesome as to compel us to abandon this temporarily adopted position, i.e. that the LIB index *recapitulates* the F Scale: it does not. The important thing is to establish a point of balance in this hypothetical symposium. This can be struck by pointing to the closeness of *three* of the thirteen F Scale items to those of the LIB index, whilst at the same time noting that this, in itself, would not be sufficient to generate a correlation as high as the one actually obtained. The correlation must be only moderately discounted in order to gauge correctly its substantive importance.

It might be further objected that themes of anti-intellectualism and exaggerated familial 'virtues' are nevertheless 'tied in' with ideas about the punishment of out-groups. But this is no objection. This is precisely the argument. The mistake involved in the objection arises from treating the disposition–political index relation as a fact so well known as not to require demonstration, which, whilst it is a point of view flattering to the influence of disposition (and ordinary understanding) is not well founded. 'Common knowledge' in this field is largely confined to intellectuals influenced by research into the authoritarian personality. In any case, since no prior demonstration has been made of the relation, it is a necessary part of this research enterprise.

The interpretation of correlations corrected for attenuation has to be made with some caution in this case, because of the greater variability of the tetrachoric correlation coefficient, which is employed here. The corrected correlations are displayed in Table 7.8.

TABLE 7.8 *LIB by four dispositional constructs* (*Tetrachoric correlations corrected for attenuation*) ($n = 352$)

A	LIB	$r_t = 0.14**$
F	LIB	$r_t = -1.00**$ (actually exceeds unity)
E	LIB	$r_t = -0.61**$
Angst	LIB	$r_t = 0.13*$

The fact that we are dealing in approximations is emphasized by the F–LIB correlation, where we are in the embarrassing position of having apparently discovered a perfect empirical negative correspondence, *in situ*. The implication of Table 7.8, if taken at face value, is, indeed, that we have an *embarras de richesse*: we would be in a position to predict more than 100 per cent of the variance of libertarian sentiment, given a knowledge of dispositional scores. However, the statistical anomaly is very probably the result of *conservative* estimations of the reliabilities of the scales, which would tend to over-inflate the correlations when corrected for attenuation.

Once again, this makes obvious the need for a 'personality' scale for authoritarianism which will remove the measure from direct contact with social issues; but the strength of this correlation, taken with that of the LIB index with ethnocentrism, shows libertarian sentiment to be very much a creature of disposition. The notion of libertarianism is a familiar one in its totality, of course, and it would be reasonable to expect both intention and awareness to play a part in making this relation. The high inter-item coefficients of the LIB index items, and its high reliability for so short a measure, are consistent with the view that its cohesiveness reflects the respondents' knowledge of 'what this is about'.

It is in one way unexpected to find alienation playing a positive role in promoting libertarianism, in view of the hostility of alienation to conscience radicalism, its positive relation to ethnocentrism and the similarity of the mechanisms involved in each of the political sentiments. It should be remembered that the LIB index has a good deal of punitive content, whereas the ethnocentric item halves are more mild in tone, implying no positive action other than not having one of *them* in the family. The degree of 'aggression' implied in the ethnocentrism scale items is not at all great. Possibly, two conflicting mechanisms are at work in producing the trivial positive relation between libertarianism and alienation. One may be that, since the alienated person has professed, in part, a distrust of the reigning institutions of the macro-society, and now, in the libertarianism index, is presented with a vivid picture of these bearing down in a punitive fashion on various outgroups, sometimes loosely defined, e.g. 'the enemies of this country', he instinctively steps out of the way, as it were, and opts for them to be let alone, fearing that he, another 'outsider', will be next. On the other hand, he may distrust the named out-groups and wish to discharge aggression upon them. Of these two hypothetical conflicting tendencies, the former appears to be stronger, and produces the low positive relation. The low positive relation of anxiety to libertarianism, although reliable only on the most generous criterion, is consistent with this view.

7.3.6. *Political perceptions*

Firstly, let us take perception of poverty as a special problem. There are in this instance two significant relations, which are indicated by the tetrachoric correlation when perception of poverty as a social problem is conceived as a continuum, in the same manner as the responses to the policy questions. Alienation is a minor friend of perception of a problem of poverty; authoritarianism a minor foe.

The first relation is consistent with the correlation between alienation and the established socio-economic radicalism. The second is theoretically consistent with the concept of the authoritarian, who may be expected to stereotype the poor as a blameworthy outgroup.

Authoritarianism is positively related, in a very minor but significant degree, to a perception of Communism in Asia as a danger to Australia.

Responses to the question of the danger attaching to Communism were not related to the other dispositions. For the more general question about the danger of external attack ('Do you think Australia may be in *grave danger of attack* at some time in the next ten years . . . etc.?'), there were low but reliable positive relations with every disposition. This is theoretically consistent for authoritarianism and ethnocentrism, which may both predispose to a view of a world where peril of enemy attack is perceived as customary. The relation with anxiety, which implies projection of the subject's personal insecurity onto the conception of the external world, is also theoretically consistent. In fact, the question is not so much why such a relation should be found here for anxiety, as why it was *not* found in relation to perception of 'danger' in Asian Communism. The answer may lie in the non-specificity of the 'attack' question, which is worded in very general terms with a slightly sinister innuendo, if an innuendo is sought for.

The positive relation of alienation here is a paradox, since alienation is related to 'dovish' sentiment (DL). The difficulty is not great, since both correlations are low. We have hypothesized a 'reception' of ALP policy orientation on external affairs by the alienated, who score high on the ER index, indicating an allegiance to the ALP's position on domestic policy. On the more general question of attack as it is phrased, implying the possibility that the attack may be unexpected or sudden, the ALP has, perhaps sensibly, no firm view to hand down. The alienated may therefore be inclined to be influenced by their sense of uncertainty in the social world, and to project it onto the conception of the external world in the same way as those high in anxiety.

There is a slight but reliable tendency on the part of authoritarians to 'trust' Britain, in the event of an emergency, in the sense intended by the relevant question.

No other dispositional correlations are significant. 'Trust in the USA' is more general. Low but significant relations obtained between 'trust in the USA' and alienation and authoritarianism, negative in the first case, positive in the second.

The authoritarian's trust in Australia's most powerful ally is easily explicable, the opinion being heavily laden with 'conventionalist'

138

sentiment. The negative relation with alienation springs, conjecturally, from reception of the ALP's tendency to play down, at this stage, the importance of the American alliance, and a tendency to generalize distrust in the same manner as in the case of anxiety.

7.4. Variations in correlations

Having set out the central tendencies of the influence of the four psychological dispositions on political opinion, and noted some of the variety evident in the relationships, the analysis will now be directly addressed to the uncovering of complexities. Table 7.9 exhibits the correlations between all four dispositions and the four political indices within each social class. Constancies will be noted first. Authoritarianism and ethnocentrism are the foes of conscience radicalism and libertarianism in both classes. Alienation in each class is the friend of the established socio-economic radicalism. Ethnocentrism is also hostile to conscience radicalism. These five correlations are the major connections established between dispositions and political opinion, and to find them undisturbed by variations in class identification is a strong indication of their regularity.

The inconstancies are to be found in the less reliable levels of lower correlation. Where an inconstancy has no manifest rationale, it will be dubbed an 'eccentricity'. The latter, as we shall see, are more numerous when variations in correlation by education are examined. The four inconstancies suggested in Table 7.9 are the following:

(i) The alienation–conscience radicalism correlation is significant only in the middle class. The difference in magnitude between the correlations in each class is significant. We thus have no reliable evidence of hostility of alienation to radicalism on conscience issues in the working class. This finding, or rather lack of one, is reminiscent of the depression in the A–E relation, reliably determined in the less educated group. In that case, it was suggested that frustration is more liable to lead to retreat than aggression at the less educated level. Social frustration may have a greater potential for inhibiting sympathetic, nurturant identification with the *other* in the middle class. Another possibility is that the issues of conscience are less salient generally to the working class, opinions on them less stable and that the influence of alienation is dispersed without it having much effect on what is an area of minor concern.

(ii) Alienation is significantly related to libertarianism in the working class only, where the relation is positive. This accords with the 'I may be next' hypothesis advanced to explain the apparent general relation at Section 7.3.5. Apprehensiveness of authority might

TABLE 7.9 *Correlations between four psychological scales and political indices within social classes* (*Tetrachoric correlations*)

		Middle class (n = 215)	Working class (n = 108)
A	ER	0·36**	0·25**
	CR	−0·37**	−0·11
	DL	0·06	0·12
	LIB	0·05	0·26**
F	ER	−0·09	0·18
	CR	−0·27**	−0·41**
	DL	−0·02	−0·34**
	LIB	−0·54**	−0·54**
E	ER	−0·04	0·06
	CR	−0·36**	−0·44*
	DL	0·02	−0·18
	LIB	−0·36**	−0·36**
Angst	ER	0·06	0·10
	CR	−0·09	0·22**
	DL	0·11	0·03
	LIB	0·03	−0·07

well be more pronounced in the working class.

(iii) Authoritarianism is significantly related to 'dovishness' (DL) in the working class only, where the relation is negative. It is hypothesized that there is less informed opinion at the working class level, that views are selectively received from above, and that selection at this less informed level is governed more by disposition. Authoritarians, in keeping with their generally hostile tendency, select 'hawkish' views.

(iv) There is a curious apparent relation, positive and significant, between anxiety and conscience radicalism in the working class. The relation in the middle class is negative but not significant.

Inspection of the relevant questionnaires suggests that many of these anxious working-class respondents find a general sympathy for the 'little man', seeing in him both themselves and others. A fitter of 56–65 says of the ALP, for which he votes: 'In the main, [they] have the little people at heart.' He explains his votes as follows: 'They support little people and the working class, including those not in the employed or monied bracket.' He scores near the maximum on the CR index (and on the libertarianism index). This diffusion of sympathetic sentiment seems to be associated with 'worry' over the position of both the subject and others. The relation between CR and anxiety in the working class may be reciprocal.

We turn now to variations in correlation by educational level, exhibited in Table 7.10.

TABLE 7.10 *Correlations between four psychological scales and political indices at three education levels (Tetrachoric correlations)*

		Lower ($n = 127$)	Middle ($n = 118$)	Higher ($n = 105$)
A	ER	0·35**	0·11	0·44**
	CR	−0·13	−0·27**	−0·30**
	DL	0·29**	0·30**	−0·17
	LIB	0·43**	0·08	0·04
F	ER	0·04	−0·30**	−0·12
	CR	−0·27**	−0·40**	−0·53**
	DL	−0·05	−0·11	−0·17
	LIB	−0·52**	−0·50**	−0·46**
E	ER	−0·11	0·08	−0·36**
	CR	−0·27**	−0·46**	−0·47**
	DL	0·29**	−0·11	−0·11
	LIB	−0·24**	−0·25**	−0·40**
Angst	ER	−0·01	0·08	0·18
	CR	0·07	0·01	0·04
	DL	0·14	0·16	−0·14
	LIB	−0·07	0·26**	−0·07

Four of the five major general correlations, the negative relations between authoritarianism and ethnocentrism, on the one hand, and conscience radicalism and libertarianism, on the other, are not disturbed when educational level is varied. These four great impulses are present at every level of education. There is indeed a slight suggestion that they are more powerful at the higher level, but no differences in the magnitudes of these correlations are significant.

It is sometimes assumed that dispositional influences are greatly reduced at the higher level. Whilst liberal political views are more common at this level and the two 'negative' dispositions less common, as the data of Chapter 5 and 6 have demonstrated, there is no evidence that the *connection* between the 'negative' dispositions and conservative views is dissolved at this level, or even reduced.

The other major finding, the moderate but reliable general relation between alienation and the established socio-economic radicalism, is disturbed at the middle-educated level, where it is trivial and non-significant. This eccentricity is discussed below.

The relative independence of the DL index of psychological correlates is again evident, although some minor and irregular ones are to be observed.

There are, in all, seven inconstancies evident in Table 7.10, most of them trivial. They are discussed below.

(i) Alienation is not significantly related to ER at the middle educated level.[1] This 'eccentricity' has a suggested explanation which has a substantive significance for the position of the middle educated. As has been remarked, inspection of the relevant questionnaires reveals that they are often self-consciously aware of their 'middling' position. In a society where most people have a noticeably rising standard of living, their position is not an easy one. They are educationally qualified to gain good incomes (as is noted in Appendix A) but through lack of drive, opportunity or overburdening commitments may fail to keep up, become 'losers'.

The lack of the A–ER relation at this level stems, I suggest, partly from the different 'meanings' of alienation at the lower and higher levels of education. At the lower level, it is likely to be an *imposed* disposition, through socialization into alienation, in the extreme case, or caused by the manifestly frustrating social conditions or working-class social experience, in one way or another. At the higher level, it is more likely to be an intellectual stance, partly *chosen*, as has been suggested in the case of students. It may arise out of uncertainty of social verities or a highly critical normative judgement of the larger and smaller social worlds. There are, of course, at this level also any number of possible paths to alienation, but it is suggested that they result in a disposition more commonly *recognized* in its totality by

[1] The difference between the lesser of the two significant positive relations (at the lower education level) and that at the middle-educated level is significant ($p < .05$) by the application of the Fisher z_r transformation test, and the overall discrepancy approaches significance when the chi-square test is applied to a collapsed frequency table of the whole sample.

the subject. At this educational level, he has the social assurance and intellectual expertise to perceive a socio-political solution (partial, to be sure) in a radical stance on the ER issues. Conversely, at the lower level, grouches against society are less likely to result in an intellectual step to ER, but rather a firmer *acculturation* to working class political norms, that is, the radical domestic policy of the ALP. At the middle level of education, however, there is often neither the acculturation to working class political norms nor intellectual expertise, and so alienation is more likely to be experienced as a *personal dilemma* without political implications. An outspoken radicalism of the 'Labor' sort might, indeed, endanger the social status of the subject, who is often in a transitional political phase, shedding, or moving further away, from the collectivist politics of the working class to the individualist stance of the middle class.

Here is another fitter and turner (36–45), identifying himself as middle class, high in alienation. He earns over $60 per week, and votes Liberal. He is asked 'If you could choose just *two* matters for *more government attention* . . . which *two* would you choose?' They both illustrate his very moderate 'individualist' position.

A National Health Scheme – something that covers more than dental care, and general coverage of hospital fees, etc. I think perhaps the person who throws away his money on gambling and drinking, and has nothing, gets more help in time of need than a person who saves steadily and runs into trouble and it is all gone. A National Health Scheme would protect this second person.

Closer watch on gross profiteering – especially chemists – this is not done by grocers and the little man. When you need medicines, they mark up the profits. This is not fair to the average man.

In this case, a 'middle-class' protest rather than espousal of ER – which he rejects *in toto* (i.e. he scores zero on this index) – results from his social concerns. He epitomizes the suggestion made above. It can also be illustrated by the following response to the same question, reflecting the apoliticism of the *petit bourgeois*. The speaker is an 'average middle-class' widow of 55–65, with an income of less than $15 a week, again a Liberal voter.

Nothing that comes to mind. I think they're doing a good job. I'm on an invalid pension and I think it's marvellous what's being done for us. I don't know why people complain. As far as child endowment is concerned, when I was bringing up my children, I didn't have it, and managed. People expect too much help these days.

The interviewer commented 'This respondent was very adamant about the fact that age and invalid pensions are adequate . . . This seems, to me, contrary to what most people think.' The respondent is very high in alienation, and scores zero on ER.

The two cases above are extreme ones, of course, and serve only to illustrate a trend which is countered by many respondents who score high both in alienation and ER (or low on both). The point is that the two conflicting tendencies in the middle-educated group seem to produce the near-zero correlation.

(ii) Alienation is positively related to libertarianism in the less educated sample only. The explanation afforded above for this correlation in the working class is also plausible here.

(iii) Another inconstancy is the rather low but significant prediction of alienation to 'dovishness' at the lower- and middle-educated levels, but not at the higher-educated level. Alienation here possibly promotes defence leftism seen as isolationism, or, at the lower level, there is a 'reception' of ALP policy. At the higher-educated level, 'dovishness' has other sources.

(iv) Authoritarianism is negatively related to ER to a moderate degree in the middle-educated sample, but in no other. Once again, it is suggested that this apparent eccentricity stems from the *transitional* character of the politics of the middle-educated group. At this level, 'conventionalist' and 'ego-defensive' persons are sometimes inclined to distance themselves from the working class by rejecting radical views and associations. Here is the second fitter and turner mentioned above in relation to the first inconstancy, asked to name two 'good things' about the Liberal Party.

They have handled the unions well. I work in a factory but I don't like to see the government back down to the unions. I can't think of any special instances offhand, though.

An authoritarian infusion is also hinted at in his view of what may be 'wrong' with the Labor Party.

The main obvious thing is the split in Labor – I mean the ALP and DLP. I think this is bad. Anything divided is weak.

Sometimes the middle-educated authoritarian, whilst rejecting Labor policies, is a reluctant, backward-looking ALP voter, for 'individualist' reasons. An electricity council inspector (36–45), 'common ordinary working class I suppose', who is radical only on age pensions, says of his reasons for voting ALP: 'Only that I think they are more interested in the worker as a person . . . I don't agree with withdrawal from Vietnam but [I] vote Labor anyway.' He is very high in authoritarianism, endorsing all the punitive half-items.

(v) Ethnocentrism has a substantial and significant negative relation to ER at the higher education level only. This seems to be relatively straightforward in theoretical terms. The ethnocentric person at the higher educated level is deviant, an unusual bigot. It is not surprising to find him expressing an unusually pronounced opposition to Labor domestic policies, perceived as those of an alien 'lower' class.

(vi) Ethnocentrism has a positive relation to defence leftism, 'dovishness', at the lower-educated level only. This is *prima facie* extraordinary, but easily explained. Since the DL issues have much to do with the American alliance, a 'left' position at this educational level is often just plain anti-American. An English lady in Glen Iris (Melbourne's paradigm middle-class suburb), although she votes Liberal, is a case in point. Of things 'wrong' with the Liberal Party, she says: 'They haven't a proper foreign policy. They blindly follow another country – the USA.' She is very high in ethnocentrism. A typist clerk of 46–55, an ALP voter, near the maximum in ethnocentrism, says when asked to name things 'wrong' with the Liberals: 'Their defence attitude. They're too Americanized.'

An ethnocentric plasterer (36–45) with left views on the DL index, finds these matters for 'more government attention': 'They should take over the offshore natural gas completely, and the car industries, and kick out the Yanks.' A loquacious pensioner (56–65) again high in ethnocentrism and defence leftism, found the Liberals 'buttering up America too much. We need dollars but too much was spent on Johnson's trip. Sure we need American help and we need American dollars but in my mind that money what went on all those flags and things, could have been put to better use for the nurses.[2] Waste of money, all of it.' The explanation for this eccentricity in correlation virtually leaps off the pages of the questionnaires.

(vii) Anxiety is positively associated with libertarianism, at the middle-educated level only.[3] In this group aspirations to success

[2] Nurses were asking for more pay at the time.

[3] This eccentricity is amongst the most reliable, being significant ($p < .02$) when tested by chi-square.

involve respectability rather than prestige. This requires the subject to put a clear distance between himself and *outré* groups of low status, homosexuals, beatniks, Communists. But one badge of high status is tolerance. The upwardly aspiring middle-educated person is thus in an awkward position, wishing to deplore 'bad behaviour' *comme il faut*, but at the same time striving to exhibit a high-minded liberalism. Libertarian sentiment may thus be ambiguously perceived, in his particular *ambience*, either as a suspect sympathy with disreputable groups, or as a praiseworthy tolerance. According to this hypothesis, therefore, the political opinion creates the disposition, and not vice versa.

In affording theoretical explanations for these seven inconstancies in correlations between dispositions and political opinion, the social position of the person has often to be considered. Not only an understanding of the general social environment and the nature of subjective dispositions, but also a comprehension of the significance of the social location of the subject and the ways in which his views may be formed at various social levels is necessary, if the variety in the relations are to be explained. Many nuances are exhibited by the relationships, and great complexity. Having attempted to understand some of this complexity, the reader may be left with the false impression that the relationships are so various that few reliable predictions from disposition to political opinion can be made. This is not so, for two reasons.

The first is that, as we noted before this extensive consideration of inconstancies, there are a number of striking constancies to be found. These lie in the special vulnerability of conscience radicalism and libertarianism to psychological influence, especially by authoritarianism and ethnocentrism, which produces apparently invariant general relations, moderate when the correlations are uncorrected for attenuation, very strong when they are corrected. There is also a fairly reliable relation between alienation and a radical position on socio-economic questions.

The second reason for confidence in the possibility of reliable prediction is that, once the fact of an inconstancy in a relation is established, and its location noted, the prediction can take into account an unusual correlation, or lack of one, in a particular locale. More research is clearly necessary to substantiate many of the conjectured theoretical explanations for particular inconstancies, but these, too, if shown to be reliable, can qualify prediction so that it is apt to the situation being considered. What is most clear is that a narrowly political, psychological or sociological approach to the understanding of the relation of disposition to opinion is bound to fail. The researcher must have recourse to an armoury of techniques to facilitate and expand the analysis until it is capable of matching the complexity of reality.

7.5. Conclusion

We have established that two of the three main dimensions of radicalism, conscience radicalism, and the established socio-economic radicalism are susceptible to high and moderate degrees of influence, respectively, by psychological dispositions. Opinions on the third dimension, the 'left'–'right' continuum in foreign and defence policy are more independent of dispositional influence, but do not altogether escape it. A fourth continuum of political opinion, libertarianism, is strongly influenced by disposition. The principal interrelations are displayed in Figure 7.1.

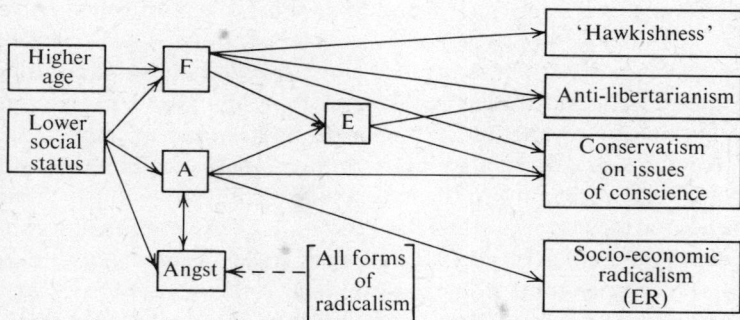

Figure 7.1. The principal interrelations between psychological dispositions and political attitudes.

What do these findings displayed in Table 7.1 amount to? All these dimensions relate to matters of *policy*, and it is therefore reasonable to suppose that dispositions (a) create a motive force for radicalism or conservatism in their respective domains at the highest level, that is, they influence decision makers and leaders of opinion as well as the mass public, and (b) that they create 'climates of opinion' in the mass public which invite forward policies or negate and impede them. We have also shown that perceptions of political situations are influenced by psychological disposition.

But two objections could be raised with considerable force if we were to go so far as to suggest that political *events* related to the implementation of these policies are strongly influenced by psychological dispositions. The first is that, as we noted in first introducing discussion of psychological influence in Chapter 3, economic interest groups, through their influence on political parties and governments, play a large part in determining the course of events in economic policy. Likewise, external forces in international relations often compel actions in defence and foreign policy.

The second objection is that, even in so far as one may gauge their influence in the *electorate*, policy opinions, and hence dispositions influencing policy opinions, play a relatively small part in the voter's choice. True, party record as well as promise may be weighed in terms of policies implemented or proposed and so policy considerations may have more weight with the mass public than may at first appear. The 'political' public, also, is more alive to them, and by personal contact may influence less interested voters. Speakers on the mass media may also increase the actual impact of policy considerations. But one striking finding is that in exploring the correlates of voter's choice of party, only alienation is a disposition apparently capable of altering the balance between the major parties. Domestic economic policy issues, on which opinions are related to alienation, are given a much higher rating in importance by voters than defence and foreign policy. Moreover, these two dimensions of policy were, at the time of the major survey, the only two which differentiated the major parties. The ALP and the LCP were not seen to be much different in respect of conscience radicalism and libertarianism. The dispositions influencing radical opinion, therefore, were operative at the margin of policy determination, and it cannot plausibly be argued that they were central.

However, three important considerations should be borne in mind. The first is that through the erosion of anti-liberal dispositions by rising affluence and levels of education, conscience radicalism and libertarian sentiment are likely to become more widely diffused, and issues connected with them to increase in importance. The second is that, as this occurs, the major parties may seek to differentiate their positions on these continua in the eyes of the mass public, and indeed, since 1966, have taken steps to do so. The ALP is presenting itself as the champion of radical opinion in both cases. It follows that the influence of disposition on vote, and, ultimately, the determination of policy, will become more central. Thirdly, this empirical study has been conducted at a time of relative calm, in a stable democracy. In critical episodes, when, for example, basic liberties guaranteed by the state are at hazard, or democratic regimes are threatened by extreme mass movements with an ethnocentric basis, then psychological dispositions may be paramount in influencing the course of events, although still only some of several important factors in any actual situation. One such situation was the collapse of the Weimar Republic in Germany in 1933, considered in Chapter 9. It would not be possible to describe the collapse of the Weimar régime without engaging in an analysis which emphasized the themes of alienation, authoritarianism, ethnocentrism and anti-libertarian sentiment. The mechanisms connecting these, obtainable by empirical investigation in periods of quiescence in stable democracies, can be useful in forming a repertoire of analytical devices for such critical episodes. Indeed, they are of crucial importance, if the analyst of political history is to accomplish his essential task, which is not to be able to 'know' something in its totality, but to be able to say 'I see'.

8 Political conversation in a small group

8.1. Introduction

This chapter is an *excursus*. It consists, in the main, of a speculative discussion of a political conversation amongst a small group of voters after the elections. One purpose of it is to illustrate the complexity of the structure and function of political attitudes (and their relations with dispositions) in situations of actual personal interaction. Another is to show how such contrived situations may be used to generate hypotheses testable on the larger sample (none of these subjects was included in the final voter sample).

Some general problems in attaching a specific meaning to the location of a subject on a continuum by assigning a scale score to him are discussed.

Some data consistent with one hypothesis are advanced. A brief discussion follows of ways in which the influence of psychological dispositions on opinion may be deflected.

8.2. A political conversation

This conversation was recorded in December 1966, two weeks or so after the federal elections. The venue was an office of a market research firm. The writer chaired the discussion, which was tape-recorded. All five of the participants had voted Liberal, and been interviewed before election day. They were invited to participate in a discussion either because they had at that time confessed 'a lot' of interest in politics (in the case of three) or had fallen into one of the two questions designed to identify 'opinion leaders' (all five).

The purpose of contriving these circumstances was partly to illustrate the complexity of expressed attitudes in actual social interaction and partly to see whether any hypotheses capable of being tested with data from the total sample of about 400 might be suggested. Accordingly, the participants were pushed on to as many 'sensitive' topics as possible, the chairman aspiring to the conflicting demands both of neutrality and the role of *agent provocateur*. The in-

150

terpretation of the fragments of conversation offered below is therefore highly speculative, and is meant to be.

To introduce the participants (the unbracketed data is from their questionnaires):

Mr A.*:[1] A shoe factory manager, aged 46–55. Education: Intermediate Certificate (taken at about age 15). Married, no children under 17.

Described himself as 'average middle-class'. 'No church, just a Christian.' Father a farmer. (Tough face, self-concept rough but just? Working-class manner.)

Mr B.: Manager of a civil engineering firm, aged 46–55. Senior Technical College Engineering Diploma. Married, one child under 17.

Described himself as 'average middle-class'. Non-churchgoing Congregationalist. Father a 'senior' engineer.

(Dressed carefully and formally, socially assured, relaxed.)

Mrs A.: Home duties, aged 36–45, educated to Matriculation (taken at about age 17). Wife of a graduate engineer, his father being a farmer. Two children under 17. Once again, 'average middle-class'. A Catholic churchgoer. Fortuitously, the same surname as Mr A. (Elegant, charming, physically attractive.)

Mr C.: Sales manager in an electronics firm, aged 26–35. Had a Trade Certificate and had undergone further technical training. Married, with two children under 17. Described himself as 'upper middle-class'. A non-churchgoing Presbyterian. His father a sergeant in the army.

(Confident, middle-class demeanour; aggressive in discussion.)

Mr D.*: Employed as a metallurgist, a part-time student pursuing an Engineering Diploma, aged 26–35. Married, with one child under 17; refused absolutely to place himself in any social class. A churchgoing Presbyterian.

(Awkward, shy, spoke in a hushed voice in the direction of the right lapel of his yacht club jacket.)

All but one (Mr D*) said they seldom talked politics. The tone of the conversation was often like that of a managerial meeting: issues were discussed in a practical fashion and principles struck a jarring note when they cropped up. Mr A* and Mr D* seemed eager to be socially acceptable to the other three, who were not at all anxious about their own status, and were faintly patronizing.

Two conflicting groups emerged in the course of an hour: on the one hand, Mr A* and Mr D*, who might be described *post hoc* as punitive and dependent; and on the other, Mr C and Mrs A (non-punitive and independent). Mr C bore the brunt of such hostility as developed. Mr B preserved throughout a position of social leadership and withdrew from violent argument. All except Mr C over-

---

[1] Watch Mr A* and Mr D*; The asterisks will be retained throughout the chapter.

stated their agreement with one another's views; he alone intervened from time to time to disagree.

The conversation was marked by some sketchy anecdotes from the personal histories of both Mr A* and Mr D*, which were evidently intended to add conviction to their opinions. The early experiences of both men seemed to lie heavily upon them, and to colour their views. The remaining three were reticent, apparently untroubled, and never implied they had been taught wisdom by experience.

Picking over the conversation on tape, in retrospect, led to the following suppositions:

1. Although at one on socio-economic and party political issues, the discussants exhibited such divisions on non-economic issues as to suggest two camps: the 'punitive, dependent' pair of Messrs A* and D*, who spoke feelingly of their own histories, sometimes reduced complex problems of causation to the conspiratorial machinations of persons, admired strong leaders, were somewhat racially prejudiced, one in favour of hanging, both for violence generally, and anti-libertarian. They were of lower status. In contrast to this pair, Mrs A and Mr C either had no personal problems, or sat on them without difficulty; were sceptical of heroes, ascribed social problems to systematic causes capable of being remedied, were libertarian and assured of their own social position. Mr B hovered pensively between them, his support valued and sought by both sides.

2. Both Mr A* and Mr D* revealed their dispositions with caution: sometimes only by the violent language surrounding a 'liberal' formal opinion. They often abandoned punitive opinions when they found they were sailing too close to social rejection.

It is suggested here that these two were trying to *shrug off* a somewhat authoritarian disposition in the face of middle-class social pressure, through the adoption of liberal opinions on particular issues. They were nevertheless haunted by social disasters narrowly avoided. Their basic dispositions accommodated liberal opinions with some difficulty.

The two speculative interpretations advanced above may now be illustrated from the voices. Two dots indicate a pause; three an omission.

Mr D* on his early life:
I spent the first part – the first eighteen years of my life in a small town called Hay in New South Wales . . . in the smaller country towns you have the townspeople, and you have the so-called squatters, or cockies. *Now*, in the

smaller country towns there is a very, very strong, and very cliquey groups [sic] . . . the landowner has their clubs in each of the different towns, and they stick to their group and that's it. They only come to town to shop.

Mr C: I disagree with that. I believe the division is greater in the city than it is in the country. [Uproar]

Mr D* [shouting]: This is a statement of what I've seen, and lived in . . [more calmly] they have their own dances, their own ball, they have the Country Club race meeting, picnic races and that sort of thing, and you've got to be *in* there to *get* there and that's – that's it.

Despite attempts to change the topic, Mr D* returned frequently and bitterly to the theme of social rejection in country towns.

Mr A* reveals a little of his early life in discussing the ALP. The group as a whole is pessimistic about the party's future. Mr A* exceeds them all in pessimism.

Mr A*: . . . I'd go along with this but I – I – I – can't see, I can't foresee – and I was a member of the Labor Party . . .

Mr C: But I think it *must* [put its house in order] to survive. I can't see any future for the Labor Party unless they do something to resolve their problems.

Mr A* [desperately]: I can't see it! I genuinely can't see it!

Mrs A deplores class distinction by the Labor Party.

Mr C: They try too much to project this image of being for the working man, and the working man just doesn't exist . . look at the people!

Mr A* is asked for his view:
I'd go along with Mrs A . . . just as well you're not my wife! [all laugh]. Ugh, go along with it strong – I think it's a matter of growing up . . . I think this is the big failing in the Labor Party and why I can *never* see it coming good, because the people that control it are – like the shop steward that's got a vote at work and I've got to kid to him to be a shop steward anyway – he hasn't got any brains . . .

. . . The need for it [the ALP] is gradually diminishing.

Mr A* links the 'diminishing need' for the ALP to his new paternal role. For Messrs B and C, and Mrs A, it is a matter for other people.

Both Mr A* and Mr D* have their political heroes. The others are sceptical, and sometimes disdain particular politicians.

Mr A* is asked whether the DLP will ever succeed in convincing people 'that they're not sectarian' (his phrase).

Mr A* [pauses]: I think they could, yes! . . . If they get coves like Benson . .[2]

Mr C: Benson's not DLP.

[2] Captain Benson, a retired merchant sailor, had won a seat as an Independent candidate at the elections, after being expelled by the Victorian ALP because of his membership of a 'right-wing' body, the 'Defend Australia Committee'.

Mr A* [raises his voice]: No, I'm just saying if they can incorporate coves *like* this – leaders and *men* – like Benson – I think they could go places!

Mr D* [in a whisper]: I think I'd agree with that one too.

Mr A*: . . . you speak to very few people – even Labor Party men – that don't respect Benson. This is the type of person they've got to get – someone that's shown a bit of courage in their bloody time, and! – a Mason if necessary, just to get this stigma out of their – their party that this is controlled by the Roman Catholic church.

Mr D* greatly admired President Johnson, and felt that Mr Calwell created 'an *uneducated* image, for want of a better term' which led many to lose respect for him as a potential national leader.

Neither Mr C nor Mrs A admired Johnson. Mrs A felt that the publicity given to the President's visit was:

an implicit help to the Liberal Party and I felt that the less – well I just don't think he had a right to come over, I think he meddled in our politics.

So too, Mr B:

Well, I, I don't think too much of President Johnson – he's a bit of a larrikin,[3] although I – from my brief acquaintance with America I – have a very high regard for Americans generally – I think they're hard workers – particularly for Texans, I had a good time in Texas, but President Johnson I think is a . . [vehemently] he's just a politician and a wheeler-dealer . .

Mr C: Exactly.

Mr B: . . and a real larrikin, in a way . . As to his coming to Australia . . it was just a political *move*, I think – thought he'd help a bit, and help himself, and help Harold[4] . . [quiet laughter from Mr C at the mention of 'Harold'].

Mr B is asked what sort of an impression Mr Holt made when travelling with President Johnson.

Mr B: Oh, that made me slightly sick.

A debate on whether or not social class differences exist in Australia had the more authoritarian pair thinking in personal terms of class enemies. Mr D*'s grim recollections have been set out.

Mr A*: I think there's a very small percentage – possibly one and a half per cent – that consider themselves high society. Outside that, nought.

The others, however, saw social differences as generated in an impersonal, systematic way, and not as the creature of supposedly exclusive groups. Mr B even discovers in himself a little Marxist residue:

[3] An Australian idiomatic expression for 'hooligan', but with a milder tone.
[4] Harold Holt, then the Prime Minister and Leader of the Liberal Party.

Mr B: . . . I think there's another division too. I think there's the division be-tween the people who work for their living on – on wages, and the people – the capitalists, if you like, who own the m – the, the sources, or the means of production.

 . . . not that they're wealthy people necessarily . . .

Discussion of migrants and migration policy revealed some sur-prising dissonance between the professed general attitudes and par-ticular opinions accommodated within the one person. Notably Mr B:

I don't know whether we're going to talk about the colour – the White Aus-tralia policy – but I would have views on that, too.

Well I would think that we should preserve the White Australia policy . . . That's not to say that there are some, perhaps some Asians – Asiatics – that would – wouldn't perhaps be permissible. From my view, I think that if we need to build up the country . . *population* quickly we may have to accept a sort of a quota of perhaps Asians, but [pause] they're not really coloured in the sense that I was thinking about: I mean they are and they aren't.

Chairman [baffled]: In what way are they not?

Mr B: Well I mean I'm thinking the – that dark coloured people are . . *pres-ent* . . problems, but there is less trouble with – even where intermarriage occurs with, say, Malaysians and people like that.

Chair: How about Malaysian Indians? When you say dark people are you thinking of Africans?

Mr B [suddenly]: Well I was thinking about negroes, of course.

Stereotypes seem to be stretched to breaking point here: Asians, Malaysians especially, are made, perhaps, honorary whites. Messrs A* and D* declare themselves for a quota system of Asian migration, but nevertheless fail to avoid a fight with Mrs A and Mr C, who want to open the floodgates. Mr C dislikes the idea of any quota system except one based on education.

On the issue of capital punishment, battle was joined on the ques-tion of whether a convict (Ryan) who had shot dead a warder in a bid to escape from prison should have been hanged. Mr A* thought it was imperative to hang him, for administrative reasons – the good management of the prison. Mr B vacillates, and is temporarily attracted to the abolitionist view by Mr C, who reminds him of a case where an innocent man was hanged. Mrs A says she is opposed to capital punishment in any circumstances. Mr D*, still having trouble in grabbing life by the tail, has a special point of view:

There is always that little bit of doubt . . no matter how sure – how much evi-dence there is in favour of the person's guilt. To take that person's life is so final . . .

155

This is final. No matter what comes up in the future you can't bring this person back.

However, I wouldn't – I wouldn't be against, say, physical punishment, I wouldn't – I wouldn't be against Ryan getting, ah, two lashes a day for the rest of his life, as a deterrent, or anybody else in a similar category, because this can always be stopped. But to take the person's life, I feel it's – so final.

It is not the violence but the finality to which Mr D* is implacably opposed. Rejection, after all, played a notable part in his early life.

The final question was whether or not the Communist Party should be banned. By now everyone was heated. Mr A* shuttled rapidly between permissiveness and a sharply-felt need for counter-violence:

I don't think you can outlaw any political party. I think education, standard of living, can keep them in their place. But certainly if they get, ah, start getting power in a certain direction, give them the option – say that's where you want to live you just go there and live there! Don't treat them with kid gloves *all* the time. If they can hit hard, well hit hard back! And no-one should scream if one of them is sent back to – over to China . . .

Mr B, Mrs A and Mr C are all convinced that social conditions will prove an adequate impediment to the growth of Communism in Australia and find legal measures wrong in principle.

Mr A* states a contingency:
If they can get a cell, in a union, they can tie this country up in two minutes.

Mr D* comes to his assistance:
I'm not talking about suppressing, I mean forcing into the open.

Mr A*: Yeh.

Mr D*: Force them out – force them out into the open, where everybody can see what's going on.

Mrs A: [confused] How do you do [that]? – but I mean – look – what do you do? – they *are* in the open.

Mr D* [reluctantly]: Well, yes and no.

[Uproar]

Mr A* [to the aid of Mr D*]: They're not in the open! No fear! They've got their meetings – underground meetings – don't worry about that!

Mr D*: And they've got their own little schools! [like those squatters?]

Mr A*: And they've got their own school and cadre and own education.

Mr C: [sceptically] You could say that about the Labor Party and the Central Executive,[5] couldn't you?

Here the tape ends, with the two factions at last shouting at, and

[5] The controlling committee of the ALP organization in the state of Victoria.

down, each other. Mr C, and later also Mrs A, were moved easily to a spirited defence of liberal values; Mr B approaches his own opinions with caution and detachment. But Mr A* and Mr D* have invested a lot of emotional capital in a view of society potentially beset by crisis and emergency, and are loath to give it away.

8.3. A hypothesis

We will now check this onrush of speculation and proceed with our exercise in method. The purpose is to counterpoint imaginative insight with hard data. We are fortunate enough to have some reliable information about the participants in this discussion, through their interviews. The five participants in this discussion were also given political questionnaires after its conclusion. We are thus in a position (a) to throw some light on what was going on during the discussion; and (b) to see whether any of the processes which emerged in the group discussion have any *generality*; that is, can be discovered in the wider sample.

In taking out ideas from the recorded conversation to face the crowd of data from the survey, only a very minor confrontation is planned. Much of the conversational transaction, it was suggested, was related to obtaining, often in an oblique way, social acceptance; and it is to this point that the exercise will be directed.

Table 8.1 shows authoritarianism (F) scores for each member of the group, and their radical or conservative position on three issues, as shown in their written questionnaire before and after[6] discussion.

For the sample as a whole, the median F score was 13·5. Although the relative magnitude of the F scores is as expected, only Mr B is above the sample median. Three are normal (9–14) in authoritarianism, two low. The three issues are ones connected with conscience radicalism which were touched upon in the conversation.

What is chiefly interesting here is the extraordinary instability of the views of Mr A*, whose outlook has undergone a sea-change since he was interviewed a month before. Taken together with the suppositions elaborated above, these data suggest that 'upwardly mobile' persons of working-class origin may, in the process of seeking social acceptance, adopt liberal opinions on such conscience issues as those above; *or* adapt their views to those of whatever group they aspire to join, perhaps a conservative one. In *either* case their current opinion

---

[6] The first questionnaire was that administered about a month earlier; the second immediately after the discussion.

would stem less from dispositions, such as authoritarianism, and more from infection of opinion, so to speak, from the groups in which they seek acceptance. It follows that for the upwardly socially mobile group, the correlation between F scores and opinions on particular issues, especially those susceptible to dispositional influence, should be lower than it is for the socially fixed.

TABLE 8.1

Participant	F Scale score[7] (0–26)	White Australia Before	After	Aid to Asia Before	After	Capital punishment Before	After
Mr D* ⎫ Middle ⎧	12	Cons.	Rad.	Cons.	Rad.	Cons.	Rad.
Mr A* ⎪ range ⎨	9	Rad.	Rad.	Rad.	Rad.	Cons.	Cons.
Mr B ⎭ ⎩	14	Rad.	Rad.	Rad.	Undec.	Rad.	Cons.
Mrs A ⎫ Low ⎧	2	Rad.	Rad.	Rad.	Rad.	Undec.	Rad.
Mr C ⎭ ⎩	6	Rad.	Rad.	Cons.	Cons.	Rad.	Rad.

The data discussed in Chapter 5 indicate that there is a reliable negative relation between both social class identification and education, on the one hand, and authoritarianism, on the other. But whilst the relation is reliable, its magnitude is not great, and there are many high scorers amongst the middle-class and the educated. Table 7.3, in Chapter 7, indicates a moderate negative relation between the conscience radicalism index and authoritarianism. The CR index (of five items) incorporates opinions on the three issues mentioned above in Table 8.1. There is no reliable relation found between conscience radicalism and class, and the relation with education is significant only when the 'higher' and 'lower' groups are compared (excluding the 'middle' group).

These data indicate that it is most unsafe to generalize in small group settings from class identification to authoritarian orientation or opinions. A shift to a liberal opinion may be some help, or no help at all, in gaining acceptance in a particular small group. The process of *bargaining for acceptance* which seemed to emerge in the recorded

---

[7] The designation of the raw F scores is as for quartiranges, the first being designated low, the second and third 'middle range'. The standardization data are in Appendix C.

group discussion involved pressure to a change in a liberal direction in that particular group: the general point, however, seems that to be acceptable, one may have to change in *either* direction. If this is true, then the opinions of the upwardly socially mobile, and their confessed prejudices, should be uncertainly related to authoritarian disposition. Hence we expect a low correlation.

An 'upwardly socially mobile' group was extracted from the sample as follows. Those 'average' or 'upper' middle class, but without higher formal education ('Leaving' or above) were identified, and of these those with higher than average income ($3000 to more than $12,000 p.a.) were retained. They numbered 45.

Amongst this group, the F–CR correlation is indeed lower, as Table 8.2 demonstrates. But the difference between the correlation in this group is not *significantly* different from the rest of the sample.

TABLE 8.2   *Relations between CR scores and F scale scores (Tetrachoric correlations)*

Upwardly mobile	r_t	F–CR = 0.18 (n.s.)	(n = 45)
All others	r_t	F–CR = 0·39**	(n = 305)

However, a more detailed scrutiny of the data revealed the following: on two issues, hanging and economic aid, the negative relation between the radical position and authoritarianism is absent in the upwardly mobile group. The differences on these issues between the correlation in the upwardly mobile group and that in the rest of the sample is significant in both cases.

This finding is important, since these two issues are amongst the more salient of the CR group.

The data thus seem to suggest that the process of bargaining with one's opinions on the way up acts to some extent as a solvent on their connection with psychological dispositions. It is not that authoritarians must appear liberals in order to rise; rather one must be prepared to exchange internal psychological formative pressures for external social ones.

The process appears to reflect one of Greenstein's[8] maxims: 'If . . . the disposition that is strong is to take one's cues from others, the effects of personal variation on behaviour will be reduced.'

[8] F. I. Greenstein, 'The Impact of Personality on Politics: An Attempt to Clear Away the Underbrush', *American Political Science Review*, 61, (1967), pp. 629–41.

To make a general point, in the larger, 'socially stable' part of the sample, the fact of psychological influence in the area of conscience radicalism is possibly a result of the absence of a definable self-interest in this area. There are thus no class or interest group sanctions to be wary of. Here again, one of Greenstein's principles[9] seems to be relevant: 'The impact of personal differences in behaviour is increased to the degree that sanctions are not attached to certain of the alternative possible causes of behaviour.'

The point that has been made about the apparent deflection of psychological influence amongst the upwardly socially mobile, is, of course, that, in their case, there *are* social sanctions waiting in the wings. They must have a careful eye to the opinions held in the groups they aspire to join; they are involved in a game situation, where the dice are opinions, and the reward chips, signals of social acceptance.

8.4. The deflection of psychological influence

Apart from the rather special pressures on the upwardly mobile, there are two major contingencies which may deflect psychological influence on opinion. Neither has come very much to the fore in this book.

The first is institutional affiliation, especially to political parties. Affiliation to socialist organizations, which usually propound liberal opinions on racial harmony, for example, may well dampen the effects of working-class authoritarianism in such societies as contemporary Britain. But since, at the time of this survey, the ALP had not emphasized its radical position on issues of conscience (except hanging) it exhibited little influence in the mass public on these.

The second is what may be termed 'moral' or 'intellectual' control by the subject of his own authoritarian impulses. This concept presupposes an authoritarian personality structure in a process of transmutation, with the super-ego, particularly that component of it dubbed the ego-ideal, playing an active role in persuading, as it were, a compliant ego to mitigate expressions of hostility. This is likely to be a lengthy and difficult process, since the hypothetical defence mechanisms of the ego which may underpin ethnocentrism as a stratagem (namely anti-intraception, projectivity and stereotypy) are unconscious.

[9] *Ibid.*

The moral deliberations of Mr B, in our recorded conversation, are perhaps a case in point. The hesitancy he displays, taken with his air of command over proceedings, suggests that he has come to an awareness of his authoritarianism in the first place through social interaction. He is introspective and self-critical (deviant characteristics in an authoritarian, but perhaps ones acquired in the course of coping with social difficulties), even audacious: he himself raises the issue of 'colour – the White Australia policy'. But he does so in order to put forward what is in fact a liberal opinion, after staking out a formally conservative general position. He has adopted the substance of liberalism whilst retaining the conservative form. The first requirement of his 'moral control', and perhaps 'moral control' in general, appears to be some anti-authoritarian element in the super-ego; the second, deliberate contest with anti-intraception.

The pressure (and opportunities) for this kind of 'moral control' of authoritarianism might be expected to be most marked amongst those with tertiary education, mixing in middle-class circles.

The two modes of 'deflection' of psychological influences discussed above are, of course, different in kind: the first is through an external, social influence; the second refers to the deflection of the influence of one kind of psychological disposition (authoritarianism) by other 'internal' psychological mechanisms.

8.5. 'High' and 'low' scoring

Reflection on the conversation reported above leads me to two further considerations, the first a speculation, the second perhaps better termed a rumination.

(i) It was something of a surprise to find that the two 'punitive', 'dependent', 'more authoritarian' contestants in the conversational struggle were, in fact, scorers in the *middle range* of the F distribution. What an argument between very low and very high scorers might have been like is an interesting question. The two 'middle range' subjects nevertheless exhibited what seem unquestionably authoritarian views *at times* (such as Mr D*'s proposal that the convict discussed should be lashed *every day*). At other times, they are not authoritarian in their views. In the middle range, therefore, we may speculate that, rather than finding deepening shades of grey, so to speak, there are *spasms* of authoritarianism.

This is, in a way, not out of accord with theoretical expectations, since the work done in the field has been much more concerned with the elaboration of the personality mechanisms of the authoritarian, those of the liberal being somewhat neglected. Most of the theoretical substance of the F Scale used here is to be found, therefore, in the authoritarian item-halves, the non-authoritarian ones being more in the form of after-thoughts or replies, and, taken together, less coherently related to a body of central principles. The zero point of the scale thus resembles a nullity rather than a liberal, and, as we allow our gaze to travel along the scale towards its higher reaches, we see something like an authoritarian ghost taking more and more concrete shape, being solid and fully rounded at the maximum score.

In the central range of scores, therefore, there may be as much *ambivalence* as neutrality.

(ii) The second point has a general bearing on scale scoring, and so on the general methodology of research with scales. The question of whether the zero end of a scale designates the opposite pole from its maximum, or a neutral point, has seldom been raised. It is an important one. It seems reasonable to suppose that the lower scores on this paired-alternative F scale, 'fuzzy' though the non-authoritarian item-halves may be, do not reflect *authoritarianism* in a minor degree, but an inclination *opposed* to authoritarianism. Just where the watershed, i.e. the true neutral point, may be, is likely to be contentious, but the desirability of treating anti-authoritarian persons as arithmetically *negative* in their scores seems to me to be clear.

One tenable solution to this problem might be to use the information we have about the empirical distributions and to use quartile scores, negative for the first and second, positive for the third and fourth. Thus, using the standardization data set out in Appendix C one might translate the raw authoritarianism scores in these terms to ones with a minimum of -2 and a maximum of $+2$.

The same procedures are defensible for the ethnocentrism and alienation scales, if these are to be treated as capable of defining polar opposites.

If a standard procedure admitting negative scoring had been in vogue for the past two decades, we might have seen fewer cases where authoritarianism and its correlates had been researched amongst undergraduates and other unsuitable samples, since their preponderantly negative scores would have made their inappropriateness abundantly obvious. To go looking for fascist tendencies, in the manner of much reported research, amongst university students, in English-speaking countries, is like measuring kangaroos in the hope

162

of quantifying tigers.

This suggestion can only be raised with diffidence at this stage of the argument of this work. However, the fact that data from a large, representative urban sample have been obtained and presented makes possible its easy implementation. It seems particularly appropriate to the description of individuals through use of the scales developed in this book in later research.

8.6. Conclusion

This *excursus* has been, in part, designed to show how contrived circumstances may be useful in throwing up hypotheses capable of being tested in larger samples. One, in particular, that upwardly mobile persons may be less susceptible to dispositional influence than to group pressures in forming their opinion on issues of conscience, has been shown to have some limited evidential support in the larger sample. Other considerations have been raised speculatively, with a view to future research. We shall now point to the pith of its argument and demonstrate the mode and extent of the general analytic utility of its findings.

9 Conclusion; the psychology of Nazism

9.1. Introduction

A cartographical enterprise requires adequate instruments. A major part of this book has been devoted to showing why the instruments in previous use for the measurement of some dispositions have been inadequate, and in constructing more adequate ones. The dispositional measures of authoritarianism, ethnocentrism and alienation, the construction of which is set out in Appendix C and which are described in Chapter 4, are held to be adequate for investigation and are offered for research use. In employing correlational and factor analysis in identifying political constructs, we have evolved more modest indices.

However, the process of enquiry through which these instruments were developed clarified the structure of political opinion itself. Indeed, the structure has a clarity almost unlooked for; and one of the political dimensions identified, conscience radicalism, exhibits a constancy over time, a cohesiveness and rootedness in psychological dispositions which suggest that it will persist as a disparate attitude. Sociological considerations suggest it will grow in importance.

Of the four psychological dispositions whose influence on one another and on political opinion has been investigated, it is anxiety which has proved the most disappointing. Although it appears to have a low positive relation to each of the four sentiments of radicalism, and to a very general perception of threat, its relations with other dispositions and political attitudes has been less than might have been expected. This research was initially inspired by an interest in the implications of insecurity and aggression. It seems now that, far from being at the core of mechanisms of hate and distrust, anxiety cowers in a corner by itself, so to say, and that confident men possessed of complex social frustrations are closer to a central symbol of the aggressive type. This is not to say that latent or *repressed* anxiety has no role: on the contrary, there is persuasive evidence from in-depth analyses, dwelling on the themes of externalization and ego-defence,[1] which cannot be ignored. But here we have been concerned chiefly with the function of relatively manifest anxiety.

In exploring the interrelations of dispositions, their influence on political attitudes and the structure of political attitudes, this study has declared its 'contextualist' persuasion, has been concerned to acknowledge the potentiality of intention, and, at almost every stage of the analysis, has argued, implicitly as well as explicitly, the necessity of *Verstehen* in social enquiry, both as a tool of research and a method by which the results of research can be interpreted. A few of the most salient findings are noted below, as a prelude to consideration of the critical question of prediction from disposition to action, and from action to a sequence of historical events.

9.2. Psychological dispositions and political attitudes; constancies

The five major constancies in the correlation of psychological dispositions and political attitudes are the following:

(i) Authoritarianism is negatively related to conscience radicalism.

(ii) Authoritarianism is negatively related to libertarianism.

(iii) Ethnocentrism is negatively related to conscience radicalism.

(iv) Ethnocentrism is negatively related to libertarianism.

(v) Alienation is positively related to socio-economic radicalism.

All these relations are substantial, and only the last exhibits any disturbance when variations in correlation between different social class and educational groups are considered.

Of the four psychological dispositions, it is alienation, conceived as social estrangement, which is the most various in its function, being a precursor of ethnocentrism, a friend of socio-economic radicalism, a foe of conscience radicalism, a minor ally of a 'left' position in defence and foreign policy, and, in a very minor degree, an associate of libertarianism. It is in contemplating this disposition that the unexpected is most in evidence; 'wherein', to quote one clinical usage of the term itself, 'familiar persons and situations appear strange: it is the opposite of *déjà vu*'.[2] Its most significant role is in its prediction to ethnocentrism, which seems a result either of the familiar frustration–aggression mechanism, or the generalization of social distrust. But its effects go beyond this, as the illustrative case of 'John'

[1] M. Brewster Smith, 'A Map for the Analysis of Personality and Politics', p. 23.

[2] H. B. English and A. C. English, *op. cit.*, p. 22.

suggests: the world is not the place 'John' thinks it to be, nor, one might go on to say, is it the place he is trying to *create*. At its most extreme, alienation may generate a paranoid world-view, and its creative potential may assume a sinister significance, inventing hostile intentions and imputing them to innocents.

9.3. Psychological dispositions and political interpretation

The independent predictions of both authoritarian personality tendency and alienation to ethnocentrism are empirical findings of very substantial analytical utility to the political scientist. It may be as well, in standing back to contemplate the potential influence of dispositions on political attitudes, to take a case which illustrates clearly the utility of the knowledge of the interrelations of dispositions themselves. Ethnocentrism is a disposition of considerable political importance, being relevant to the social disharmony or, *in extremis*, social disintegration, and, when the cultural conditions are ripe for them, capable of generating extremist mass movements of great destructive force.

Thus far in this book, its themes, both in substance and technique of enquiry, have relied heavily on the 'hard data' of empirical research, and, to a lesser extent, loosely spun conjecture on situations actually observed. Now, a critical question must be confronted. Put very baldly, it is this: are the insights derived from psychological scale technology useful in interpreting *macro-politics*? Upon the answer to this question hangs the usefulness of almost the entire analysis; must we creep or can we march?

To anticipate my conclusion, under some conditions, we can, I think, *march*, brandishing psychological explanation as *primary*. In order to demonstrate this possibility, I propose an entry into a critical historical episode, probably well known to the reader: the rise of Nazism and the nature of Nazi anti-Semitism in Germany in the thirties and forties. This plunge will not aim to be at all extensive, merely suggestive of the potential magnitude of the value of psychological concepts in macro-political interpretation. The promise made at the close of the Introduction was of a 'move upwards' to a consideration (in the light of psychology) of critical historical episodes. The illustration now proposed constitutes this shift in perspective.

Before making this, it might be salutary to recall that the general utility of psychology to political science has, on and off, been in con-

166

siderable doubt. As Greenstein has said,[3] in a *cri de coeur*:

If the political scientist persists in his determination to make systematic use of psychology, he is likely to experience . . . discouragement. Much of the research and theory he encounters will seem singularly irrelevant to explaining the kind of complex behaviour which interests him . . . Psychologists' insights seem irrelevant to political scientists, for the good reason that many psychologists do not conceive of their science as one which *should* attempt to explain concrete instances of social behaviour, but rather as a means of understanding general principles underlying that behaviour.

The political scientist is often puzzled as to how to *apply* the findings of psychology, which is nomothetic in its bias, having as its purpose the production of generalizations. Whilst the political scientist is rarely purely idiographic in his concern, that is, trying to portray a political situation in all its idiosyncracy, he is sufficiently of the two contrasting worlds of social analysis as to be uncomfortable, or even at a loss, in using the tools of either.

Let us consider briefly the circumstances of the fall of the Weimar Republic, to see how difficulties of this kind can be resolved. The later period of Weimar, and that of the National Socialist régime, are, of course, ones where the influence of psychological dispositions had *un jour de fête*. Indeed, they provided an impulse to the psychological interpretation of political events which had its beginnings in the very distinguished work by Fromm,[4] and is still active, particularly in the analysis of the fate of European Jewry.[5] The dominant themes have been of a malignant alienation, especially in the middle class, and of a diffusion of authoritarian personality characteristics in the German national culture of the time.

The illustrative case to be presented, in order to show how psychological insights are necessary to an understanding, is that of the German Jews, as they were seen by their fellow Germans, and as they saw themselves, in the twilight of Weimar. Their self-conception was, in the main, based on a realistic appreciation of experience; the conception of them advanced by the Nazis was that of a social cancer,

---

[3] F. I. Greenstein, 'Personality and Politics: Problems of Evidence, Inference and Conceptualization,' *American Behavioural Scientist*, 11 (1967), p. 40.

[4] E. Fromm, *The Fear of Freedom*. The most recent study of the psychological climate of Weimar is by P. Gay, *Weimar Culture: The Outsider as Insider* (London, 1968).

[5] M. Wangh, 'National Socialism and the Genocide of the Jews', *International Journal of Psychoanalysis*, 45 (1964), pp. 386–95.

destroying the nation. It bore little relation to actuality.[6] Jews were in socially exposed positions in petty commerce, the theatre and the professions, but not in a position of great economic or political power. Confronted by this extraordinary conception of themselves as a group, the Jews tried to reason on the basis of an ordinary logical interpretation of experience, attempting to engage on this basis the sympathy of their fellow Germans. A political scientist resistant to the employment of the data of psychology might have taken the same view as they did. In June 1933, the Zionist paper *Jüdische Rundschau* appealed in the following terms[7] to the German public:

The National Socialists, in their demonstrations, designate the Jews as 'enemies of the state'. That designation is incorrect. The Jews are not enemies of the state. The German Jews desire and wish for the rise of Germany, for which they have always invested, to the best of their knowledge, all their resources, and that is what they wish to continue to do.

Hilberg's[8] account of earlier events runs as follows:

[In April] The *Central-Verein Zeitung*, organ of the Jewish assimilationists, had published an editorial, born out of despair, which contained Goethe's famous line of frustrated love: 'If I love you, what business is it of yours?' The Zionist paper *Jüdische Rundschau* thereupon published a reply which stated with defiance: 'If I love you, then it *is* your business. The German people should know: a historical alliance, hundreds of years old, cannot be severed so simply.' But it *was* severed.

What the German Jews could not understand, and what nomothetic research can tell us, is this: it was *not* the Jews the Nazis hated. They were not concerned with the *actuality* of the German Jewish community, in its real relations with the state. What they hated was intrinsic to themselves, their *idea* of the Jew. In the Jew was the paradigm of the intrusive foreigner, the alien corrupting the national *Volk*. Ethnocentrism is not a disposition reflecting a realistic appreciation of the out-group. It reflects a *stereotype* of the out-group, and the more extreme its causal antecedents, alienation and authoritarianism, the more extreme is ethnocentrism, which incorporates derogatory mistake. What the Nazis were arguing was for the German people to abandon a conception of the Jew based on the

[6] For a contemporary account in plain language of the position of the Jews in German society, see S. H. (Sir Stephen) Roberts, *The House that Hitler Built* (London, 1937), pp. 258–67.

[7] Quoted in R. Hilberg, *The Destruction of the European Jews* (Chicago, 1961), p. 30.

[8] *Ibid.*, p. 30.

logic of ordinary experience, and to put in its place a stereotype which bore no relation to reality, indeed contradicted it. *But it was one in which they themselves believed.* Here is Hitler epitomizing those dispositions apparently possessing the audience to whom he addressed himself: authoritarianism, alienation and ethnocentrism. He is at the dinner table, on 23 January 1942 (the following is a steno-graphic record of his private conversation).[9] He is speaking of the Jews:

> A good three or four hundred years will go by before the Jews set foot again in Europe. They'll return first of all as commercial travellers, then gradually they'll become emboldened to settle here – the better to exploit us. In the next stage, they become philanthropists, they endow foundations. When a Jew does that, the thing is particularly noticed – for it's known that they're dirty dogs. As a rule, it's the most rascally of them who do that sort of thing. And then you'll hear these poor Aryan boobies telling you: 'You see, there *are* good Jews.'

Here, he is urging his audience to put the opposite construction to the normal one on a datum of experience: an ostensibly generous act is really cunningly selfish. Indeed, more than usually so: 'it's the most rascally of them who do that sort of thing'. What is real is what is 'known' *a priori* '. . . they're dirty dogs'. But this 'knowledge' is not based on external reality; it is a paranoid reconstruction of elements of external reality, with a great deal added. It springs from *within* the personality of the highly ethnocentric subject. Even the Jews' own consciousness of their motives and actions can be disregarded in the light of this 'knowledge'. Here is Hitler speaking on the night of 1–2 December 1941:[10]

> Ten years ago, our intellectual class hadn't the least idea of what a Jew is.
>
> Obviously, our racial laws demand great strictness on the part of the indi-vidual. *But to judge of their value, one mustn't let oneself be guided by indi-vidual cases.*[11] It is necessary to bear in mind that in acting as I do I am avoiding innumerable conflicts in the future.
>
> I'm convinced that there are Jews in Germany who've behaved correctly – in the sense that they've invariably refrained from doing injury to the German idea . . . *Probably many Jews are not aware of the destructive power they represent.* Now, he who destroys life is himself risking death. That's the secret of what is happening to the Jews. Whose fault is it when a cat devours a mouse? The fault of the mouse, who has never done any harm to the cat?

[9] H. R. Trevor-Roper (ed.), *Hitler's Table Talk, 1941–1944* (London, 1953), p. 236.

[10] *Ibid.*, p. 140–1.

[11] My stress, here and below.

This 'knowledge' from the inner springs of personality functioning extends far and wide. On 18 October 1941,[12] Hitler ruminates: 'It's a queer business, how England slipped into the war. The man who managed it was Churchill, that puppet of the Jewry that pulls the strings.' The murder of the Jews in the concentration camps is never mentioned in the 'Table Talk', only deportation. The real nature of the 'Final Solution' had been disclosed to a small group of higher bureaucrats by Heydrich on 20 January 1942 at a conference at Gross-Wannsee.[13] But on 23 January 1942, Hitler is saying this:[14]

One must act radically. When one pulls out a tooth, one does it with a single tug, and the pain quickly goes away. The Jews must clear out of Europe. Otherwise no understanding will be possible between Europeans. It's the Jew who prevents everything. When I think about it, I realize that I'm extraordinarily humane. At the time of the rule of the Popes, the Jews were mistreated in Rome. Until 1830, eight Jews mounted on donkeys were led once a year through the streets of Rome. For my part, I restrict myself to telling them they must go away. If they break their pipes on the journey, I can't do anything about it. But if they refuse to go voluntarily, I see no other solution but extermination. Why should I look at a Jew through other eyes than if he were a Russian prisoner-of-war? In the p.o.w. camps, many are dying. It's not my fault. I didn't want either the war or the p.o.w. camps. Why did the Jew provoke this war?

How much this tells of the subject who is speaking, and how little of the Jews! To discuss the world of the concentration camps, of the 'SS state', would be to enter a nether region beyond the scope of this illustration, where, perhaps, the alienated imagination, in a monstrous historical episode, had created a physical alternative to the rejected society, with its own complex 'language rules'[15] to avoid even the mention of 'killing' in surroundings of general slaughter. This world must be accorded its own psychopathology, to grapple with an explanation of its *grands grotesques*. Here there is an *enclosed* character to deviant behaviours, which often, as in the faces in the demonic paintings of Hieronymus Bosch, exhibit an apparent serenity in a grossly eccentric environment.

Let us return to the theme of the illustration, that of attitudes to the Jews in the late Weimar period. Nomothetic research can show

[12] H. R. Trevor-Roper, *op. cit.*, p. 72.

[13] G. Reitlinger, *The Final Solution: The Attempt to Exterminate the Jews of Europe, 1939–1945* (London, 1953), pp. 96ff.

[14] H. Trevor-Roper, *op. cit.*, p. 235–6.

[15] Cf. R. Hilberg, *op. cit.*, pp. 555ff.

how ethnocentrism can come about as a result of disturbing social conditions, via the stepping stone of alienation, and also how it can emerge from the personality dynamics of the authoritarian. But it also tells us *what it is*, i.e. essentially a disposition of the subject, not of the object, the target group. To be sure, the actual relation of the two in a given society is also relevant: the target group here, the Jews, were seen by some as the paradigm of the foreigner, being actually the descendants of a wave of migration from the East; so that one can regard anti-Semitism, in part, as the result of a dysfunctional relation between the society and the minority group. But most of the dysfunction arises because of the characteristics of the society and of the ethnocentrism within it.

What I think the foregoing illustration indicates is that there is a striking degree of correspondence between the available 'soft' data of the time (for example the insightful but impressionistic analysis by Fromm) and 'hard' data, based on quantification, at a later date in a proximate culture-system. Indeed, even Fromm's notion that lower-middle-class ethnocentrism is likely to be more volatile under conditions of stress is supported by the statistical data indicating variations in correlation between social groups (see Chapter 5, pp. 97–8).

In short, research with dispositional scales is, *at the least*, a vital complement to intuitive political psychology. The latter relies too heavily on merely persuasive argument; the former, if carefully employed, may enable political psychology to reach that further shore where one can erect theoretical structures capable of empirical validation or invalidation. The empirical test may, of course, be oblique: for example, in the case above, there is the gap in time, *inter alia*. But the potential in this for advances in method is considerable.

It is important to make it clear, in a general way, what is *not* argued here. Obviously, the collapse of the Weimar Republic, and the fantastic sequence of historical events which followed, cannot be deduced from a knowledge of the interrelations of the dispositions we have discussed. What *is* being argued is that the historical situation cannot be *understood* without this knowledge. But notice that even the generalizations of nomothetic analysis have to be understood *within* the given culture. Why the *Jews* should have been the target group for extreme prejudice requires special explanation, that is, complementary idiographic research.[16] That the anti-Semitic

[16] An example of this is a work by P. G. J. Pulzer. *The Rise of Political Anti-Semitism*

stereotype was of the foreigner, not so much, as in English-speaking countries, the unscrupulous money-grubber, is also important, because it clarifies the reason for the centrality of anti-Semitism: the Jew was the symbol of the alien, and therefore, putatively, the natural foe of the organic *völkisch* nation-state which the Nazis sought to create. Why they sought to create such a state is itself a question which requires a delicate analysis of the idiosyncrasies of the historical situation, such as that of Erikson.[17] The generalizations afforded by nomothetic analysis are modulated by the particularities of the socio-historical situation in a given culture. The idiographic and nomothetic approaches to an understanding of politics are therefore complementary, not opposed.

9.4. Dulce domi: some implications of social stress and social stability

This work has been principally an enquiry into the darker tides in the human psyche, which have bedevilled statecraft in recent history and led millions into despair, moral catastrophe and physical loss. The imaginative life of the German people, for example, after the recovery of their national identity, has often dwelt poignantly on such themes as false hopes and faith terribly betrayed. For most peoples, reminiscence, the loosely governed and sometimes fugitive journey into time remembered; humour, the enjoyment of the idea of the absurd; and even nostalgia, the faint or acute sense of the loss of good times, or their often imperfect and idealized archetypes, are the elements from which 'home' is built in human imaginative life. 'Men', Milovan Djilas has said, 'live in dreams and in realities.' Whilst the British and the French may enjoy each of these elemental pastimes and, along with regrets, gather pride, reassurance and a sense of wellbeing from them, the Germans can till only ground which, latterly, has been left barren or treacherous by the Nazi experience. The British (especially the English) play with plural ideas of what it is 'to be English', or a regional variant, as do the French. But the Germans have had the unenviable task of defining, anew, what it is to act as a German. It is unenviable partly because, although traits like thoroughness and honesty are quickly associated with the idea of things German, a German cannot easily make a reflective excursion through the last hundred years of national history without feeling at least some disquiet, or a pain so intense as to tempt him to turn

in *Germany and Austria* (New York. 1964).

[17] E. H. Erikson, *Childhood and Society*, second ed. (New York, 1963), ch. 9.

sharply away from this as a recreation. The concept of the absurd had been actualized in a most horrifying way. It suggests what is black and forbidding rather than *whimsical*; not something amusing because it is impossible.

The result of this powerful inhibition has been a dearth of good German films or written works of fiction which do not dwell despondently on the past, and an emphasis on things 'European'. Part of the legacy of the experience of living under a bizarre ethnocentric régime is a residual tendency to a mental focus on the doings of what Dahrendorf[18] has called the 'normal' (the *cynosure*) group – healthy males between twenty-five and forty.

This, in a degree, deprives four out of five adults in West Germany – women, those older, those younger, the sick, the foreign worker – of full regard for their rights and individuality. A circumspect attention to the full implications of individuality is intrinsic to the liberal tradition. The central task of West German liberal élites has therefore been to erase the critical line of demarcation which distinguished those to be treated with special consideration and those with lesser rights, *de facto*, to ensure that everybody is given due deference to their status as individuals, and to establish, as *received* ideas in West German society, the notions of the French Enlightenment. From being the party regarded as representing those *outside* the dominant tradition, and even a nursing school of potential traitors, the Social Democrats (and now their Free Democrat partners) are now the standard bearers of individualist ideas, those with imaginative sympathy for others. When the then Chancellor of the Federal Republic, Willy Brandt, received the Nobel Peace Prize in Oslo in December 1971, he spoke of the letters he had received in the past few weeks:

. . . from Heads of State and school-children, from happy and tormented people, from a relative of Anne Frank, from prisoners. Among the first letters was one from a lady whose life has not been easy and who reminded me of the story of the Red Indian boy asking his father as they came out of the cinema: 'Do we never win?'[19]

The instinctive emotional alignment with the under-dog, which these remarks suggest, is in head-on collision with ethnocentrism.

The remaking of the German culture-system is no trivial task – indeed, the replanning of a culture-system of *any* kind has to be

---

[18] R. Dahrendorf, *Society and Democracy in Germany* (London, 1968), pp. 347ff.

[19] Press and Information Office of the Federal Republic of Germany, *Peace Policy in Our Time* (Bonn, 1972), p. 16.

regarded as a gigantic endeavour. In the West German case, it is being achieved through a symbiotic relation between liberal élites and, especially, the younger group in the political public. The wider implications of the process, as they become apparent, will assist in an understanding of the bases of social integration and flexible fraternization. In this book, I have been preoccupied with the reverse side of the coin.

9.5. A note on the method of political science

Cross-cultural research, to establish whether the intercorrelations between dispositions and attitudes discovered in this thesis, in the Australian urban context, are general to other cultures or not, is a desirable future prospect. What one might say, indeed must say, on the basis of the work done here, is that social conditions which are liable to engender alienation, conceived as social estrangement, or which conduce to the diffusion of authoritarian personality characteristics, are surrounded by a penumbra of ominous potentiality. They exacerbate ethnocentrism. Thus to launch an immigration programme during an economic recession is a dangerous enterprise, not merely because it will increase competition for jobs, but because, if a wave of unemployment increases alienation, as would seem highly likely, a growth of irrational antagonism to migrants will follow. One of the main lessons of this research is that, rather than attempting to predict to attitudes directly from social conditions, it is preferable to consider first the step from social conditions, understood in their particularities, to dispositions, likewise cautiously measured, before attempting to prophesy the structure of opinion on particular issues. Empirical research, heavily qualified by the operation named *Verstehen*, is the *sine qua non* of such social analysis.

A final note on the method of political science and, in particular, of political psychology might here be usefully offered. Of the social sciences, political science is the most various in its method. Indeed, it happens that it has not one methodology, but several. It is sometimes difficult to distinguish it from history, except for its generally contemporary bias. It is therefore appropriate that, for some purposes, it should adopt the methodology of that discipline. At other times, methods more like those of the natural sciences, on the empirico-mathematical model, are useful. This is not confusion; it is simply that, in a discipline addressed to the analysis of affairs of state, the subject matter is as large in scope as life itself, and the variety in techniques of analysis must be broad in order to match the difficulty of the subject. In the treatment of disposition and political opinion in this book, one methodological lesson has emerged with paramount force: it is that, in political psychology, many methods of analysis must be conjoined, and that statistical techniques must be married to a human understanding, before they can be used to display the subject in all its intricacy.

1. Introduction

The major survey, the matter of which is reported and discussed in Chapters 4 to 7, is that of the sample of voters in Melbourne and Sydney interviewed in October–November 1966 ($n=400$), taken just before the federal elections for the House of Representatives in that year.

The questionnaire administered was a long one. It is not reproduced in full in this book, since the many responses were not put to use. The substance of it, beginning with political questions, proceeding to the dispositional scales, and concluding with 'background' data for each respondent, has already been displayed, chiefly in Chapters 4 and 6.

Since the interview varied from ninety minutes to four hours, considerations of expense dictated that more time be given to the interview itself rather than the discovery of the location of the interviewee. This meant some lack of precision in the accuracy of sampling, but with the compensating advantage of being able to administer long and reliable scales for the psychological dispositions. It is nevertheless important to test the accuracy of sampling by comparing some sample characteristics with available parameters for the relevant populations, and this is the main purpose of this appendix.

In refining the instruments for the voter survey, use was made of a captive sample of low-grade (fourth division) Commonwealth public servants, which is described in Appendix C.

The voter survey of 1966 was funded by the Australian National University and carried out by a Melbourne polling organization, Australian Sales Research Bureau. It was possible, in this survey, to control sampling procedures closely.

2. Non-random samples

A statistical note may be offered here on the technique of applying tests of significance (in this research, mainly the chi-square test) to non-random samples. Since these tests are, in principle, intended to test differences between independent random samples, it follows that the generalizations which they make possible are, strictly, generalizations to *hypothetical universes of content* of which the samples are random samples. The population to which one generalizes is thus a hypothetical, not an actual one. However, if one can (and this appendix does) demonstrate a close identity between the hypothetical and actual populations, by showing that the characteristics of the non-random sample are closely related to population parameters, then

177

the sample has approximately the same function as an (admittedly superior) random sample would have had. However, this special meaning of the tests of significance should be kept in mind.

The model of all the sampling techniques described in this chapter is that of stratified cluster sampling.[1] The 1966 voter sample is a close approximation to it.[2] It is moderately large, sufficiently so to permit small disproportionalities to reach significance. Although it is confined only to the two biggest cities in Australia, there is a general uniformity in Australian urban life which make it seem likely that the trends to be discerned in it apply to urban Australia generally.

3. The Melbourne–Sydney sample of 1966

3.1. *Method of interviewing and sampling*

Interviewing commenced in Melbourne on 5 November 1966 and in Sydney on 6 November 1966. The period of the survey ran up to election day, 26 November. By a mischance, three interviews in Melbourne were completed after the election.

The intention was to obtain 200 completed interviews in Melbourne and 200 in Sydney. Forty locations within each of the two metropolitan areas were designated, spread over each city on the basis of the 1961 census data, but arbitrarily discounting the inner-city area in both cases by 25 per cent to allow for the non-voting migrant population. Interviewers were instructed to proceed from a particular intersection (the location designated), in a given direction in a specified street. They were asked to administer the questionnaire to the first five willing voters living in that street, provided that not more than one voter in each household was to be interviewed, and that for each quota of ten interviews, they should try to obtain equal numbers of women and men.

The sample was confined to persons eligible to vote and fluent in English.

In an effort to obtain a correct proportion of young people, who are often under-sampled in procedures of this type, interviewers were instructed to give first preference to a voter under 30 years, if one was present. In the absence of a voter under 30 years, any willing voter was interviewed, without discrimination as to age. Of the 400 interviews completed, some had missing responses on one or more of the political policy items ($n=5$) and some had missing responses on one or more of all the dispositional scale items ($n=22$). Since the factor analyses required an identical sample for each correlation, all those interviews with one or more blanks on the political policy items were excluded from the analysis of political policy items, and subsequent breakdowns by background data. The maximum size of the sample used in the 'political' analysis was therefore 395.

An identical consideration led to the exclusion of the 22 interviews with one or more blanks on all the dispositional scale items. Members of the min-

---

[1] See L. Kish, *Survey Sampling*, pp. 49–53 and pp. 164–6.

[2] A procedure for drawing a precise sample of the Australian electorate and its application is to be found in M. Kahan and D. Aitkin, *Drawing a Sample of the Australian Electorate*, Occasional Paper No. 3, Department of Political Science, Research School of Social Sciences, Australian National University (Canberra, 1968).

ority groups mentioned in the ethnocentrism scale were also excluded from the dispositional analyses, as the items of the ethnocentrism scales referred to themselves, and responses could not, in principle, measure an attitude to an out-group. These numbered 23. The sample used for the dispositional scale analysis, excluding these two groups, was 355. If all questionnaires with any blanks on the political policy or dispositional items were excluded, the sample was 352. The sample size is indicated in every table. Its representativeness is not seriously affected by the reduction, as the tables below demonstrate, except that, of course, the small proportion of the sample (approximately 5 per cent) who are actually members of the Jewish, Greek or Italian minority groups are not included when the sample is reduced to 355. However, this deficiency is more than compensated by the increased clarity of the analysis, a consideration which outweighed the small drop in representativeness and sample size.

3.2. *The representativeness of the sample*

Table A.1 compares the sample percentages intending to vote or having voted for the various political parties with the sum of the actual votes of both metropolitan areas reported by the Commonwealth electoral officer.[3]

The DLP vote is somewhat under-represented, and the LCP vote somewhat over-represented. The general balance of the samples of both sizes is adequate to our purposes.

TABLE A.1　*Vote in 1966 (percentages)*

	LCP	ALP	DLP	Other
Sample ($n = 395$)	52·9	38·9	5·3	2·9 = 100%
Sample ($n = 355$)	52·7	39·2	5·5	2·6 = 100%
Actual	47·8	39·3	8·5	4·4 = 100%

The sample figures exclude those undecided or refusing to answer this question.

Only figures for the entire population, juvenile and adult, are available for religious affiliation. Census figures for the proportion in each age group were categorized on a slightly different basis from those in the sample. Table A.2 sets out data for religious affiliation. Here again, overall representativeness is adequate. Table A.3 exhibits data for age groups.[4]

[3] *House of Representatives Elections – 26 November 1966. Summary of Votes for Political Parties*, unofficial notes circulated by F. L. Ley, Commonwealth Chief Electoral Officer, 27 January 1967.

[4] The census data are to be found in Commonwealth Bureau of Census and Statistics, *Census of Population and Housing, 30th June 1966, Commonwealth of Australia* (Canberra, no date), Vol. 4, *Population and Dwellings in Local Government Areas, Part 1, New South Wales* (pp. 18–19, 216–17 for the 'Sydney Statistical Division') and *Part 2, Victoria* (pp. 20–1, 208–9 for the 'Melbourne Statistical Division').

179

The younger groups are slightly oversampled, and the elderly are under-sampled. Neither of these discrepancies suggests that the sample is less than adequately representative.

The attempt to obtain about equal numbers of men and women was successful.

These data, taken together, suggest that the sample is representative of the sociological and political characteristics of the parent population to a degree adequate to our purposes.

4. Further characteristics of the 1966 sample

The sociological characteristics of the sample give some evidential bases for the following trends: the electorate is becoming better educated; the proportion of Catholics in the community seems likely to increase, and, as the better educated younger generation grow older and accumulate status and possessions, the proportion of the electorate declaring itself 'middle class' will rise sharply. The three 'status' variables, education, class identification and householder's income, are moderately to strongly related to each other, but in no case does the relation approach identity. They occasionally exhibit differential relations with political opinion.

TABLE A.2   *Religious affiliation (percentages)*

	Sample (n = 395)	Sample (n = 355)	Census
Church of England	30·1	32·0	37·7
Presbyterian	12·5	13·3	9·2
Methodist	9·2	9·6	6·8
Catholic	31·9	30·6	32·3
Other Christian	8·4	8·2	11·3
Non-Christian	2·8	0·6	1·5
No religion	5·1	6·7	1·2
	= 100%	= 100%	= 100%

TABLE A.3   *Age Groups (percentages)*

	21–35	36–55	56 and over
Sample (n = 395)	34·4	44·3	21·3 = 100%
Sample (n = 355)	35·5	43·7	20·8 = 100%
Census	20–34	35–54	55 and over
	32·1	40·5	27·4 = 100%

1. Statistics as a necessity

It will be clear from even a casual glance through the text that this book cannot be understood without a grasp of the concepts and procedures described briefly below. A good general reference is that by Guilford.[1] In understanding factor analysis, the most sophisticated technique employed, a handy starting point is to consider 'cluster' analysis. Fruchter's[2] discussion of this is one of the simplest to follow. A standard text for factor analysis is that of Harman.[3]

2. Significance

In plain language, to say that a finding is 'statistically *significant*', is to assert, after the application of a routine test, that it is reliable. A feature of the sample thus points to (signifies) a *real* feature of the population from which it is drawn. If one is examining, say, the relation of sex to hair colour, and found that males, in the sample, tended to have darker (or lighter) hair than females, in a degree that could be obtained only one time (or less) in twenty by chance alone, convention allows one to call the result 'significant'. To put it another way, if one were sampling at random from a population in which no relation of hair colour to sex difference existed, one would achieve 'significance' (in error) 5 per cent of the time.

The idea involves a bet: one finds a discrepancy in hair colour by sex, and knowing that if a test of significance shows the probability of the discrepancy being due to chance to be once in twenty or less, one makes a bet and treats the difference in hair colour as reliable.

Two things to note: firstly, since significance is (properly) more easy to obtain in large samples, i.e. low but reliable tendencies in the populations can be more certainly identified than in small samples, the degree of significance is not *a test of the strength of the relationship*: it merely suggests that such-and-such a relationship exists (but to an unknown extent). Thus 'highly significant' means 'highly reliable'; but *not* necessarily closely connected.

Secondly, it is not to be confused with the term 'significant' when used non-statistically, e.g. 'It is significant that Mr X has been seen in the company of Miss Y a lot lately.' Therefore, I have never used the single term 'significant' with the latter meaning in this book. Since the constant repetition of

[1] J. P. Guilford, *Fundamental Statistics in Psychology and Education*, third ed. (New York and Tokyo, 1956).

[2] B. Fruchter, *Introduction to Factor Analysis* (New York, 1954), pp. 12–17.

[3] H. H. Harman, *Modern Factor Analysis*, revised ed. (Chicago and London, 1967).

the term 'significant' is tiresome, I have occasionally used parallel words like 'reliable', or, for '*highly* significant', 'reliable' (or 'significant') 'at a high level of confidence'.

The most common test of significance for a two-way table is called 'chi-square'. The level of probability of a finding about a population being true is expressed as a proportion of one (or unity) e.g. the expression $p < 0.01$ means that the discrepancy in the sample would occur by chance less than one time in a hundred.

3. Correlation

Put simply, this means togetherness. If measures of height and weight of a group of persons tend to be related, then one can calculate the degree of 'togetherness' and express it by a correlation *coefficient* (or index).

This is so constructed as to vary from -1.00 through 0 to $+1.00$. In the example above, it would be unlikely that taller men would be lighter, in absolute terms; more probably, they would be heavier; so the correlation would be positive.

By convention, a correlation coefficient of 0.20 is considered low; 0.40 is deemed moderate; 0.60 strong; and 0.80 high. The same goes for those with *negative* values.

The three kinds of correlation coefficient referred to in this book are the 'product-moment' correlation, for which the code is simply r; the phi coefficient, which is numerically equal to the product-moment when the two variables being related have only two possible values, the code being the Greek letter φ. It has the disadvantage of having a low maximum if one of the two variables has an uneven 'response split' e.g. 70% 'yes', 30% 'no'. Another correlation coefficient that is used is the 'tetrachoric'.[4] Despite its interesting name, it is simply an estimate of the product-moment when one is stuck with a four-cell table of two continuous variables, such as anxiety and alienation. It does not suffer from the awkwardness of low maxima if response splits are uneven, and indeed, tends to the opposite error, although not to the same degree. However, Jenkins[5] has produced a formula for 'deflating' it in this event (see the first note to Chapter 5). It is designated r_t.

4. Shared variance

If two variables correlate, they 'overlap' to a specific degree. The degree of overlap can be easily calculated by taking the correlation coefficient, expressed in two digits, shifting the decimal point one place to the right, squaring it and treating the resulting value as a percentage: e.g. 0.20 indicates an 'overlap', or shared variance, of only 4 per cent; whilst 0.50 indicates a shared variance of 25 per cent. Thus the actual importance of a correlation

---

[4] All estimates of the tetrachoric coefficient in this book have been arrived at by the use of Davidoff and Goheen's table reprinted in A. L. Edwards, *Statistical Methods for the Behavioural Sciences* (New York, 1955), p. 510 and corrected for marginal splits at points away from the median by Jenkins' method.

[5] W. L. Jenkins, 'An Improved Method for Tetrachoric *r*'. *Psychometrika*, 20 (1955), pp. 253–8.

does not vary directly with its value; higher values are more important than lower values to a greater extent than may at first appear.

5. Correcting for attenuation

The administration of the same dispositional scale to the same group of persons twice, with an interval of perhaps two weeks in between, enables one to calculate the test–retest correlation, or in statistical terms, the 'reliability coefficient'. (This can be estimated by other means.) If one multiplies this, expressed in two digits, by ten, squares it, and treats the squared value as a percentage, one obtains that proportion of the variance which is systematic, the rest being commonly called 'error variance'. Obviously, one can be contemplating a peach-tree, worrying over a girlfriend, or simply not caring much, when doing a test. If a test has a low reliability, it often means that the scores will not tend to be constant or are governed by extraneous things. A reliability of 0.50, for example, indicates only 25 per cent of its variance is systematic. Now, if one knows the reliabilities of two scales being intercorrelated and wishes to know *how much of the systematic variance is shared*, then one adopts the technique of 'correcting for attenuation', which excludes all 'error variance' by postulating reliabilities that are perfect, i.e. +1.00. The correlations which are then calculated are often a better guide to the real strength of the relation between the two variables, but have to be interpreted with caution.

6. Factor analysis

A brief outline, in lay language, of what this is about is hazardous, but should be offered. Broadly, given a table (sometimes vast) of correlations between variables, the researcher sometimes suspects that the pattern of relations suggests that underlying factors are in operation, governing the values of the correlations. If one had four variables, a snuffly/non-snuffly nose, fever, hand tremor and sweaty palms, the pattern of correlations might well suggest that the first two go together, and so do the last two. The 'background' factors might be, in the first place, a cold in the head, in the second, anxiety.

'Varimax' factor analytical procedures, which are those employed in this volume, *assume* that the background factors are unrelated ('orthogonal', or, geometrically, at right angles to each other). To offer a spatial metaphor, suppose that three clusters of variables are hanging in space in clouds, in a way dictated by their intercorrelations. The 'varimax' analysis spins a central three-pronged structure until each prong is thrust, as nearly as is possible, through the middle of each cloud. This is called 'maximizing the variance on each factor', or more reassuringly, 'rotating to simple structure'. Of course, not only three, but any *appropriate* number of factors may be stipulated. How many are 'appropriate' is sometimes hard to determine.

Factor analyses are now almost invariably carried out by a computer, because of the labour otherwise involved. The factor loadings which are printed out opposite each variable resemble correlation coefficients in appearance, i.e. they vary from −1.00 to +1.00.

7. Testing the significance of differences in correlations

Suppose one has two different samples, one male and the other female. The correlation between physical attractiveness (measured by some ingenious scale) and anxiety amongst males is −0.20; amongst the females, −0.40. Are the females really more worried (about their appearance?) than the males? One needs a test of the significance of the difference between two correlation coefficients to help provide an answer. The standard one for this purpose is called the Fisher Z_r transformation test.

But chi-square could also be used. Suppose one labelled anxious, plain females and non-anxious, plain males as Group I, (supporting the hypothesis) and non-anxious, attractive females plus anxious, attractive males Group II (also supporting the hypothesis). Group III would consist of non-anxious, plain females and anxious, plain males; and Group IV, attractive, non-anxious males, plus attractive, anxious females (both groups negate the hypothesis). This 'collapse' of the variables enables the construction of a four-cell (or four category) table and the testing of the hypothesis by the chi-square test of significance.

8. Quartile scores

If the number of cases falling at each score on a scale (on a single variable) are shown on a graph, this is called a frequency distribution. The point on the scale below which a quarter of the cases fall is called the first quartile, and the space between 0 and that point, 'the first quartirange'. The second quartile point is that below which half the cases fall, and is identical with the 'median'. The third quartile point is that below which three quarters of the cases fall.

Quartile scores are simply *translations* of the raw scores on the sole principle of which quartirange of the distribution the raw score fell within; they therefore have only four values.

APPENDIX C *Constructing the scales for authoritarianism, ethnocentrism and alienation*

What follows is a necessarily brief account of an application of the solutions to the problems in the measurement of dispositions proposed in Chapter 4. Three forced-choice measures of authoritarianism, alienation and ethnocentrism were constructed in two stages, the first employing a captive sample of public servants, the second a sample of metropolitan voters. Standardization data for the three scales are set out in Tables C.4, C.6, C.8 and C.10, at the conclusion of this appendix. Tables C.5, C.7, and C.9 give item characteristics.

1. Stage I

1.1. Subjects

155 fourth division public servants, consisting of 86 linesmen-in-training at the PMG's Schools of Lines in Melbourne and Sydney and 12 additional trainees at the School of Lines in Melbourne; 34 clerical assistants in Melbourne; and 23 PMG clerks-in-training at Sydney.

1.2. Materials

(i) Candidate alienation items: 30 forced-choice items were administered, constructed *ad hoc* to reflect the various sentiments of alienation discussed in Chapter 4. Those which survived statistical analysis are to be found in Exhibit 4.1, Chapter 4. Their manifest content was intended to relate to the sentiments of alienation as follows:
  (i) Powerlessness; impersonal agency:
     nos. 1, 2, 4, 5, 7, 9, 10, 11.
  (ii) Powerlessness; personal agency:
     nos. 3, 6, 8, 12.
  (iii) Meaninglessness:
     nos. 16, 17, 18.
  (iv) Normlessness:
     nos. 13, 14, 15.
  (v) Isolation:
     nos. 19, 20, 21, 22, 24.
  (vi) Self-estrangement:
     no. 23.
This classification did not pre-suppose that the items would cluster empirically in precisely the same way, if clusters were discernible; it was merely intended as a logical basis for their inclusion in the scale. The perception of their groupings by respondents could, and did, diverge somewhat from the classification above.

(ii) Candidate authoritarianism items: 26 forced-choice items were administered, consisting of 26 original F Scale items and 26 reversals drawn from the various reversed scales or constructed *ad hoc*, with the intention of providing reversed half-items which had a 'tone' similar to the positive halves. Those which survived the procedures of the statistical refinement set out below are given in Exhibit 4.2, Chapter 4.

(iii) Candidate ethnocentrism items: 25 forced-choice items were administered, constructed *ad hoc* to suit the special requirements of Australian ethnocentrism. Those surviving the method of refinement are set out in Exhibit 4.3, in Chapter 4.

(iv) An anxiety measure: This consisted of 20 items randomly abstracted from Cattell's 40-item IPAT measure of anxiety,[1] under the constraint of preserving the proportion contributed by each of the sub-scales. This is a 'balanced' instrument. Because these scale items are available only to members of a recognised association of psychologists, they cannot be exhibited; but some standardization data are set out in Table C.10.

1.3. Procedure

(i) Administration method: The scales were administered to groups at one sitting, each respondent filling in a questionnaire on which the scale items appeared, by himself. At the head of each scale were instructions urging him to avoid an 'undecided' response. Greeks, Italians, Jews and respondents with incomplete questionnaires were removed, leaving a sample of 155.

(ii) Method of analysis: each item pool for the three scales, authoritarianism, ethnocentrism and alienation, was considered separately.

To gain admission to the first two scales, a candidate item had to satisfy the following requirements:

(a) The 'split' in the sample had to be 80/20 or better.
(b) The percentage 'undecided' had to be low: 10 per cent or less.
(c) The correlation with the raw score on other candidate items had to be statistically significant at the 0.05 level, i.e. for $n=155$, 0.16 or more.

In order to gain admission to the Alienation (A) Scale, a candidate item had to satisfy the following requirements:

(a) The split in the sample had to be 85/15 or better. This is a slightly more liberal requirement than for the F and E Scales, and can be justified by the much higher mean item–total score coefficient (even when covariance with anxiety is partialled out).
(b) The percentage 'undecided' had to be 10 per cent or less.
(c) The first-order item–raw score coefficient had to be significant.
(d) The item–raw score coefficient had to remain significant when the covariance of each item and the raw score on the remaining items with the anxiety measure was withdrawn, by the method of partial correlations.

These steps, with exception of the last for the A Scale, represent a conventional correlational analysis, which is designed to ensure that each item functions adequately in making discriminations. Step (d) for the A Scale is an innovation.

[1] R. B. Cattell, *IPAT Self-Analysis Form* (Melbourne, 1957).

1.4. Results

These operations excluded 10 of the candidate F Scale items, leaving 16; 7 of the candidate E Scale items, leaving 18; and 4 of the 30 candidate A Scale items, leaving 26.

1.5. Discussion

The small number of items which the step (d) for the A Scale excluded (two) show that there is a substantial degree of cohesiveness between the items, which cannot be attributed to their covariance with anxiety. It does not prove that alienation is a unitary construct, since it was not yet established that the items do not form disparate and independent clusters within the putative A Scale.

2. Stage II

2.1. Subjects

Subjects were 355 voters in Melbourne and Sydney, drawn from an original 200 in each city. The sampling and interviewing methods have been explained in Appendix A.

2.2. Materials

The remaining A, F and E candidate items were administered, together with the 20-item adaptation of the IPAT anxiety measure, along with many political questions.

2.3. Procedure

(i) Administration method: this is set out in Appendix A, and Section 4.10 of Chapter 4.

(ii) Method of analysis:

(a) A factor analysis was carried out of all interrelations of the 60 A, F and E candidate items in company with the 20 anxiety items. A four-factor solution, employing varimax procedures with orthogonal rotations and the insertion of communalities in the diagonals, was specified. The purpose of this was to examine the degree to which the constructs were empirically distinguishable. Extensive cross loading would have destroyed the hypothesis that the constructs were disparate. To explore the variety in the data more fully, varimax principal components analyses, extracting 6 and then 10 orthogonal components, were later carried out. Some aspects of the principal components analyses are described in Chapter 5; they were used, in part, to develop sub-scales.

(b) The 24 items of the A Scale which emerged from the above operations and which also survived the procedure to develop sub-scales were factor analysed (using varimax procedures) stipulating five orthogonal factors. The items loading more heavily on each factor were treated as sub-scales related to the five factors. The first-order relations of each of these sub-scales to anxiety and ethnocentrism were examined, and their relation with each other, when the common

187

variance with anxiety was removed by the method of partial correlations, was determined. This was a further test of the discreteness and unitary character of the alienation construct. These results are displayed in Tables 4.1, 4.2 and 4.3 of Chapter 4.

(c) Three scales, which would reflect a positional response set, if one existed, were computed from the A, F and E Scales. The respondent scored 1 each time he chose the *first* option of a pair of half-items, and 0 if he did not do so. Product-moment relations between Positional Response Set Scales 1, 2 and 3, drawn from the A, F and E Scales respectively, were then computed. The order of magnitude of the correlations would indicate whether or not this set was present, and if so, whether it was of negligible, low or substantial magnitude.

TABLE C.1 *Correlations between positional response set scales* (*Product-moment*)

	1	2	3
1	1·00	0·17**	0·13*
2		1·00	0·12*
3			1·00

The inference to be made from the Table C.1 is that whilst positional response set in fact *exists* as an authentic source of infection, the scales are negligibly contaminated by it.

TABLE C.2 *Factor loadings of all candidate A, F and E items, and anxiety items*

		I (Alienation)	II (Eth.)	III (Anxiety)	IV (F)
Candidate A items, nos	1	0·34	0·10	0·13	0·01
	2	0·35	0·02	0·07	0·10
	3	0·42	0·15	0·09	0·11
	4	0·31	0·15	0·18	0·14
	5	0·36	0·24	0·09	−0·13
	6	0·43	0·13	0·09	0·00
	7	0·34	0·05	0·31	−0·09
	8	0·46	−0·14	0·08	0·02
	9	0·36	0·01	0·15	0·09
	10	0·47	0·03	0·18	−0·06
	11	0·47	0·08	0·30	0·02

TABLE C.2 (*continued*)

		I (Alienation)	II (Eth.)	III (Anxiety)	IV (F)
Candidate A items, nos	12	0·49	0·10	−0·01	0·03
	13	0·55	0·03	−0·07	−0·12
	14	0·35	0·15	−0·10	0·03
	15	0·42	0·11	−0·10	−0·02
	16	0·24	0·08	0·18	−0·05
	17	0·41	0·10	0·19	−0·07
	18	0·42	0·05	0·15	−0·22
	(a)	0·15	0·03	0·16	0·07
	19	0·46	0·12	0·02	0·18
	20	0·41	0·14	0·03	−0·07
	21	0·46	0·09	0·06	0·14
	22	0·33	0·08	0·34	0·12
	23	0·42	0·08	0·20	−0·09
	24	0·24	0·09	0·28	−0·01
	(b)	0·20	0·07	0·38	−0·07
Candidate F items, nos	1	0·12	0·07	−0·10	0·50
	2	−0·01	0·05	−0·04	0·40
	3	0·05	0·05	0·07	0·36
	4	−0·16	0·11	0·06	0·31
	5	0·00	0·05	−0·03	0·31
	6	−0·01	0·08	−0·06	0·45
	7	0·05	0·03	−0·05	0·37
	8	0·09	0·26	−0·14	0·23
	9	−0·04	0·04	−0·13	0·57
	10	0·11	0·30	−0·06	0·17
	11	−0·01	0·21	−0·07	0·29
	12	−0·02	0·08	0·04	0·37
	(c)	0·18	0·14	0·04	0·30
	13	0·02	0·24	0·03	0·30
	(d)	0·23	0·14	−0·01	0·06
	(e)	0·09	0·14	0·08	0·16
Candidate E items, nos	1	0·04	0·43	0·15	−0·02
	2	0·14	0·27	−0·26	0·05
	3	0·14	0·56	0·08	0·04
	4	−0·03	0·63	0·10	0·23
	5	0·13	0·40	0·04	0·18
	6	0·10	0·46	0·01	−0·06
	7	0·12	0·44	0·07	−0·09
	7	0·06	0·62	0·09	0·07
	9	0·12	0·27	−0·22	0·02
	10	−0·05	0·68	0·13	0·30
	11	0·19	0·44	0·03	0·10
	12	0·12	0·54	0·09	0·16

TABLE C.2 (*continued*)

		I (Alienation)	II (Eth.)	III (Anxiety)	IV (F)
Candidate					
E items, nos	13	0·11	0·34	0·09	0·21
	14	−0·03	0·45	0·06	0·25
	15	0·25	0·31	−0·03	0·07
	16	0·30	0·37	−0·08	0·18
	17	0·25	0·37	−0·03	0·12
	18	0·12	0·20	0·04	0·33
Anxiety					
Items, nos	1	0·15	0·07	0·13	0·21
	2	0·07	−0·09	0·27	−0·28
	3	0·11	−0·06	0·14	−0·49
	4	0·20	0·03	0·33	−0·25
	5	0·01	−0·03	0·44	−0·16
	6	0·06	−0·03	0·26	−0·03
	7	0·04	0·04	0·34	0·04
	8	0·27	−0·06	0·34	0·06
	9	0·29	0·08	0·20	0·08
	10	−0·05	−0·03	0·35	0·06
	11	−0·02	0·15	0·37	0·22
	12	0·01	−0·03	0·40	−0·38
	13	0·12	0·00	0·51	−0·04
	14	0·05	−0·01	0·14	0·31
	15	0·25	0·06	0·25	0·14
	16	0·14	−0·05	0·16	0·19
	17	0·14	0·04	0·46	0·06
	18	0·02	0·06	0·41	−0·14
	19	0·03	0·05	0·39	−0·14
	20	0·03	0·07	0·26	0·09

(d) A conventional correlational analysis was then performed to determine the reliabilities of each scale; the mean inter-item correlations; and the relation of each F item with ethnocentrism. Medians, quartiles, means and standard deviations were also determined. These standardization data are set out in Tables C.4 to C.10.

(e) Product-moment correlations between all four scales were then computed (see Table 4.4, Chapter 4).

2.4. *Results:*

The result of the four-factor varimax analysis of the 80 scale items is set out in Table C.2.

The principal components analyses extracted at first 6 components, and then 10. The latter was treated as the most convenient device for the definition of sub-scales.

As all items were required to belong to one or other of these, as meaningful elements of a construct, the 10 principal components also governed the final admission of all candidate items to the A, F and E Scales. Items (a) and (b) of the candidate alienation items were more closely related to what was dubbed the 'intra-punitive' sub-scale of anxiety, than to the sub-scales of the A Scale; items (c) and (d) more to the 'extra-punitive' sub-scale of anxiety than to the sub-scales of the F measure; item (e) more closely related to the anti-Semitism Scale of the E Scale than to either of the F Sub-scales. These items ((a) – (e)) were therefore excluded from *all* scales and sub-scales.

The anxiety measure was retained in its original form.

3. Additional data in validation of the Alienation Scale

Whilst it is noted in Chapter 4, Section 6, that no 'universally acceptable' criterion groups are available in the case of alienation, so that one cannot validate the scale in the same way as one might, for example, validate a neuroticism scale against a hospitalized sample of anxiety neurotics, certain identifiable groups may be useful in testing the alienation scale. These are convicts and hospitalized psychiatric patients. In both cases external circumstances impose a condition of powerlessness in relation to life-goals, at least temporarily, and unless the latter are very substantially reduced; both are likely to feel isolated from those who share their values; the nature of the administration of goals and psychiatric hospitals may engender normlessness, especially in the former; in these circumstances, and in this company, the patients and prisoners are likely to feel a sense of meaninglessness; and it seems not unreasonable to hypothesize self-estrangement.

The Alienation Scale has been administered to groups of convicts and mental patients, and students at a tertiary institution by Mr Brian Ross.[2] The samples must first be described.

(a) Prisoners

These were all male, in two gaols in New South Wales: Long Bay in Sydney, where the sample of prisoners is described by Ross as 'hard core', with an age range of 18–45, and Bathurst Gaol, where the prisoners were recidivist and, in most cases, under 30.

(b) Psychiatric patients

These were in two groups of mixed sex; one in Broughton Hall, in Sydney, a voluntary-patient psychiatric clinic, where the sample was in the majority neurotic, the remainder psychotic; the other in the psychiatric ward of a general hospital, Prince Henry's, in Sydney, where again most were neurotic, some psychotic. The age range of the psychiatric patients tested was 16–65.

[2] With whose permission these data are reproduced. They are drawn from a personal communication of 23 September 1968. At the time of communication, Mr Ross was located at the District Hospital, Bourke, New South Wales, as psychologist attached to the 'Human Ecology of the Arid Zone Project' of the University of New South Wales.

(c) Students

These were trainee teachers at the Australian School of Pacific Administration, Sydney, being prepared for positions in schools in Papua and New Guinea. They were intended to serve as a group whose norms would approximate those of the normal adult population, which was, in fact, the case. Their age range was 18–32.

The scale was administered to the students, psychiatric patients and Long Bay prisoners in January–February, 1968; to the students once again in June 1968, and to the Bathurst prisoners in September 1968. The normative data obtained are given in Table C.3. along with means and standard deviations from the Melbourne–Sydney adult sample reproduced from Table C.4.

TABLE C.3   *Criterion group validation data for the Alienation Scale*

Group	Mean	Standard deviation	Sample size
Prisoners	21·64	12·15	$n = 83$
Patients	20·69	10·43	$n = 58$
Students	12·81	10·58	$n = 99$
Representative voter sample	12·35	8·79	$n = 355$

These data indicate that the Alienation Scale validates well against these criterion groups. The test–retest coefficient (product-moment) of the Alienation Scale (students, $n=99$, February–June 1968) was 0.689.

This is a satisfactory reliability coefficient for re-administration after an interval of four months, and closely approximates the reliability coefficient obtained by the parallel forms method (0.681, as exhibited in Table C.4).

4. The construct validity of the Ethnocentrism Scale.

The Ethnocentrism Scale items are displayed in Exhibit 4.3 of Chapter 4.

The ethnocentrism item-halves of items 5, 6, and 7 are supposed to reflect derogatory mistake in the case of Italians. Item 5 ('street brawls') obtains its currency from press reports of street brawls between Italian migrants and Australians in the late 1940s and early 1950s. In the main, what are now Italian neighbourhoods are peaceful, and Italians have a comparatively low rate of violent crime in Australia.

Item 6 ('turn the districts they live in into slums') appears the reverse of the truth. Down-at-heel neighbourhoods, such as Carlton, in Melbourne, have often in fact been rescued from slum status by the regeneration of their residential and shopping facilities, and the opening of a multiplicity of good cafes by Italian migrants since the mid 1950s.

Item 7 ('admire elegance and good manners') is of course hard to verify, but is apparently true in relation to aspiration. Italian migrants tend often to be deferential to Australians.

Item 11, derogatory of Greeks ('seem to be content with a lower standard of living than most Australians') is contrary to the account of industriousness and attempts at upward social mobility given by Price.

Item 12, derogatory (by implication) of Southern Europeans generally ('will take over the country') is intended to be violent in tone and wildly untrue, as Southern Europeans mainly enter the lower ranks of the manual work force, and are not prominent in non-migrant organizations. Greeks have a greater tendency than Italians to aspire to higher education, but they are not numerous in universities.

Items 15–18 refer to derogatory misconceptions of Jews.

Item 15 ('have too much power and influence') is, in its literal sense, unverifiable, since what is 'too much' must be a value judgement. If it is loosely construed to mean a 'great deal of influence', or a 'dominant influence', it does not seem to be true, since, whilst Jews are disproportionately numerous in petty commerce, the professions and academic life, they do not command much influence in banking, big industry, the stock exchange or politics.

Item 16 ('if Jewish people are interested in education, it is probably so they can use it to make more money') has an *element* of truth, as one quickly sees if one substitutes 'Australians' for 'Jewish people'. However, as in Jewish communities elsewhere in the world, the traditional Jewish reverence for scholarly endeavour and 'high' culture is evident. There is ardent patronage of the theatre, and support of chamber music organizations, for example. The other half of this item ('place great value on education and culture') is a fairer statement.

Item 17 ('are less honest and public-spirited than most') is in its first part the least verifiable derogatory statement, except through some highly unlikely programme of situational tests. To endorse it, however, would seem to entail at least a hazardous extension of impressions gained from limited experience. The latter part ('[less] public-spirited') is contradicted by the many honours bestowed on notable Jews for public service, such as the one-time Governor-General, Sir Isaac Isaacs.

On Item 18 ('seem to keep their money for their own charities') there is contrary public evidence. Each year, in Melbourne, the press publishes donations given in places of public worship on Hospital Sunday, when money is raised for all hospitals, secular and religious. In 1966, the year of the survey, the five Hebrew congregations gave more, in absolute terms, than the total of Catholic contributions to this appeal, and an amount comparable with that of each of the three major Protestant denominations. Thus Jewish people gave, proportionately, a much greater amount than others.[3]

Of the other items of the Ethnocentrism Scale, no. 1 is a 'soft' lead-in mentioning 'migrants', so that the intention of the scale is not too loudly proclaimed. Items 2 and 3 refer to intolerance of Italians; item 4 to social distance from Italians. Items 8 and 9 refer to intolerance of Greeks; item 10 to social distance from Greeks. Item 13 refers to intolerance of Jews; item 14 to social distance from Jews.

Nine of the eighteen items of the Ethnocentrism Scale thus have some delusional content, and the scale therefore reflects an important element of the underlying syndrome; distortion in perception of the external world.

---

[3] *The Age* (Melbourne, 24 October 1966).

5. Standardization data and item characteristics of the Alienation, Authoritarianism, Ethnocentrism and Anxiety Scales.

(These are drawn from one 1966 votes sample, numbering 355)

TABLE C.4 *Standardization data for the Alienation Scale*

Reliability (parallel forms method)	0·681	
Range (possible)	0–48	
Mean	12·35	
Standard deviation	8·79	
Median	10·5	

Quartiles	Raw score	% sample
High	18–48	25
Middle range	11–17	22
	6–10	31
Low	0–5	22
		= 100%

TABLE C.5 *Item characteristics of the Alienation Scale*

Item no.	% 'alienated' response	% 'can't decide'	Mean correlation with other items (φ)
1	11	0	0·17**
2	37	3	0·13*
3	8	1	0·19**
4	36	3	0·15**
5	15	1	0·18**
6	22	2	0·17**
7	16	1	0·17**
8	10	5	0·18**
9	39	2	0·16**
10	17	1	0·17**
11	21	1	0·26**
12	30	3	0·19**
13	36	3	0·19**
14	37	6	0·14**
15	60	3	0·15**
16	52	3	0·12*
17	11	3	0·19**
18	15	3	0·19**
19	34	1	0·19**
20	28	1	0·18**

TABLE C.5 (*continued*)

Item no.	% 'alienated' response	% 'can't decide'	Mean correlation with other items (φ)
21	26	1	0·18**
22	14	1	0·17**
23	11	1	0·19**
24	10	1	0·14**
			0·17**[a]

[a] Mean inter-item correlation.

TABLE C.6   *Standardization data for the Authoritarianism Scale*

Reliability (parallel forms method)	0·509
Range (possible)	0–26
Mean	12·85
Standard deviation	5·49
Median	13·5

Quartiles	Raw score	% sample
High	17–26	26
Middle range	14–16	24
	9–13	26
Low	0–8	26
		= 100%

TABLE C.7   *Item characteristics of the Authoritarianism Scale*

Item no.	% 'authoritarianism' response	% 'can't decide'	Mean correlation with other items (φ)	correlation with E scale (φ)
1	82	2	0·17**	0·22**
2	69	3	0·16**	0·08
3	55	20	0·12*	0·18**
4	65	4	0·14**	0·12*
5	51	3	0·13*	0·12*
6	39	1	0·16**	0·14**
7	54	9	0·16**	0·11*
8	37	3	0·14**	0·27**

195

TABLE C.7 (*continued*)

Item no.	% 'authoritarianism' response	% 'can't decide'	Mean correlation with other items (φ)	correlation with E scale (φ)
9	46	3	0·17**	0·12*
10	21	1	0·10	0·28**
11	28	9	0·15**	0·11*
12	29	4	0·16**	0·10
13	34	3	0·17**	0·35**
			0·15**[a]	0·17**[b]

[a] Mean inter-item correlation
[b] Mean correlation with E scale

TABLE C.8   *Standardization data for the Ethnocentrism Scale*

Reliability (parallel forms method)	0·787	
Range (possible)	0–36	
Mean	11·58	
Standard deviation	7·74	
Median	10·5	

Quartiles	Raw score	% sample
High	17–36	23
Middle range	{11–16	26
	{ 6–10	28
Low	0–5	23
		= 100%

TABLE C.9   *Item characteristics of the Ethnocentrism Scale*

Item no.	% 'ethnocentric' response	% 'can't decide'	Mean correlation with other items (φ)
1	28	2	0·19**
2	67	4	0·13*
3	17	2	0·24**
4	27	2	0·26**

TABLE C.9 (*continued*)

Item no.	% 'ethnocentric' response	% 'can't decide'	Mean correlation with other items (φ)
5	22	7	0·21**
6	24	15	0·20**
7	34	10	0·19**
8	17	3	0·26**
9	54	5	0·13*
10	27	3	0·29**
11	25	11	0·22**
12	25	3	0·26**
13	8	3	0·19**
14	34	3	0·20**
15	29	10	0·18**
16	30	6	0·21**
17	13	6	0·21**
18	46	19	0·14**
			0·21**[a]

[a] Mean inter-item correlation

TABLE C.10 *Standardization data for the Anxiety Scale*

Reliability (parallel forms method)	0·552	
Range (possible)	0–40	
Mean	11·66	
Standard deviation	6·05	
Median	11·5	
Quartiles	Raw score	% sample
High	17–40	29
Middle range	12–16	23
	8–11	26
Low	0–7	22
		=100%

APPENDIX D: *Constructing the political scales*

In order to obtain the relationships between the 22 items (Table 6.1 in Chapter 6), all responses were collapsed to two categories, those 'undecided' being allotted to the smaller of the remaining two. (The initial procedure for Q.7, which gave four possible responses, has been described.) Product-moment coefficients (numerically equivalent to the phi coefficient when there are two values for each variable) were then computed.

Five varimax factor analyses were carried out, stipulating from two to six orthogonal factors. For technical reasons, a three-factor solution was unavoidable. These were, firstly, that a two-factor solution was misleading, since, if one examined the intercorrelations of the items loading on the second factor, they formed two *statistically* disparate clusters, one having to do with conscience issues such as hanging, the other with issues in defence and foreign policy. Secondly, since the factors extracted under these procedures tend to become weaker as one progresses, it was decided to exclude a solution which extended to a factor without substantive meaning. This required a three-factor solution, since when four factors are extracted, the last, and weakest, exhibits a minority of significant inter-item correlations for those items which are loaded noticeably on it. All loadings of 0.02 or more were regarded as 'noticeable'. The average inter-item coefficient amongst these approximated zero. A four-factor solution, or one postulating a greater number of factors, is thus untenable, if the factors are required to have substantive meaning.

TABLE D.1 *Factor loadings of all policy items*

Item nos	I	II	III	
1	0·39	0·31	0·10	(Education spending)
2	−0·10	0·21	0·20	(Aid to church schools)
3	0·13	0·05	0·63	(Defence spending)
4	−0·28	−0·03	0·60	(Troops for Vietnam)
5	−0·17	−0·06	0·51	(Conscripts for Vietnam)
6	−0·06	−0·19	0·31	(Conscription in direct attack)
7	0·05	0·09	0·52	(Defence ties with USA)
8	0·07	−0·15	0·50	(Atomic weapons)
9	0·02	0·65	−0·12	(Aid to Asia)
10	−0·02	0·57	−0·16	(Relax White Australia)
11	−0·09	0·53	−0·07	(Aid to Indonesia)
12	0·15	0·36	0·18	(New Guinea)
13	0·63	0·04	−0·08	(New Government enterprises)

TABLE D.1 (*continued*)

Item nos	I	II	III	
14	0·68	−0·14	−0·23	(Nationalization of monopolies)
15	0·10	0·18	−0·21	(Controls on US investment)
16	0·41	0·04	−0·31	(Economic planning)
17	0·54	−0·26	−0·04	(Strict economic planning)
18	−0·02	0·04	−0·16	(Capital gains tax)
19	0·07	0·56	−0·18	(Abolish death penalty)
20	0·43	0·03	0·02	(Child endowment)
21	0·47	0·05	0·01	(Age pensions)
22	0·34	0·14	0·21	(Republic)

The factor loadings for the three-factor solution are displayed in Table D.1. Factor analysis, unlike cluster analysis, does not force an item into one category, so Table D.1 conveniently exhibits cross-relationships when these are apparent. However, they are relatively rare.

The signs (+ or −) of the loadings should be interpreted as in the following examples: factor III, as discussion elsewhere indicates, represents a 'hawkish' sentiment on foreign policy. Item 3 (defence spending) is positively loaded on this factor, and item 15 (controls on US investment) is negatively loaded on it. Thus 'hawks' want to spend more on defence and *not* impose special controls on US investment, nor introduce economic planning (item 16). The meaning of a cross-loading may be illustrated as follows. Factor I is best described (see discussion in Chapter 6) as the 'established socio-economic radicalism'. Item 4 (troops for Vietnam) loads negatively on Factor I and positively on Factor III. Thus sending troops to Vietnam is in accordance with 'hawkish' sentiment and out of sympathy with socio-economic radicalism. Acquiring atomic weapons (item 8) is 'hawkish', but loads negatively on factor II (representing conscience radicalism), and so is in opposition to the latter.

The 'items', or questions, are set out in full in Chapter 6, and standardization data, along with item characteristics of the libertarianism index, are displayed in Tables D.2 to D.4. The scoring method is set out on pp. 107 and 113.

TABLE D.2 *Standardization data for the political index ER* (Item nos: 1, 13, 14, 16, 17, 20, 21, 22)

Range (possible)	0–16	
Median	6·5	
Quartiles (n = 352)	Raw score	% sample
High	11–16	20
Middle range	{ 7–10	30
	{ 5–6	22
Low	0–4	28
Reliability (split-half method) (n=395)=0·433		=100%

TABLE D.3 *Standardization data for the political index CR* (Item nos: 9, 10, 11, 12, 19)

	Raw score	% sample
Range (possible)	0–10	
Median	4·5	
Quartiles ($n = 352$)	Raw score	% sample
High	8–10	26
Middle range	5–7	24
	3–4	24
Low	0–2	26
Reliability (split-half method) ($n=395$) $=0\cdot351$		$=100\%$

TABLE D.4 *Standardization data for the political index DL* (Item nos: 3, 4, 5, 6, 7, 8, 15)

	Raw score	% sample
Range (possible)	0–14	
Median	6·5	
Quartiles ($n = 352$)	Raw score	% sample
High	9–14	25
Middle range	7–8	20
	5–6	23
Low	0–4	32
Reliability (split-half method) ($n=395$) $=0\cdot403$		$=100\%$

TABLE D.5 *Standardization data for the libertarianism index LIB*

	Raw score	% sample
Range (possible)	0–12	
Median	5·5	
Quartiles ($n=352$)	Raw score	% sample
High	8–12	32
Middle range	6–7	17
	3–5	24
Low	0–2	27
Reliability (split-half method) ($n=395$) $=0\cdot492$		$=100\%$

Item nos.	Mean correlation with other items (φ)
1	0·29**
2	0·24**
3	0·21**
4	0·16**
5	0·17**
6	0·25**

Dispositional scales and agreement tendency: how far has research been corrupted?

1. Acquiescent response set and the F scale

The empirical evidence is suggestive of a *low* covariance between balanced F scales and measures of ARS in some samples, and so of a minor degree of intrinsic association, but one not sufficient to account for the major contribution, *almost equal to that of content*, of ARS to the variance on all-positive F scales.[1] Most of the influence of ARS on the all-positive F scale seems therefore likely to be extrinsic, i.e. specific to the format and not the *content* of the scale items, and hence to represent 'contamination'.

2. Acquiescent response set and the correlates of the F scale

Whether, and in what ways, research on the correlates of authoritarianism has been corrupted by the contamination of the all-positive F Scale by ARS depends on two factors:

(a) Whether or not other all-positive, or predominantly positive, self-report measures are similarly contaminated by ARS; and

(b) the personality correlates of ARS itself.

Both are capable of spuriously raising or *lowering* relationships.

2.1. Scales of the Minnesota Multiphasic Personality Inventory (MMPI) and ARS

The MMPI scales[2] differ strikingly in the proportion of items keyed 'true' and 'false'. Where all, or nearly all, are keyed in one direction, it is possible that ARS may influence scores. Item-reversal studies (which examine the correlation between a positive scale and its 'reversed' counterpart) are capable of establishing a *prima facie* case for ARS contamination. However, research of this kind, reviewed by Dicken[3] has 'yielded high correlations

[1] See A. Hughes, 'Problems and Solutions in the Measurement of Psychological Dispositions', in Australian Unesco Seminar, *Mathematics in the Social Sciences in Australia* (Canberra, 1972), pp. 467–72; A. Couch and K. Keniston, 'Yeasayers and Naysayers: Agreeing Response Set as a Personality Variable', *Journal of Abnormal and Social Psychology*, 60 (1960), pp. 151–74, and L. J. Chapman and R. D. Bock, 'Components of Variance due to Acquiescence and Content in the F scale Measure of Authoritarianism', *Psychological Bulletin*, 55 (1958), pp. 328–33.

[2] S. R. Hathaway and J. C. McKinley, *The Minnesota Multiphasic Personality Inventory* (The Psychological Corporation, New York, 1943).

[3] C. Dicken, '"Acquiescence" in the MMPI: A Method of Variance Artifact?', *Psychological Reports*, 20 (1967) pp. 927–33.

between original and reversed items and/or scales, evidence which contradicts the acquiescence hypothesis'. Moreover, Block[4] has shown that the factorial structure of the MMPI remains the same when acquiescence-free scales are factored. It seems that little, if any, of the variance of the original MMPI items can be attributed to ARS.

It might be conjectured that MMPI items are less likely to attract ARS than F scale-type items because they are shorter, less obscure, and more immediately relevant to the experience of the respondent.

In this area, contamination of the all-positive F scale is thus likely to have *lowered* rather than *raised* systematic correlations between personality factors and authoritarianism, except for those with the personality correlates of ARS itself.

2.2. *Anxiety Scales and ARS*

The Taylor Manifest Anxiety Scale (TMAS),[5] which is predominantly (39 of 50 items) positive, seems uninfected by ARS. Chapman and Campbell,[6] in an item-reversal study, found a high correlation between positive and reversed scales of the same order as the reliability of each. Adams and Kirby[7] achieved similar results in a study of the same kind, and also found a zero relation between ARS and content scores derived from the TMAS, suggesting no intrinsic covariation.

The MPI (Maudsley Personality Inventory)[8] 24-item Neuroticism scale is all-positive, but a factor-analytical study by Eysenck[9] suggests that it, too, is uncontaminated by ARS. The ARS factor was derived from positive and reversed F scales, and had a negligible loading on the Neuroticism scale.

The reasons for the lack of ARS contamination of these is presumably the same as for the MMPI scales, which they closely resemble.

2.3. *Ethnocentrism Scales and ARS*

The evidence here suggests that ethnocentrism scales have some covariance with ARS, but less than the all-positive F scale. Chapman and Campbell[10]

[4] J. Block, *The Challenge of Response Sets: Unconfounding Meaning, Acquiescence and Social Desirability in the MMPI* (New York, 1965), esp. chs. 2 and 5.

[5] J. A. Taylor, 'A Personality Scale of Manifest Anxiety', *Journal of Abnormal and Social Psychology*, 48 (1953), pp. 285–90.

[6] L. J. Chapman and D. T. Campbell, 'Absence of Acquiescence Response Set in the Taylor Manifest Anxiety Scale', *Journal of Consulting Psychology*, 23 (1959), pp. 465–6.

[7] H. E. Adams and A. C. Kirby, 'Manifest Anxiety, Social Desirability or Response Set', *Journal of Consulting Psychology*, 27 (1963), pp. 59–61.

[8] H. J. Eysenck, *The Maudsley Personality Inventory* (London, 1959).

[9] H. J. Eysenck, 'Response Set, Authoritarianism and Personality Questionnaires', *British Journal of Social and Clinical Psychology*, 1 (1962), pp. 20–4.

[10] L. J. Chapman and D. T. Campbell, 'The Effect of Acquiescence Response Set upon Relationships among the F Scale, Ethnocentrism and Intelligence', *Sociometry*, 22 (1959), pp. 153–61.

found no evidence for ARS covariance in one mode of analysis; but simultaneously report evidence of a different kind from the same sample, which suggests some ARS contamination. Peabody[11] found high correlations between positive and reversed anti-Semitism Scales, and evidence of only minor double-agreement tendencies.

2.4. *The Dogmatism Scale and ARS*

The Rokeach Dogmatism scale[12] which is all-positive, seems to be related to ARS to about the same extent as the all-positive F Scale.

Couch and Keniston[13] found a moderate relation (.40) between their OAS (Overall Agreement Score) measure and the Dogmatism scale, partly attributable, in their view, to intrinsic covariance. Peabody[14] found only low correlations between positive and reversed Dogmatism scales, and substantial indications of double agreement.

The data for the dogmatism measure correspond closely with those for F scales, and suggest extrinsic contamination. McBride and Moran[15] found judged item ambiguity to be as closely related to double-agreement on the Dogmatism scale as on the F scale. Rokeach[16] has advanced conceptual arguments as to why ARS might be expected to play only a minor role, if any, in influencing Dogmatism scale scores, but little empirical evidence. His proposals are chiefly that the variety of the correlates of the dogmatism measure would be hard to account for on purely response set grounds, and that a set to fake only *reversed* items may account for Peabody's data. The first of these arguments is insufficient to negate the hypothesis of *some* ARS contamination of the positive measure, and the second is less parsimonious than the hypothesis he attacks.

The correlation between the Dogmatism scale and the positive F scale may well be inflated by ARS contamination of both instruments.

The various measures correlated with the F Scale thus seem to be ranged along a continuum of ARS susceptibility, strong in the case of measures of complex social attitudes, moderate in prejudice scales, and weak in personality indices.

The ways in which research into the personality correlates of the F syndrome might have been corrupted are considered below.

[11] D. Peabody, 'Attitude Content and Agreement Set in Scales of Authoritarianism, Dogmatism, Anti-Semitism and Economic Conservatism', *Journal of Abnormal and Social Psychology*, 63 (1961), pp. 1–11.

[12] M. Rokeach, 'Political and Religious Dogmatism: An Alternative to the Authoritarian Personality', *Psychological Monographs*, 70 (1956), no. 18, pp. 1–43, whole no. 425.

[13] A. Couch and K. Keniston, 'Yeasayers and Naysayers'.

[14] D. Peabody, *op. cit.*

[15] L. McBride and G. Moran, 'Double Agreement as a Function of Item Ambiguity and Susceptibility to Demand Implications of the Psychological Situation', *Journal of Personality and Social Psychology*, 6 (1967), pp. 115–18.

[16] M. Rokeach, *The Open and Closed Mind* (New York, 1960), pp. 405–7, and M. Rokeach, 'The Double Agreement Phenomenon: Three Hypotheses', *Psychological Review*, 70 (1963), pp. 304–9.

3. The significance of the contamination of the F scale by acquiescent response set

The significance of ARS contamination of the F scale emerges in four main ways.

(i) Research into the correlates of authoritarianism may be corrupted by covariance of positive F measures and others with ARS. The danger of this is particularly marked in the case of complex attitudinal measures with social referents, such as all-positive alienation and anomia scales.

(ii) Contamination of the all-positive F scale by ARS is likely to have *lowered* rather than *raised* systematic correlations between personality factors and authoritarianism, except for those with the personality correlates of ARS itself.

(iii) It is also possible for researchers to have unknowingly described the correlates of ARS, when reporting the correlates of a positive F measure, since ARS seems to be *a stable personality trait with its own correlates*. Couch and Keniston[17] found their criterion measures of ARS (the OAS) to be related positive and significantly to a large number of sub-scales of the MMPI, including those measuring prejudice and dependency, and to those scales of Cattell's 16 PF measure which contribute to his anxiety factor, in a sample of sixty-one undergraduates. The importance of the fact that these are amongst the most commonly found correlates of the F syndrome, as measured by positive scales, hardly requires emphasis. As the MMPI itself does not seem to be much infected by ARS, these correlates of ARS are unlikely to be artifacts of the research procedure. Of particular importance are the association of weak ego strength and anxiety with ARS.

The relation of the OAS to the Cattell anxiety measure was tested only obliquely, but one can infer that it would probably have been of the order of 0.40. The reliability of the OAS was reported to be 0.85. The correlation of the anxiety measure with a 'pure' measure of ARS might therefore be expected to be of the order of 0.45, i.e. they would share about 20 per cent of their variance. The contribution of ARS to the total variance of the all-positive F scale seems likely to fluctuate from sample to sample, but generally to be between 20 and 40 per cent. Between 4 and 8 per cent of the variance would thus be likely to be shared by such an anxiety measure as this, as a result of the covariance with ARS. This would generate correlations of the order 0.20 to 0.30. Correlations between all-positive F scales and anxiety measures within this range may thus be attributable to contamination of all-positive F by ARS, *even when non-positive measures of anxiety have been employed.*

Kirscht and Dillehay[18] in their review of the literature relating the F syndrome to anxiety and neuroticism found no studies relating balanced or forced-choice F scales to anxiety, and no studies with the positive F scale whose outcome could not be accounted for, in the light of the analysis here, by covariance with ARS.

[17] A. Couch and K. Keniston, *op. cit.*

[18] J. P. Kirscht and R. C. Dillehay, *Dimensions of Authoritarianism: A Review of Research and Theory* (Lexington, 1967).

There is thus no substantial evidence for an intrinsic relation between the authoritarian syndrome and manifest anxiety, which would lend support to its genotypical characterization as unstable, possessed of a weak ego, and confronting deep internal conflicts with defence mechanisms which are only fragile and easily overborne. The commonly employed positive measures are, indeed, probably incapable of verifying the genotypical features of the construct.

(iv) The ARS loading on the positive F scale may account, in some degree, for the correlations between the items themselves. This threw doubt on the cohesiveness of the syndrome, and so even on the stability of the construct viewed phenotypically.

Peabody[19] having noted evidence presented by Campbell *et al.*[20] of the poverty and primitiveness of political attitudes in the general population, and the low proportion of their national sample (12 per cent) showing evidence of using any ideological dimension, concludes that 'social scientists who have been interested in the theories of authoritarianism . . . have tended to project the complexity of their own views onto their subjects'. This conclusion seems unnecessarily nihilistic, and to mistake evidence of the scarcity of *ideological* viewpoints, which are in some degree intellectually determined, for lack of evidence of the influence of psychological factors, which do not involve intellectual processes to the same extent.

However, there is some justice in his rebuke. The defects of the chief measure of authoritarianism, the consequent confusion in identifying the construct, and the perils of generalizing from samples of undergraduates, student nurses, convicts and schizophrenics to the population at large should by now be manifest. There is no avoiding the necessity of the application of an adequate measure to representative extra-mural samples, difficult to obtain as they may be.

[19] D. Peabody, 'Authoritarianism Scales and Response Bias, '*Psychological Bulletin,* 65 (1966), pp. 11–23.

[20] A. Campbell, P. E. Converse, W. E. Miller and D. E. Stokes, *The American Voter* (New York, 1960).

Bibliography

Abel, T., 'The Operation Called *Verstehen*'. *American Journal of Sociology*, 54 (1948), pp. 211–18.

Aberbach, J. D., 'Alienation and Political Behaviour', *American Political Science Review*, 62 (1969), pp. 86–99.

Adams, H. E. and Kirby, A. C., 'Manifest Anxiety, Social Desirability or Response Set', *Journal of Consulting Psychology*, 27 (1963), pp. 59–61.

Adorno, T. W., Frenkel-Brunswick, E. Levinson, D. J. and Sanford, R. N., *The Authoritarian Personality*, New York, 1950.

Aitkin, D., 'Political Review,' *Australian Quarterly*, 39 (1967), no. 1, pp. 85–95.

Banfield, E. C., *The Moral Basis of a Backward Society*, New York, 1958.

Bass, B. M., 'Authoritarianism or Acquiescence?', *Journal of Abnormal and Social Psychology*, 51 (1955), pp. 616–23.

Bell, D., 'The Rediscovery of Alienation: Some Notes along the Quest for the Historical Marx', *Journal of Philosophy*, 56 (1959), pp. 933–54.

Bergin, T. G. and Fisch, M. H., *The New Science of Giambattista Vico*, New York, 1948.

Berkowitz, N. H. and Wolkon, G. H., 'A Forced Choice Form of the F Scale – Free of Acquiescent Response Set', *Sociometry*, 27 (1964), pp. 54–65.

Bettelheim, B., 'Obsolete Youth', *Encounter*, 33 (1969), no. 3, pp. 29–42.

Blauner, R., *Education and Freedom*, Chicago, 1964.

Block, J., *The Challenge of Response Sets: Unconfounding Meaning, Acquiescence and Social Desirability in the MMPI*, New York, 1965.

Campbell, A., Converse, P. E., Miller, W. E. and Stokes, D. E., *The American Voter*, New York, 1960.

Campbell, E. and McCandless, B., 'Ethnocentrism, Xenophobia and Personality', *Human Relations*, 4 (1951), pp. 185–92.

Cattell, R. B., *Handbook for the IPAT Anxiety Scale (Self Analysis Form)*, Melbourne, 1957. Published by the Australian Council for Educational Research by arrangement with the Institute for Personality and Ability Testing, Champaign, Illinois, USA. Available only to members of recognised associations of psychologists.

Cattell, R. B., *IPAT Self-Analysis Form*, Melbourne, 1957. Published by the Australian Council for Educational Research by arrangement with the Institute for Personality and Ability Testing, Champaign, Illinois, USA. Available only to members of recognized associations of psychologists.

Cattell, R. B., Saunders, D. R., and Stice, G., *Handbook of The 16 Personality Factor Questionnaire*, Champaign, 1967. Available only to members of recognized associations of psychologists.

Certcov, D., 'Alienacion Social y Enfermedad Mental', *Acta Psiquiatrica y Psicologica de America Latina*, 17 (1971), pp. 401–9.

Chapman, L. J. and Bock, R. D., 'Components of Variance due to Acquiescence and Content in the F Scale Measure of Authoritarianism', *Psychological Bulletin*, 55 (1968), pp. 328–33.

Chapman, L. J. and Campbell, D. T., 'Absence of Acquiescence Response Set in the Taylor Manifest Anxiety Scale', *Journal of Consulting Psychology*, 23 (1959), pp. 465–6.

Christie, R. and Jahoda, M. (eds.), *Studies in the Scope and Method of 'The Authoritarian Personality'*, Glencoe, 1954.

Christie, R. and Cook, P., 'A Guide to Published Literature relating to "The Authoritarian Personality" through 1956', *Journal of Psychology*, 45 (1958), pp. 171–99.

Christie, R., Havel, J., and Seidenberg, B., 'Is the F Scale Irreversible?', *Journal of Abnormal and Social Psychology*, 56 (1958), pp. 143–59.

Clayton, M. B. and Jackson, D. N., 'Equivalence Range, Acquiescence and Overgeneralization', *Educational and Psychological Measurement*, 21 (1961), pp. 371–82.

Collingwood, R. G., *The Idea of History*, London, 1946.

Commonwealth Bureau of Census and Statistics. *Census of Population and Housing, 30 June 1966, Commonwealth of Australia*, Canberra, no date.

Commonwealth Bureau of Census and Statistics, *Official Year Book of the Commonwealth of Australia*, no. 52, Canberra, 1966.

Coser, L. A. and Rosenberg, B., *Sociological Theory*, New York, 1964.

Couch, A. and Keniston, K., 'Yeasayers and Naysayers: Agreeing Response Set as a Personality Variable'. *Journal of Abnormal and Social Psychology*, 60 (1960), pp. 151–74.

Crisp, L. F., *The Parliamentary Government of the Commonwealth of Australia*, third ed., London, 1961.

Dahrendorf, R., *Society and Democracy in Germany*, London, 1968.

Davidoff, M. D. and Goheen, H. W., 'A Table for the Rapid Determination of the Tetrachoric Correlation Coefficient', *Psychometrika*, 18 (1953), pp. 15–21.

Davies, A. F., *Australian Democracy*, Melbourne, 1958.

Davies, A. F., *Private Politics: A Study of Five Political Outlooks*, Melbourne, 1966.

Davies, A. F. and Encel, S. (eds.), *Australian Society: A Sociological Introduction*, Melbourne, 1965.

Dean, D. G., 'Alienation: its Meaning and Measurement', *American Sociological Review*, 26 (1961), pp. 753–8.

Dicken, C., '"Acquiescence" in the MMPI: A Method Variance Artifact?', *Psychological Reports*, 20 (1967), pp. 927–33.

Dicks, H., 'Personality Traits and National Socialist Ideology', *Human Relations*, 3 (1950), pp. 111–54.

Edwards, A. L., *Statistical Methods for the Behavioral Sciences*, New York, 1955.

English, H. B. and English, A. C., *A Comprehensive Dictionary of Psychological and Psychoanalytical Terms*, New York, 1958.

Erikson, E. H., *Childhood and Society*, second ed., New York, 1963.

Eysenck, H. J., 'Response Set, Authoritarianism and Personality Questionnaires', *British Journal of Social and Clinical Psychology*, 1 (1962), pp. 20–4.

Eysenck, H. J., *The Maudsley Personality Inventory*, London, 1959. Available only to members of recognised associations of psychologists.

Eysenck, H. J., *The Psychology of Politics*, London, 1954.

Eysenck, H. J. and Eysenck, S.B.G., *Manual of the Eysenck Personality Inventory*, London, 1964. Available only to members of recognized associations of psychologists.

Ferguson, G. A., *Statistical Analysis in Psychology and Education*, London, 1959.

Fromm, E., *The Fear of Freedom*, London, 1942.

Fruchter, B., *Introduction to Factor Analysis*, New York, 1954.

Gay, P., *Weimar Culture: The Outsider as Insider*, London 1968.

Goldthorpe, H. J., 'Attitudes and Behaviour of Car Assembly Workers: A Deviant Case and a Theoretical Critique', *British Journal of Sociology*, 17 (1966), pp. 227–44.

Goot, M., *Policies and Partisans: Australian Electoral Opinion, 1941 to 1968*, Occasional Monograph No. 1, Department of Government and Public Administration, University of Sydney, Sydney, 1969.

Greenstein, F. I., 'Personality and Politics: Problems of Evidence, Inference and Conceptualization', *American Behavioral Scientist*, 11 (1967), pp. 38-53.

Greenstein, F. I., *Personality and Politics*, Chicago, 1969.

Greenstein, F. I., 'The Impact of Personality on Politics: An Attempt to Clear Away the Underbrush', *American Political Science Review*, 61 (1967), pp. 628–41.

Greenstein, F. I., 'The Need for Systematic Enquiry into Personality and Politics: Introduction and Overview', *Journal of Social Issues*, 24 (1968), pp. 1–14.

Guilford, J. P., *Fundamental Statistics in Psychology and Education*, third ed., New York and Tokyo, 1956.

Gusfield, J. R., *Symbolic Crusade: Status Politics and the American Temperance Movement*, second ed., Chicago, 1969.

Hancock, W. K., (Sir Keith), *Australia*, Brisbane, 1961 (first ed., 1930).

Harman, H. H., *Modern Factor Analysis*, revised ed., Chicago and London, 1967.

Harper, R. J. A., 'Survey of Living Conditions in Melbourne – 1966', *Economic Record*, 43 (1967), pp. 262–88.

Hathaway, S. R. and McKinley, J. C., *The Minnesota Multiphasic Personality Inventory*, The Psychological Corporation, New York, 1943. Available only to members of recognized associations of psychologists.

Hilberg, R., *The Destruction of the European Jews*, Chicago, 1961.

Himmelweit, H. T., 'Frustration and Aggression: A Review of Recent Experimental Work', in T. H. Pear (ed.), *The Psychological Factors of Peace and War*, London, 1950, pp. 159–91.

Bibliography

Horne, D., *The Education of Young Donald*, Sydney, 1967.

Huck, A., *The Chinese in Australia*, Melbourne, 1967.

Hughes, A., 'Authoritarian Orientation, Alienation and Political Attitudes in a Sample of Melbourne Voters', *Australian and New Zealand Journal of Sociology*, 3 (1967), pp. 134–50.

Hughes, A., 'Political Review', *Australian Quarterly*, 41 (1969), no. 2, pp. 98–108.

Hughes, A., 'Political Review', *Australian Quarterly*, 41 (1969), no. 4, pp. 15–24.

Hughes, A., 'Problems and Solutions in the Measurement of Psychological Dispositions', Australian National Advisory Committee for Unesco, *Australian Unesco Seminar: Mathematics in the Social Sciences in Australia, University of Sydney, May 1968*, Canberra, 1972, pp. 463–504.

Hughes, A., *Psychological Dispositions and Political Attitudes*, unpublished doctoral dissertation, Australian National University, Canberra, 1971.

Hughes, C. A., 'Political Review', *Australian Quarterly*, 36 (1964), no. 1, pp. 92–105.

Hughes, C. A. and Graham, B. D., *A Handbook of Australian Government and Politics, 1890–1964*, Canberra, 1968.

Israel, J., *Alienation: From Marx to Modern Sociology*, Boston, 1971.

Jackson, D. N. and Messick, S. J., 'A Note on Ethnocentrism and Acquiescent Response Sets', *Journal of Abnormal and Social Psychology*, 54 (1967), pp. 132–4.

Jenkins, W. L., 'An Improved Method for Tetrachoric *r*', *Psychometrika*, 20 (1955), pp. 253–8.

Jones, M. B., 'The Pensacola Z Survey: A Study in the Measurement of Authoritarian Tendency', *Psychological Monographs*, 71 (1957), no. 23, whole no. 452.

Jupp, J., *Arrivals and Departures*, Melbourne, 1966.

Jupp, J., *Australian Party Politics*, Melbourne, 1964.

Kahan, M. and Aitkin, D., *Drawing a Sample of the Australian Electorate*, Occasional Paper No. 3, Department of Political Science, Research School of Social Sciences, Australian National University, Canberra, 1968.

Kamenka, E., *The Ethical Foundations of Marxism*, Lonon, 1962.

Keniston, K., *The Uncommitted: Alienated Youth in American Society*, New York, 1960.

Kirkpatrick, S. A. and Pettit, L. K. (eds.), *The Social Psychology of Political Life*, Belmont, California, 1972.

Kirscht, J. P. and Dillehay, R. C., *Dimensions of Authoritarianism: A Review of Research and Theory*, Lexington, 1967.

Kish, L., *Survey Sampling*, New York, 1965.

Knöpfelmacher, F. and Armstrong, D. B., 'The Relation Between Authoritarianism, Ethnocentrism and Religious Denomination among Australian Adolescents'. *American Catholic Sociological Review*, 24 (1963), pp. 99–114.

210

Lafitte, P. *The Person in Psychology: Reality or Abstraction*, London, 1957.

Laski, H. J., *Communist Manifesto: Socialist Landmark*, London, 1948.

Lasswell, H. D., *Psychopathology and Politics*, New York, 1960 (first ed., 1930).

Lewis, O., *La Vida*, London, 1967.

Lipset, S. M., 'Democracy and Working-class Authoritarianism', *American Sociological Review*, 24 (1959), pp. 428–501.

Lipset, S. M., *Political Man: The Social Bases of Politics*, London, 1960.

Lutterman, K. G. and Middleton, R., 'Authoritarianism, Anomia and Prejudice', *Social Forces*, 48 (1969–70), pp. 485–92.

McBride, L. and Moran, G., 'Double Agreement as a Function of Item Ambiguity and Susceptibility to Demand Implications of the Psychological Situation', *Journal of Personality and Social Psychology*, 6 (1967), pp. 115–18.

McCary, J. L. (ed.), *Psychology of Personality: Six Modern Approaches*, New York, 1956.

McClosky, H., 'Conservatism and Personality', *American Political Science Review*, 52 (1958), pp. 27–45.

McClosky, H. and Schaar, J. H., 'Psychological Dimensions of Anomy', *American Sociological Review*, 30 (1965), pp. 14–40.

McClosky, H. and Schaar, J. H., 'Reply to Srole and Nettler', *American Sociological Review*, 30 (1965), pp. 763–7.

McDill, E. L., 'Anomie, Authoritarianism, Prejudice and Socio-Economic Status: An Attempt at Clarification', *Social Forces*, 39 (1960–1), pp. 239–45.

May, R. S., *Federalism and Fiscal Adjustment*, Oxford, 1969.

Mayer, H. (ed.), *Catholics and The Free Society: An Australian Symposium*, Melbourne, 1961.

Medding, P. Y., *From Assimilation to Group Survival*, Melbourne, 1968.

Miller, J. D. B., *Australian Government and Politics: An Introductory Survey*, second ed., London, 1959.

Murray, R. A., *The Split: Australian Labor in the Fifties*. Melbourne, 1971.

Neal, A. G. and Rettig, S., 'Dimensions of Alienation among Manual and Non-Manual Workers', *American Sociological Review*, 28 (1963), pp. 599–608.

Neal, A. G. and Rettig, S., 'On the Multidimensionality of Alienation', *American Sociological Review*, 32 (1967), pp. 54–64.

Nettler, G., 'A Further Comment on "Anomy"', *American Sociological Review*, 30 (1965), p. 762.

Oeser, O. A. and Hammond, S. B. (eds.), *Social Structure and Personality in a City*, London, 1954.

Overacker, L., *The Australian Party System*, London, 1952.

Peabody, D., 'Attitude Content and Agreement Set in Scales of Authoritarianism, Dogmatism, Anti-Semitism and Economic Conservatism', *Journal of Abnormal and Social Psychology*, 63 (1961), pp. 1–11.

Peabody, D., 'Authoritarianism Scales and Response Bias', *Psychological Bulletin*, 65 (1966), pp. 11–23.

Peabody, D., 'Two Components of Bi-Polar Scales: Direction and Extremeness', *Psychological Review*, 69 (1962), pp. 65–73.

Pear, T. H. (ed.), *The Psychological Factors of Peace and War*, London, 1950.

Press and Information Office of the Federal Republic of Germany, *Peace Policy in our Time*, Bonn, 1972.

Price, C. A., *Jewish Settlers in Australia*, Canberra, 1964.

Price, C. A., *Southern Europeans in Australia*, Melbourne, 1963.

Pulzer, P. G. S., *The Rise of Political Anti-Semitism in Germany and Austria*, New York, 1964.

Rank, O., *The Myth of the Birth of the Hero*, New York, 1959.

Ranulf, S., *Moral Indignation and Middle Class Psychology, A Sociological Study*, second ed., New York, 1964.

Ray, J. J. and Sutton, A. J., 'Alienation in an Australian University', *Journal of Social Psychology*, 86 (1972), pp. 319–20.

Reitlinger, G., *The Final Solution: The Attempt to Exterminate the Jews of Europe, 1939–1945*, London, 1953.

Reserve Bank of Australia, *Statistical Bulletin*, Canberra, 1967.

Roberts, A. and Rokeach, M., 'Anomie, Authoritarianism and Prejudice: A Replication', *American Journal of Sociology*, 61 (1956), pp. 355–8.

Roberts, S. H. (Sir Stephen), *The House that Hitler Built*, London, 1937.

Rokeach, M., 'Political and Religious Dogmatism: An Alternative to the Authoritarian Personality', *Psychological Monographs*, 70 (1956), no. 18, whole no. 425.

Rokeach, M., 'The Double Agreement Phenomenon: Three Hypotheses', *Psychological Review*, 70 (1963), pp. 304–9.

Rokeach, M., *The Open and Closed Mind*, New York, 1960.

Rorer, L. G., 'The Great Response-Style Myth', *Psychological Bulletin*, 63 (1965), pp. 129–56.

Rotter, J. B., 'Generalized Expectancies for Internal versus External Control of Reinforcement', *Psychological Monographs*, 80 (1966), no. 1, whole no. 609.

Sanford, F. H., *Authoritarianism and Leadership*, Philadelphia, 1950.

Sanford, R. N., 'The Approach of the Authoritarian Personality', in McCary, J. L. (ed.), *Psychology of Personality: Six Modern Approaches*, New York, 1956, pp. 261–82.

Santamaria, B. A., 'Struggle on Two Fronts: The DLP and the 1969 Election', *Australian Quarterly*, 41 (1969), no. 4, pp. 33–42.

Santamaria, B. A., '"The Movement": 1941–1960 – an Outline', in Mayer, H. (ed.), *Catholics and the Free Society: An Australian Symposium*, Melbourne, 1961, pp. 54–103.

Schutz, A., 'Concept and Theory Formation in the Social Sciences', *Journal of Philosophy*, 51 (1954), pp. 260–7.

Seeman, M., 'On the Meaning of Alienation', *American Sociological Review*, 24 (1959), pp. 783–91.

Seeman, M., 'The Urban Alienations: Some Dubious Theses from Marx to Marcuse', *Journal of Personality and Social* Psychology, 19 (1971), pp. 135–43.

Shils, E. A., 'Authoritarianism: "Right and Left"' in R. Christie and M. Johoda (eds.), *Studies in the Scope and Method of 'The Authoritarian Personality'*, Glencoe, 1954.

Siegman, A. W., 'A Cross-Cultural Investigation of the Relationship between Ethnic Prejudice, Authoritarian Ideology, and Personality', *Journal of Abnormal and Social Psychology*, 63 (1961), pp. 654–5.

Smith, M. Brewster, 'A Map for the Analysis of Personality and Politics', *Journal of Social Issues*, 24 (1968), pp. 15–28.

Srole, L., 'A Comment on "Anomy"', *American Sociological Review*, 30 (1965), pp. 757–62.

Srole, L., 'Social Integration and Certain Corollaries: An Exploratory Study', *American Sociological Review*, 21 (1956), pp. 709–16.

Taylor, J. A., 'A Personality Scale of Manifest Anxiety', *Journal of Abnormal and Social Psychology*, 48 (1953), pp. 285–90.

Trevor-Roper, H. R. (ed.), *Hitler's Table Talk, 1941–1944*, London, 1953.

Truman, T., *Catholic Action and Politics*, Melbourne, 1959.

Truman, T., *Ideological Groups in The Australian Labor Party and Their Attitudes*, University of Queensland Papers, Department of History and Political Science, Vol. 1, no. 2, Brisbane, 1965.

Wangh, M., 'National Socialism and The Genocide of the Jews', *International Journal of Psychoanalysis*, 45 (1964), pp. 386–95.

Wiggins, N., 'Individual Viewpoints of Social Desirability', *Psychological Bulletin*, 66 (1966), pp. 68–77.

Zeman, Z. A. B., *Nazi Propaganda*, London, 1964.

Zuckerman, M. and Norton, J., 'Response Set and Content Factors in the California F Scale and the Parental Attitude Research Instrument', *Journal of Social Psychology*, 53 (1961), pp. 199–210.

Index

Abel, T., 6n

Aberbach, J. D., 40–1, 57

acquiescence, *see* agreement response set

acquiescent response set (ARS), *see* agreement response set

Adams, H. E., 202

Administration method for chief dispositional scales developed, or employed, herein 59–61, 63

Adorno, T. W., 3, 9, 30n, 31n, 45n, 47n; *see also* authoritarian personality tendency

aggregative analysis, 2–3

agreement response set (ARS), 31–63, 45–51 and esp. 201–5; and all-positive scales, 32–6, 201–3; Couch and Keniston's measure of ARS, 203–5; unable to influence scores on paired alternative scales, 50; and the California F scale, 45–8, 201–5; *see also* attitude and dispositional scale construction; psychological dispositions; response sets

Aitkin, D., 22n, 178n

alienation, as a felt *sentiment* of social estrangement, briefly defined, 10, 52; definition elaborated, 52–8, 128–9; discussed, 29–41 *passim*, 77–82, 84–8, 165–6; Alienation Scale: items, 60–1; method of administration and scoring, 59–60; method of construction, 185–91; statistical characteristics, 65, 87–9, 185–91, 194–5; criterion group validation, 191–2; internal cohesion, 66–7, 70–1; sub-scales of 65, 70; alienation triptych, 9–11 (esp. diagram at 10), 68, 73–6, 84–8; amongst intellectuals and students, 87–90; amongst the poor, 85–7; as social scepticism, 38–41; case studies of, 78–84; disparate character of, 77–8, 185–91; relation to anxiety, 9–11, 65–7, 73, 94–9; to authoritarian personality tendency, 66–7,

95–9; to agreement response set, 33–6; to ethnocentrism, 9–11, 66–7, 73–6, 94–9; to personality correlates, 85–90; to political attitudes, 127–49; to social desirability set, 38; previous research reviewed, 29–41; social incidence, 92–3; socialization into, 85; variations in correlation with other dispositions, 95–8; whether or not plural in character, 38–9, 51–2, 56–8, 66–7; *see also* anomia; psychological dispositions; reification; student alienation

all-positive scales, described and discussed, 31–5, 201–5; *see also* agreement response set; attitude and dispositional scale construction; California F scale; psychological dispositions

alienation 'triptych', 9–11

anomia (here, synonymous with *personal* 'anomie', 'anomy'), 33–6, 53

anomie, *see* anomia

anomy, *see* anomia

'answer-system', spuriously proferred by varieties of ethnocentrism, esp. anti-Semitism, 75–6

anti-intraception, defined, 30; *see also* authoritarian personality tendency; ethnocentrism

anti-Semitism, in the Nazi imagination, 5, 75–6, 166–72; as an element in ethnocentrism, 58–9, 64, 70, 192, 197; *see also* ethnocentrism; Jewish communities, as targets for irrational hostility

anxiety, characterization of type of anxiety associated with the Cattell measure, 59; modification of the Cattell measure, 59; method of administration, 59–60; statistical characteristics of the modified Cattell scale, 197; sub-sentiments, 71; as a disposition within a system, 9–11; disparate